the
ultimate
hiker's
gearguide
Second Edition

the ultimate hiker's gearguide

Second Edition

tools & techniques to hit the trail

Andrew Skurka

NATIONAL GEOGRAPHIC

WASHINGTON, D.C.

contents

introduction

My most successful backpacking trips have been those for which I had honest, accurate, and well-informed answers to three questions: 1) What are my objectives, in terms of the time I will spend hiking relative to camping? 2) What environmental and route conditions will I likely encounter, such as temperatures, precipitation, and biting insects? 3) What gear, supplies, and skills will best help me achieve my objectives *and* keep me safe and comfortable in those conditions?

These three questions form the framework of this book. Part 1 addresses the first two questions, and Part 2 addresses the last. In Part 3, you'll find sample gear lists to use as templates and checklists.

It is not widely recognized but ought to be: There are differences in backpacking styles. One extreme is to spend most of your day hiking; camp is considered an eight-hour recharge between efforts. The other is to stay mostly in or near camp to fish, journal, earn merit badges, or relax, perhaps hiking to reach another base of operations. Most backpackers associate more strongly with one approach but ultimately prefer a balance.

No backpacking style is superior. "Hike your own hike," the refrain goes. And it is not permanent: Your style may change based on the circumstance and your company. Whatever your style, though, your tools and techniques need to be optimized for it.

Last summer, for instance, on solo thru-hikes of the Kings Canyon High Basin Route and Wind River High Route—which have extensive off-trail travel and substantial vertical relief—I packed minimal equipment and calorically dense food, hiked sustainably from dawn to dusk, and embraced the physical and mental challenges as part of the experience. In contrast, when my wife, Amanda, and I hiked the Aspen Four Pass Loop on our anniversary weekend, we carried a fully enclosed tent, Kindle, and fresh produce, and we stopped often to take photographs, brew coffee, and avoid burnout. Each trip, in its own way, was a success.

I wrote this book for backpackers who want to more fully enjoy the *hiking* component of their trips, which should be the case with all but the most devout campers. This book will most benefit beginners and intermediates who do not yet know how to pack lightly and move efficiently, and thus find hiking to be overly strenuous and unproductive. They default to camping, because it seems more fun. In the course of guiding more than 55 learning-intensive trips with

400-plus clients in the past five years I have become deeply familiar with this demographic.

This is not a "lightweight backpacking" book. I will not present arbitrary pack weight guidelines, argue that lighter is always better, turn my nose up at backpackers who carry the proverbial kitchen sink, or ignore instances of "stupid light," whereby weight-savings efforts undermine comfort and safety.

The know-how I've shared in this book was mostly gained the hard way, by making mistakes. I'm confident in the resulting recommendations but readily admit that other options may be feasible, especially in the context of your experience and preferences.

To help you assemble your kit, I have listed specific brands, products, prices, and weights, even though this will more quickly outdate the text. But I tried to focus on product *types,* not specific products, to prolong its value.

Eventually these product types will lose relevancy, but one tenet remains timeless: Carry on your back and between your ears what is appropriate for your trip objectives and the conditions.

I wrote this book for backpackers who want to enjoy hiking more.

why,

when&where

10
ARE YOU A HIKER OR CAMPER?

16
WHY I'M A HIKER

20
KNOW BEFORE YOU GO

On every backpacking trip I need clothing, footwear, shelter, a sleeping bag and pad, food and water, and various other items. But my exact selections — for instance, a short- or long-sleeved shirt, a double-wall tent or hammock, or an alcohol or canister stove — are informed by trip-specific considerations: 1) What am I hoping to accomplish during this trip? and 2) What types of conditions am I likely to encounter?

If I neglect to ask these questions, it's unlikely that I will be properly prepared. I don't care to admit how often it's happened. My pack may be too heavy for the ambitious route I had planned, or I may pack too few camp comforts for a more relaxed itinerary. Or I may mistakenly leave behind items that would have enhanced my safety and comfort, while carrying others that I never would have needed.

In this section I will discuss backpacking styles and explain how to research environmental and route conditions.

Badlands in Anza-Borrego Desert State Park, California

are you a hiker or camper?

It wasn't all going to fit, I finally acknowledged. I stepped back to reconsider my monstrously overstuffed backpack and the grocery bag of items for which I still hoped to find room. Fortunately, it was only 5:30 a.m. on a Tuesday and still dark, so I figured I had some time before anyone arrived at Georgia's Amicalola Falls State Park visitor center and discovered my neophyte status.

I discarded an extra tube of toothpaste, spare batteries, a small lantern, a box of blueberry Pop-Tarts, and my fourth pair of socks. Other items—many extraneous, in hindsight—were saved by fear of the unknown. "I don't know for sure, but I might need that," I reasoned.

This whittling act made only a small dent in my pack weight, now at 49 pounds. That may not sound awful, but imagine doing just a few flights of stairs with a bag of concrete mix strapped to your back. I squeezed in the remaining items from the grocery bag—and the grocery bag, too, just in case I needed it for something—before shouldering my backpack and heading toward the summit of Springer Mountain, where I planned to begin a three-month, 2,175-mile journey along the Appalachian Trail to its northern terminus in Maine.

"Should I have expected this to be harder?" I asked rhetorically in my journal entry for that day—May 3, 2002. I described myself as being "in the hurt shop," with a chafed crotch, sore leg muscles, and aching feet. I was depleted after covering a mere 15 miles in 7 hours, a humbling distance for a member of Duke University's Division I cross-country and track teams who, during past summers, had logged up to 80 miles per week at a seven-minute-per mile pace. And for dinner, I was content with a few handfuls of trail mix, because "It involves way too much effort to cook anything," even though my planned entrée was ramen noodles, which would have required just two cups of hot water.

Over the next week, my misery and suffering only grew. I never put it in these exact words, but many of my nightly journal entries could have been summed up with, "I want my mommy." I was more pointed on Day 7: "This sucks."

Backpacking styles

On Day 8, I called my parents from the Holiday Inn Express lobby in Hiawassee, Georgia, and explained to them that my situation was unsustainable and that I had a choice to make. If I wanted to thru-hike the entire Appalachian Trail that summer—which would necessitate a pace of about 23 miles per day—I would need to learn how to love *hiking*.

Whereas if I let go of that goal, I would have more time for relaxation and extracurricular activities, like partaking in the social scene, swimming in trailside lakes, and reading the copy of *Desert Solitaire* that I had not yet

even opened. The distance I would have hiked before school resumed was unimportant—reaching a specific destination would not be a priority.

Just a week into my first real backpacking trip, I had made an important discovery, though it took years before I could fully articulate it. Simply put, there are *styles of backpacking*, differentiated by the time and focus placed on *hiking versus camping*. Trips can be entirely hiking- or camping-centric, or some balance of the two. Backpackers who strive for opposite ratios of hiking and camping diverge in their:

> Primary trip objective;
> Knowledge of the environmental and route conditions;
> Pack weight;
> Backcountry skill level;
> Daily itinerary; and
> Preferred type of fun. Type I Fun is

Encountering a giant Sitka spruce trunk during a 500-mile hike on Alaska's Lost Coast

why, when & where

fun to do and fun to talk about later. Type II Fun is not fun to do but fun to talk about later. And Type III Fun is not fun to do and not fun to talk about later either.

In practice, "hiking" and "camping" are umbrella terms, not literal, since most backpacking trips consist of more than just these two activities. Scrambling, paddling, pedaling, snowshoeing, and skiing are additional modes of backcountry travel. And fishing, journaling, and photography are among the more popular activities in or near camp.

In the first edition of this book, I referred to backpackers who take an all-or-nothing approach as "Ultimate Hikers" and "Ultimate Campers." These terms were meaningless hyperbole, but they were at least consistent with the book's title. They also changed the conversation away from "light versus heavy," which wrongly identifies backpackers by what they *carry* instead of by what they *hope to do,* among other semantic flaws.

My labels didn't entirely hit the mark, however, because they defined types of *backpackers,* whereas I was really trying to identify *backpacking styles.* After all, a backpacker need not approach every trip the same way, even though most will associate more strongly with one style. In this edition, I will refer to the extremes with the more humble "backcountry hiking" and "backcountry camping" to avoid any confusion with day-hiking and car-camping.

Backcountry hiking

Backpackers dedicated to hiking could be described as follows:

Their primary objective is essentially to put one foot in front of the other. But it's not just about covering miles—in that case, a treadmill in an indoor gym would suffice. Rather, they wish to experience as much terrain as possible within the limited free time they have and to challenge their mind and body in a wild setting.

They are very knowledgeable about the environmental and route conditions they will likely encounter during their trip, either through past experience or through pre-trip research. This allows them to take only what they need instead of packing their fears and taking things "just in case."

They scrutinize each item they carry to minimize their overall pack weight, which is typically in the range of ten pounds without food and water for normal three-season conditions. But they are wary of "stupid light" decisions, whereby weight savings entail an unacceptable sacrifice to their comfort or safety, or to the functionality, durability, ease of use, or cost of their equipment.

They have well-developed backcountry skills, which allows them to thrive, even with minimal gear and supplies, and to rely on their brain instead of just pure brawn. For example, they are able to use a lightweight A-frame tarp instead of a dome tent because they are adept at choosing protected campsites and achieving textbook-perfect pitches. And to avoid carrying too little or too much food, they determine exactly how much they need based on their caloric consumption on previous trips.

They make constant forward progress throughout the day toward a distant destination. The key is not walking fast but walking efficiently. These "dawn-to-duskers" leave camp early, move at a sustainable pace, and pull into camp late; after an eight-hour recharge, they repeat. They use their data book, which is a bare-bones list of key landmarks and distances, to monitor their pace the way runners observe their splits during a track workout.

And they mostly prefer Type II Fun, whereby events are often more fun to talk about later than at the time they are happening. The physical and mental challenge of putting in long, hard days is a valuable part of their backpacking experience.

Backcountry camping

The opposite of backcountry hiking is backcountry camping. Backpackers who adopt this style could be described as follows:

Their primary objective is a non-hiking extracurricular activity such as birding, botanizing, gourmet cooking, hunting, leadership development, or merit badges. If they wish to hike anywhere, they will usually drop their gear at a base camp and carry lightweight day packs.

They may be knowledgeable of the environmental and route conditions, but this knowledge is not critical. They can afford to pack more than they need to ensure preparedness against anything that may come their way.

The weight of their gear and supplies is not a huge consideration since they do not carry it far. However, they don't pack "stupid heavy" by taking unnecessary junk that does not improve their camping experience and that makes worse the limited hiking they do.

They may be skilled campers (or photographers or fishermen, etc.), but their other skills are unnecessary because they can carry gear and supplies that demand few skills to use properly. These foolproof items tend to be heavy.

Their daily itinerary is relatively relaxed. Although they sometimes jump out of camp in the morning to catch the hungriest fish or the earliest light, they ensure ample opportunities to simply hang out.

They prefer Type I Fun. Their trips are fun to do and fun to talk about later. For them, backpacking should be leisure, not a challenge.

Camping by default

When I ended the phone call with my parents, I had not yet decided whether I wanted to focus that summer on backcountry hiking, backcountry camping, or something in between. But my mother had given

Where do you want to be most comfortable: In camp or on the trail?

me sound advice: "Whatever you decide, make sure it's the right decision for you." It echoed a saying that I had heard several times already on the trail: "Hike your own hike."

As I walked toward Hiawassee's outskirts so that I could hitch back to the trail, I pondered how I would describe my current backpacking style. I was camping more than hiking, not necessarily because I wanted to but because it was much easier. Many of my (equally inexperienced) fellow Appalachian Trail thru-hikers were in a similar situation.

I decided that I was a camper-by-default:

My original objective was clear, but I was unaware that my gear, supplies, and skills should be optimized for it. In light of one's objectives, there is a "right" way to backpack, and I was most definitely doing it "wrong."

I had only a vague sense of the environmental and route conditions I would encounter along the trail. I did not know that temperatures in the Smokies could still drop below freezing in May, that New Jersey had a healthy population of black bears, or that in August the mosquitoes would still be thick in Maine. Without knowing the conditions, I couldn't determine exactly what I needed, so I packed for every "what if" and "just in case" scenario, most of them extremely far-fetched. I erred on the side of caution by taking "everything but the . . . ," which is a much better Ben & Jerry's ice cream flavor than an approach to packing.

My gear selections were horribly misinformed, and ultimately I would abandon or exchange almost every item before the end of the trip. I did not understand the functions and limitations of backpacking equipment. For example, I didn't understand the nuances of "waterproof," "water resistant," and "waterproof-breathable" fabrics. I was ignorant of the pros and cons of goose down and synthetic insulations. I could not explain what I was purifying and filtering my water against (even though I was doing it) or how effective these treatments were.

Because I had so little firsthand knowledge of gear, I had to trust outdoor magazines, outdoor retail stores, outdoor education groups like the Boy Scouts and Duke University's outdoor club, and other backpackers who had done only a few trips themselves. I was also left to decipher the technical specs and marketing jargon produced by outdoor manufacturers. It never occurred to me that this information was oriented mostly toward a camping-centric experience, and that backcountry hiking required a different setup.

My skill level was very low, so my comfort and safety were dependent on the gear I carried on my back, not on the weightless backcountry knowledge I could carry between my ears. Even with all that gear, I still suffered from the mistakes I made. I lost food to rodents, miscalculated my water intake and became dehydrated, struggled to manage macerated feet and sore muscles, allowed my gear to get soaked by rain in the Smokies, and shivered through consecutive nights in the Roan Highlands because I couldn't start a fire.

My daily itinerary was unfocused. I woke up late and camped early. I wasted too much time in trail towns. I hiked too fast in the morning and was burned out by the afternoon.

And my experience was dominated by Type III Fun—it wasn't fun to do,

and it's not really fun to talk about now, even more than a decade later. Only a masochist would enjoy as much suffering as I endured early in my AT thru-hike.

I was not ashamed of being a camper-by-default. None of my family members or close friends were experienced backpackers who could have imparted their wisdom. But I knew that this identity was not consistent with walking 83 marathons in a single summer. The numbers spoke for themselves: Of the roughly 2,000 thru-hikers who start the Appalachian Trail every year, an astounding 85 percent stop their trip somewhere short of Katahdin, the high point of Maine that serves as the trail's northern terminus. The field drops off precipitously: Some quit at the first road crossing, 30 miles in; many don't make it to Damascus, a friendly trail town in southwest Virginia; and some find sufficient closure in Harpers Ferry, West Virginia, the psychological halfway point.

Some of those who stop prematurely probably discover that they need a more civilized existence that includes daily showers, a soft bed, and daily contact with loves ones. Some realize that their true passion is with backcountry camping, so a long-distance hike is simply not for them. Finally, some remain overloaded campers-by-default, and the task is simply too monumental to continue on. The remaining 15 percent of aspiring AT thru-hikers somehow learn how to enjoy hiking.

why, when & where

why I'm a hiker

A backpacking trip exclusively focused on hiking is not for everyone. But as a lifelong runner and endurance athlete, it suits me very well, and I'm unapologetic about my chosen style. My specific motivations relate to the most important things in my life—relationships with nature, with others, and with myself.

Relationship with nature

Many assume that by hiking 30-plus miles a day, I must be going "too fast" to see anything. In fact, just the opposite is true. By walking at a sustainable three miles an hour from dawn to dusk, and by carrying a featherweight pack, I can penetrate enormous swaths of wilderness, days away from the closest towns, roads, and trailheads. I've had the fortune of being in hundreds of pinch-me locations, like the north side of Denali National Park, the summit of Wind River Peak, the lower canyons of the Escalante River, and Enchanted Gorge in Kings Canyon National Park.

Perhaps more important, hiking has sparked a curiosity within me about nature. Thru-hiking the Colorado Trail piqued my interest in the mountain pine beetle, wildfire suppression, and the relationship between urban and wild spaces.

Walking along the Colorado River Aqueduct through Southern California prompted me to learn about the West's delicate water resources and infrastructure. Traveling off trail in Alaska and Yukon taught me about wildlife travel patterns. And I can't hike through any glaciated terrain without looking for moraines, ancient terminal lakes, and chatter marks.

Relationship with others

Members of a group who share a challenging objective and who depend heavily on one another for success and survival will bond more quickly and more tightly than those who don't. On challenging group trips—like the Sierra High Route with Buzz Burrell, the Alaska Mountain Wilderness Classic with Bobby and Chris, and multiple guided trips when we got in deep—I've felt a strong

Amanda on the Aspen Four Pass Loop

sense of camaraderie and partnership with those in my group. If we were neighbors or coworkers, or if we only did an easy trip together, that outcome would be less likely.

On a multiday trip, routines like work, housekeeping, and TV watching don't get between people. When I was writing the first edition of this book, several weekend trips with my then girlfriend, now wife, Amanda, helped to save our relationship, which was being overwhelmed by the manuscript. Sharing a steaming pot of tortellini and dehydrated cream sauce before retiring to a floorless tarp was not terribly romantic, but it was a refreshing break from the demands that were preoccupying me.

Relationship with oneself

This relationship is a prerequisite for the others. If I'm truer to myself, I'm in a better position to give. My trips give me reasons to wake up in the morning. I have maps to study, food to pack, passes to climb, wildlife to watch. I have a goal that demands my full focus and energy. My mind and body seem to work in a heightened state—a natural caffeine-like high.

Ambitious itineraries give me a chance to explore my mental and physical limits. Can I walk from Georgia to Maine? Do I have the fitness to average 33 miles a day for seven months? Can I ski, hike, and pack-raft 4,700 miles around Alaska and the Yukon without making a fatal mistake? I didn't know until I tried.

During these monumental efforts my "game face" is usually broken. One prime example occurred in the Canadian Arctic during a 657-mile, 24-day stretch without crossing a road or seeing another human. After finding the migration trail of the Porcupine caribou, I began to cry uncontrollably, realizing that in this vast and untamed wilderness, I was like them: While being tortured by hellacious mosquitoes, soaked by torrential rains, and stalked by grizzlies and wolves, we were all trying to stay moving, and we slept and ate only to continue our constant forward progress.

The skills I have learned out there, like good decision-making and resourcefulness, also serve me well in the Land of the Soft. But the most important takeaway has been a deep sense of humility—recognition that natural powers are at work that I will never control or fully understand, and that will prevail long after I am gone.

tried&true

how to hike "fast"

"Fast" hikers can average up to about 40 miles per day for the length of a long-distance trail. Each of their days can be reduced to the equation *Distance = Rate x Time,* where *Distance = Miles per Day* (MPD), *Rate = Miles per Hour* (MPH), and *Time = Hours per Day* (HPD). To become a fast hiker (i.e., more MPD), then, you must hike quicker or hike more.

Increase your MPH

To increase my walking speed, I can:

Work harder. At my *optimal* hiking speed, I am hiking as fast as I can without overexerting myself. This effort is physically sustainable every day, for a trip of infinite length. If I'm below this pace, I can work harder to reach it. But if I'm already at it, hiking even faster is only possible in the short term. Continued overexertion will lead to injury or chronic fatigue, or it will simply exceed my tolerance for Type III Fun.

Lighten up. I hike faster when I carry less, especially in mountainous terrain. So I keep my backpack as light as I practically can, and I try to remain physically lean, since extra body mass is just as much of a drag as unnecessary pack weight.

Increase your HPD

The real secret of hiking "fast" is simply hiking more. I'm a tortoise, not a hare; my motto is "constant forward progress" (CFP). There are four ways to increase my HPD:

Focus on pre-trip training. I prepare my muscles, tendons, feet, lungs, and heart for day-long physical activity. If I'm fresh off the couch or just out the office door, I'm instead forced to get in shape "on the trail" by starting slowly and building up.

Improve efficiency. I try to leave camp within 15 minutes of waking up. I keep oft-needed items within easy reach so that I don't have to take off my backpack. I've been known to pee while walking. I ship myself food and supplies to avoid time-consuming shopping in towns. And I try to avoid taking days off in towns by limiting my stays to 24 hours, and usually less than four.

Seize the morning. If I rise early and hike "12 by 10" or even "20 by 1"—as in 20 miles by 1 p.m.—then I have more flexibility in the afternoon. With most of my work already done for the day, I can relax, or I can keep pushing and get ahead of schedule. Whereas if I dillydally, I must spend the rest of the day playing catch-up.

Expect a challenge. A "fast" hike is rewarding and satisfying, but it's not a vacation. It can be very taxing mentally and exhausting physically. I embrace these additional difficulties as an integral part of my trip, on a par with wildlife encounters and scenic vistas.

why, when & where

tip To get an extra oomph in your stride, use trekking poles. They allow your arms to help propel you forward and upward during climbs, and to brake on descents.

know before you go

A six-week hike on the Pacific Crest Trail (PCT), starting at the U.S.–Mexico border on June 6, sounded hot to me. But I had spent very little time in Southern California and didn't know exactly how hot, so I didn't know how best to prepare. What clothing and sleeping bag should I use? How much water capacity should I have? Would the daytime heat force me to become nocturnal?

Not knowing where to look for temperature information, I sent questions to the PCT-List, an email forum: "What will be the average high and low temperatures, at the lowest and highest elevations? What about extreme temperatures?" And so on. Ten minutes later, I received a response: "Temperatures, with mean and standard deviation for both highs and lows, can be obtained from a number of stations right along the trail from the Western Regional Climate Center at *www.wrcc .dri.edu.*" (The WRCC has since been merged into the National Centers for Environmental Information.)

This was not the specific information for which I'd hoped. But in retrospect, this unspecific reply was much more valuable because it forced me to find the data on my own. And that quick lesson in self-reliance has served me well ever since.

Before venturing into an unfamiliar territory or season, I research the conditions so that I can make informed choices that will maximize my comfort and safety. It is obvious in theory that I should prepare differently for a trip in October in New York's Adirondacks than for one in April in southern Utah, for example. But by doing some pre-trip homework, I can identify exactly how my needs are different, so that I avoid being over-, under-, or mis-prepared.

I consult climate databases, topographical maps, satellite images, public land agency websites, print and online guidebooks, geotagged photo galleries, and forums and trip reports. I also reach out to knowledgeable backcountry users like park rangers, outfitters, bush pilots, and veteran backpackers who can share insights that are not publicly available. In a phone call or email, they might tell me about an unmapped spring, a fast game trail, a strong tidal current, or the feasibility of a dicey-looking pass; they

Renowned Alaskan wilderness hiker Roman Dial summits Aerial Peak.

can also confirm or add nuance to my initial research.

Below I've explained how to find information about the environmental and route conditions that affect my gear choices. Refer to Part 3 (pp. 216–233) for a selection of sample gear lists that demonstrate geographic and seasonal differences.

Temperatures

I begin planning my trips weeks or months ahead of time, long before an accurate weather forecast is available. In lieu of one, I base my decisions on historical temperature data collected at weather stations near my route.

For a short trip, I may refine my selections at the last minute based on the five- or seven-day forecast if it strongly suggests a non-average weather pattern. For longer trips, I expect a greater range of temperatures but a normal overall average.

In the United States, the most extensive archive of temperature data is hosted by the National Centers for Environmental Information (NCEI), a branch of the National Oceanic and Atmospheric Administration (NOAA). Data can be viewed or downloaded from the NCEI's website; consumer-oriented weather websites like Weather Underground may present a subset of the data, too.

why, when & where

Before a multimonth trip, I compile into a single document my notes about resupply towns, seasonal water sources, and other useful tidbits.

Elevation dramatically impacts temperatures (as well as other environmental factors like precipitation, cloudiness, and vegetation), and it must be considered when analyzing temperature data. As a rule of thumb, expect the temperature to change three to five degrees Fahrenheit per 1,000 vertical feet of change (six to ten degrees Celsius per 1,000 vertical meters). In high humidity, the change will be on the low end of this range; in low humidity, the high end of the range.

For example, suppose I was planning a one-week trip to Grand Canyon National Park in May. Weather Underground shows historical average low and high temperatures of about 30°F and 70°F. However, these observations were reported at the Grand Canyon Airport, which is on the South Rim at an elevation of about 6,500 feet; most of my route is planned along the Tonto Platform at about 4,000 feet. After factoring in elevation, I would expect average lows in the low 40s and average highs in the low 80s, or about 12.5 degrees warmer (assuming low humidity) than at the airport.

Precipitation

My clothing and shelter, the types of materials I use (e.g., polyester or wool base layers, goose down or synthetic insulation), and water availability will all be affected by the amount and frequency of precipitation I can expect during a trip.

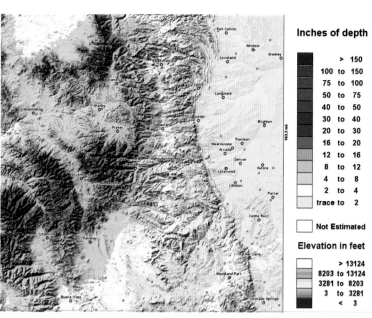

Inches of depth

	>	150
100	to	150
75	to	100
50	to	75
40	to	50
30	to	40
20	to	30
16	to	20
12	to	16
8	to	12
4	to	8
2	to	4
trace	to	2

Not Estimated

Elevation in feet

	>	13124
8203	to	13124
3281	to	8203
3	to	3281
	<	3

Colorado's current snowpack, via the National Snow Analyses' interactive map

If I expect it to be 35 degrees and raining, I pack more layers of clothing, a more protective shelter, and more fire-starting supplies.

Precipitation data is usually available alongside temperature data. At the NCEI website, I see that average precipitation in May at the Grand Canyon Airport is only 0.6 inch; the weather station at the bottom of the canyon at Phantom Ranch (elevation 2,500 feet) reports a mere 0.3 inch. In other words, it's unlikely that I'll see much (if any) rain during my trip.

If instead of a one-week trip in the Grand Canyon I was planning to thru-hike the Arizona Trail—which runs north–south across the entire state—it would be useful to find a color-coded precipitation map of Arizona. One is available through the U.S. Climate Atlas, also available at the NCEI website.

Daylight

On summer trips, there is enough daylight for about 15 hours of hiking per day, which I've found to be my sustainable limit. If I'm not hiking at night, I need only a low-powered headlamp for camp chores. And I can depend on my accelerated metabolism to keep me warm, instead of on warm clothing and a sleeping bag. In contrast, winter trips call for a high-powered light for hiking after dark, as well as warmer equipment.

Complete sun and moon data for U.S. cities and worldwide waypoints is available from the United States Naval Observatory website.

why, when & where

Ground cover

I choose different footwear for the East's leaf-covered trails than for the Southwest's soilless rocky ground. My mileage goals are less ambitious if I expect to be stumbling over Arctic tussocks, climbing over fallen ancient redwood trees, or slipping on eastern Montana's gumbo mud. If trail quality, signage, and maintenance are poor, I bring better navigational aids and more protective clothing. And I may need skis, snowshoes, or crampons for flotation or traction on Colorado's winter snowpack or for lingering snowfields on the John Muir Trail.

Quantitative information on top-soil composition is not very useful, and I've also never found a comprehensive resource for it anyway. Instead, I look at pictures and read descriptions of my planned route. Pictures of the Hoh River Trail in Olympic National Park, for example, show a well-established footpath through a temperate rain forest, the floor of which is topped with abundant and soft forest duff. Online trip reports from the Sierra High Route mention extensive alpine tundra and granite slabs and talus.

The most comprehensive data about snow coverage is available through the National Snow Analyses, a program operated by NOAA's National Weather Service. In the West, additional data is available through the Natural Resources Con-servation Service, a program of the Department of Agriculture, which maintains 600-plus SNOTEL (short for "snow telemetry") sensors that collect temperature, precipitation,

snow depth, and other data. Most of the sensors are in remote mountain watersheds, including many prime backpacking locales; real-time and historical data is available. In addi-tion to the SNOTEL sites, California's Department of Water Resources con-ducts its own snow surveys; current and historical data and data plots are available on its website.

On the National Snow Analyses website, the interactive maps feature is especially useful. Recently, for instance, I was able to discourage a friend from taking out-of-town guests to Rocky Mountain National Park for a late-spring backpacking trip. The maps clearly showed that all the backcountry campsites were still snowbound. Historical data revealed that these conditions were not exceptional.

Vegetation

For information about vegetation density and types, I look at my topo-graphical maps (which often depict vegetation with green shading), analyze satellite imagery, and find pictures and descriptions posted online. It also helps to have a basic under-standing of what types of vegetation are commonly found in an area. For example, when I was planning my first trip to Alaska, I read reports by Alaska Mountain Wilderness Classic racers who had done the Hope-to-Homer and Eureka-to-Talkeetna routes. I scanned Landsat images of the Kenai Peninsula to find walkable beaches and the "brush zone,"

When traveling at high elevations and/or on reflective surfaces, sun protection is critical.

a quagmire that separates forest from alpine. And I called Bretwood Higman and Erin McKittrick, who had done a route between Homer and Seward that was similar to the one I was planning.

Sun exposure

During my first trip along the Continental Divide through Colorado, I got scorched. My route was mostly above 11,000 feet and entirely in alpine terrain; it was a sunny weekend in June, and lingering snowfields reflected the sun so well that even the backs of my thighs badly burned. I wisely wore sunglasses and stayed well hydrated, but I should have worn more clothing and sunscreen.

The amount of sun exposure is a function of cloud cover, vegetation, elevation, surface reflectivity, and the strength of the sun (which depends on the time of day and year). These details can be obtained from topographical maps and other aforementioned resources. Some cloud cover data is also available through the U.S. Climate Atlas. National maps show that the "mean percentage of possible sunshine" in January is a gloomy 30 to 40 percent in the Great Lakes states, compared with 70 to 80 percent in sunny southern California.

why, when & where

25

Water availability

Springs and creeks are marked on topographical maps. In the East, water sources are generally reliable, except during exceptional droughts. In the West, however, many water sources dry up during the arid summer months. Before relying on a water source marked on a map, consult someone who has personal familiarity with the landscape, and check guidebooks and online trip reports for past observations.

"Water reports" are available for several long-distance trails, including the southern sections of the Pacific Crest Trail (PCT) and Continental Divide Trail, plus the entire Arizona Trail and Hayduke Trail. In the case of the PCT, the water chart is updated several times a week during peak thru-hiker season by a volunteer who collects observations via email, text, and online posts.

Wildlife & insects

The possible presence of audacious or dangerous animals—like mice, raccoons, bears, and snakes—affects how and whether I protect my food, where I cook and camp, where and when I walk, and whether I carry anything for personal defense. If not somehow mitigated, relentless swarms of mosquitoes, blackflies, and no-see-ums (or gnats) can completely ruin a trip. Bites from poisonous spiders, scorpions, fire ants, and disease-carrying bugs and ticks can have longer-lasting and more serious consequences.

If wildlife or insects are a concern, land managers usually post relevant

Porcupines and other "mini bears," such as mice and squirrels, will eat gear and food that is left unattended in high-use campsites.

part 1

nformation on their websites. The National Park Service, for example, has posted food storage regulations for Yosemite National Park to help minimize bear conflicts. The Bureau of Land Management warns about rattlesnakes in Grand Staircase-Escalante National Monument. And the U.S. Forest Service reports that the blackfly season in New Hampshire's White Mountains is between late spring and early summer. For more, or more nuanced explanation, I might call land managers or find other online resources like blogs and community forums.

With particular regard to insects, I've learned there are no hard rules. An unusually cold spring may delay the first hatch, for example. I've also encountered hellacious bugs where other backpackers did not (and vice versa) because I was apparently there at the worst time of the worst day of the worst year.

Remoteness

If something unexpected happens or if something goes wrong—like if I get caught in a freak spring snowstorm, come down with awful diarrhea, or have a group member become immobilized after hyperextending a knee—I may need to self-rescue, await an assisted rescue, and/or apply extended medical treatment. Before I leave the trailhead, I should know what types of communication devices have reliable coverage, how likely it is that I will be found by another backcountry user, how long it would

take for a search and rescue team to be mobilized, and how far it is to the closest road or town.

To gauge the remoteness of my route, I look at topographical maps and the coverage maps of mobile phone and satellite companies. I speak with land managers, recreation businesses, county law enforcement agencies, and/or other backpackers.

Natural hazards

The outdoors is not as dangerous as typically portrayed by sensationalist media stoking fear of the unknown. Nonetheless, people do get sick and injured out there, sometimes fatally. Natural hazards include unpredictable mountain weather, technical rock faces, crevasses, contaminated backcountry water sources, large bodies of water, and avalanches.

Avalanches occur mostly in the West, where the snowpack and terrain are more conducive to them, and mostly between the months of November and April. Several Northeast peaks—notably New Hampshire's Mount Washington—have avalanche-prone terrain, but it's generally a smaller concern there. A list of public and private avalanche monitoring agencies is available at *www .avalanche.org.* Every western state, except for Nevada and New Mexico, is served by at least one avalanche center that produces daily or weekly bulletins discussing current conditions and speculating about future ones; there is also an agency for New Hampshire's Mount Washington.

part ② tools &

echniques

30 CLOTHING

66 FOOTWEAR

84 SLEEPING BAGS & PADS

96 SHELTERS

122 NAVIGATION

134 TREKKING POLES

140 FOOD

158 COOKING SYSTEMS

172 WATER

184 SMALL ESSENTIALS

200 BACKPACKS

On my earliest trips, my gear was not optimized for my objectives or the conditions, and my backpacking skills were undeveloped. But through extensive trial and error, as well as research, I began to understand the underlying technologies, pros and cons, and limitations of my gear, plus associated skills like how to find five-star campsites and use a compass.

In this section I share my experiences and observations, and I recommend products that meet my standards for performance, weight, durability, value, and other key characteristics. But keep this in context: Gear and skills are merely a means to 1) achieving your trip objectives and 2) remaining safe and comfortable in the conditions you are likely to encounter.

Northern lights glow over a North American boreal forest.

clothing

I did not grow up in a backpacking family, and I never received any formal backpacking instruction. Instead, I learned to backpack the hard way: by making mistakes. Fortunately, you can learn from them. My list of clothing-related mistakes is especially long. Here are some highlights.

During a cold and wet storm in the Smokies, I became nearly hypothermic when my "water-resistant" rain gear—without sealed seams or a water-proof coating or membrane—failed catastrophically.

I got smarter, but future storms revealed other holes in my system. A two-day October rainstorm in Colorado's San Juan Mountains—for which I did not have appropriate handwear—left me with trench hands, after which my fingertips tingled for four weeks. And a ferocious gale on Alaska's Lost Coast highlighted the need for a mid-layer between my hiking shirt and rain shell. My synthetic-insulated jacket proved not to be "warm when wet," and I was left without a dry and warm layer for camp.

Blisters developed on every patch of skin—even my thighs—left exposed by my T-shirt and running shorts during a day-long stroll atop Colorado's snowbound Continental Divide at 11,000 feet. Several years later I got equally crisped while on the Pacific Crest Trail in Southern California in June, wearing a similar outfit.

Finally, mosquitoes tormented Buzz Burrell and me while thru-hiking the Sierra High Route. We were completely unprepared for them, lacking nylon pants, bug-proof shirts, or head nets. At least we had DEET.

Importance

Because I enjoy hiking sunrise to sun-down, my comfort is more dependent on my clothing than on any other product category. When conditions deteriorate, I don't want to be forced into my shelter. I need my clothing to help keep me cool when it's hot, warm when it's cold and windy, dry when it's wet, and sane when the bugs are insane; it also has to protect me against a scorching sun and abrasive brush.

My clothing is also a critical part of my sleeping system. By wearing my insulated clothing at night, I can use a lighter sleeping bag. And by carrying dedicated sleeping clothes in wet climates, I avoid ever having to sleep in soaking wet clothing.

Layering

All-day and all-night comfort is rarely possible with a single outfit. Instead, I need a clothing system composed of specialized items that can be easily adjusted and mixed and matched with changes in environmental conditions and my level of exertion. If I've assembled my clothing system perfectly, it will keep me relatively comfortable throughout the full range of conditions for which it was designed, without extraneous weight or items.

I think of my clothing system as having four distinct layers:

> Go Suit, for moisture management, skin protection (from sun, brush, and bugs), and modesty;
> Storm, for defense against wind and precipitation;
> Stop, for warmth when not on the go; and
> Sleep, for a comfortable night of recovery.

This categorization is not conventional. Normally, layers would correspond to *types* of clothing (e.g., base layer, mid-layer, wind layer, insulation layer, and shell layer). But I find this approach overly prescriptive, misleading for many sets of conditions, and lacking functional instruction; it also fails to represent an entire clothing system.

Core 13 clothing

Aside from this book, the body of writing I am most proud of is a ten-post series on my website in which I detailed 13 specific items of clothing that can be mixed and matched to create appropriate systems for every set of three-season conditions. This collection—"the Core 13"—will serve as the framework for most of this chapter;

Your clothing system should reflect the environmental and route conditions you will likely encounter during your trip. Here: cool temps, no shade, and lingering snowfields.

vapor-barrier liners, headwear, hand-wear, and eyewear are treated independently, as they are beyond the scope of the original series.

Only on a long-distance trip through multiple ecosystems could I imagine needing the entire Core 13 (but even then, I would probably exchange clothes through mail drops as needed, rather than carrying them all at once) or ever needing more than one of each Core 13 item. For a narrower range of conditions, fewer will be relevant. For instance, six are needed when hiking in August in the Colorado Rockies or on the Appalachian Trail.

If your clothing system extends beyond the Core 13, there are two explanations. First, the item could be unnecessary—either it's not warranted by the conditions or it's redundant with a Core 13 piece. Or, second, it's a niche product (e.g., a windshirt or rain kilt) that performs well in a particular set of conditions, but poorly beyond them.

Items 1 & 2: Hiking shirts

In warm temperatures with low sun exposure, I wear a short-sleeve hiking shirt. And in cooler temperatures, or when my arms need protection from scratchy brush and relentless sun, I wear a long-sleeve one. Other than sleeve length, the shirts can have identical specs.

The primary purpose of a hiking shirt is to manage moisture. First, it should wick moisture away from the skin. In warm conditions, this results in evaporative heat loss; in cool conditions, this minimizes conductive heat loss. Second, it should disperse this

A Sample Layering System: The Rockies in Summer

component	item & description	weight (oz)
go suit	**Long-sleeve shirt:** lightweight poly or merino, or blend, with chest zip	7
	Running shorts: 4- to 6-inch inseam	5
storm	**Fleece top:** 100-weight, pullover	10
	Rain jacket & rain pants: waterproof/breathable fabric	18
stop	**Parka:** hooded, 800-fill goose down	12
sleep	**Sleeping clothes:** unnecessary	0
other	**Sun hat, sunglasses, Buff, rain mitts**	8
TOTAL		**3 lb 12 oz**

part 2

What about "extra" clothes?

I never carry a redundant item of clothing: just one hiking shirt, one insulated jacket, one pair of underwear, etc. I keep these items clean through regular washing and I try to keep them dry by using shell garments. (When I can't keep them dry, I fall back on my sleeping top and bottoms, both part of the Core 13.) I try to wash my Go Suit every day. Water can remove most dirt and sweat; I only use soap in town.

Don't bring them.

moisture (i.e., increase the surface area of sweat-soaked fabric) so that it can evaporate more quickly into the atmosphere. Third, it should encourage airflow to expedite evaporation and increase convective cooling.

My hiking shirts could be described as "base layers," but that implies stylistically boring underwear, rather than sharp-looking attire. That said, I wear additional layers from my "Stop" and "Storm" categories over my hiking shirts, and my "Sleep" layers replace them when wet for improved nighttime comfort.

Fibers

Hiking shirts—and other layers in my Go Suit—should be made primarily of polyester, merino wool, or nylon. Cotton absorbs and retains a significant amount of water, hence the old adage, "Cotton kills." It's acceptable only in extreme dry heat, when prolonged heat loss is desirable. Silk and polypropylene, which were once common, are now seldom used.

Fibers can be mixed. Nylon can be added for durability; cotton for

hand, breathability, and odor resistance; and spandex for stretch and fit, though I try to avoid this fiber: It adds weight, increases water retention and dry time, and loses its elasticity with use.

Polyester is an oil-based polymer used to make plastic bottles, canoes, LCD displays, and tire reinforcements. It's also the most popular fiber for hiking shirts. Well-known polyester fabrics include Invista's Coolmax, Polartec's Power Dry, Patagonia's Capilene, and Under Armour's HeatGear. I have found that the performance of a polyester hiking shirt—and, for that matter, wool and nylon, too—depends primarily on the fabric's weight, weave, and blend, plus the garment's fit and styling. The specific manufacturer is mostly irrelevant.

Polyester has several qualities that make it an excellent hiking shirt fiber:

> It will absorb just 0.4 percent of its weight in water. (Moisture will, however, become trapped *between* the

fibers.) Thus, polyester wicks well and dries very quickly.

> It can be woven into silk-like weights, which are perfect when barely-there skin protection is needed, like against a scorching sun.

> It is relatively inexpensive. The basic REI Tech T-shirt is just $20, and discounted overstock is always available.

Of course, polyester is not perfect. First, it reeks after a mere 30-minute run, never mind a multiday outing. The stench can be reduced with anti-funk treatments, but only partially. Second, it is clammy and chilly when wet because moisture remains on the fiber surfaces, where it can make direct contact with the skin.

Merino wool is the main alternative to polyester. It was popularized as an outdoor fiber by SmartWool in the 1990s and is now also available from Ibex, Icebreaker, Patagonia, and others. Merino wool is a classification of sheep wool based on its diameter; the wool used in most hiking shirts is 17 to 19 microns. (A micron is one-millionth of a meter. The average human hair is about 100 microns.) Unlike the coarse wool used to make carpets and inexpensive sweaters (25+ microns) merino wool is soft and not itchy.

Merino wool excels where polyester does not:

> It is naturally antimicrobial and therefore more odor-resistant. To be

	polyester	merino wool
source	Oil	Sheep
common use	Athletic apparel, base layers, underwear	Base layers, underwear, fine sweaters
blends	Spandex for stretch & fit. Merino for odor resistance.	Spandex. Polyester for cost-savings & improved moisture management.
moisture management performance	Awesome. Fibers do not absorb water. Wicks well & dries fast.	Okay. Fibers absorb much more water than poly, but feels less clammy. Very breathable.
odor resistance	Usually awful. If treated, still bad.	Good. No offensive odor of its own. Like wet dog when wet.
cold-and-wet performance	Notable chilling effect	Not "warm when wet," but warmer than other fibers
cost	Low to moderate	High
durability	Good	Okay

part (2)

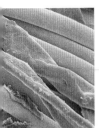

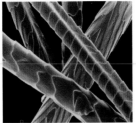

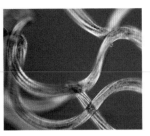

Polyester　　　　　**Merino wool**　　　　　**Nylon**

clear, after a few weeks without a shower I will still have noticeable body odor. But at least merino layers don't have an offensive odor of their own.

> When wet, it feels less clammy and less chilling. This is due to the fiber's construction: The cortex (inner core) absorbs about one-third of its weight in water, but the cuticle (outer sheath) is hydrophobic. So

when merino wool gets wet, the cortex absorbs the moisture (until it is saturated), and the cuticle feels relatively dry against the skin.

And merino fails where polyester thrives:

> It is more expensive, with a simple T-shirt starting at $65.
> It cannot be woven into silk-like weights well suited for warm climates without major sacrifices to durability. As it is, the lightest merino fabrics (which are 50 percent heavier than the lightest polyesters) will develop holes much sooner in high-abrasion and high-stress areas.

Nylon, like polyester, is an oil-based polymer. It absorbs slightly more water, but it is more durable and abrasion-resistant. The nylon fabrics used in outdoor clothing are often tightly woven, which improves bug and wind resistance but also makes the fabrics stuffy because of poor breathability. Supposedly, the tight weave also improves sun protection, but the benefit seems negligible—even a meshy polyester top will be rated to SPF 15, which means that

nylon

Oil
Outdoor pants, travel shirts, sleeping bags, & tents
Spandex. Merino. Cotton for softness & breathability.
Does not wick or dry as well as poly, but better than merino. Wovens are often hot & stuffy.
Not as bad as poly
Similar to polyester
Low to moderate
Best

it blocks more than 90 percent of the sun's UVB rays.

Fabric weights

Polyester and merino wool fabrics are available in various thicknesses. Manufacturers may describe them with adjectives like "lightweight" and "mid-weight." But for an apples-to-apples comparison across manufacturers and fiber types, it's necessary to know the exact fabric weight per square area. For example, Capilene Light-weight weighs 2.3 ounces per square yard (80 g per square meter).

Heavier fabrics provide more insulation than lighter ones, assuming the same construction. But they also retain more water: In heavier fabrics, there are more fibers to absorb moisture and more spaces between fibers where moisture can be trapped. From a comfort per-spective, this increased moisture retention is partially offset because more water can "hide" in a heavier fabric, so it's not in direct contact with the skin.

Fit & features

Hiking shirts optimized for warm weather should be loose fitting and should ventilate well to encourage the exchange of cooler outside air with warmer interior air. Look for chest zips or a button front, and

how 2

choose a hiking shirt weight

1 Determine the warmest conditions that will be encountered during the trip.

2 Consider the amount of body heat produced during maximum exertion (e.g., running versus hiking versus fishing).

3 Choose the fabric weight that will be most comfortable when you are simultaneously at maximum exertion and in the warmest conditions. If you select a layer that is too heavy, you will overheat and need to either slow down or strip down to bare skin. If you select a layer that is too light, then you will always need a secondary layer to stay warm enough. It'd be simpler to have just one layer.

a wide neck. If sun exposure is a concern, get a collared shirt.

tip By wearing my insulated layers at night, I can take a lighter sleeping bag. An added perk: I don't have to change into cold clothes in the morning.

part 2

For cooler temperatures, I prefer a semi-fitted shirt that is less drafty and that fits better under outer layers. Ventilating features are still a must, as is a longer-than-normal torso length so that my lower back is not exposed to chilly air when I bend over.

skurka'spicks
HIKING SHIRTS

For trips in the sunny Mountain West, my go-to shirt is the **Sierra Designs Long-Sleeve Pack Polo** ($80, 7 oz), which I've worn for several consecutive summers now. It has superb airflow and fast dry times; it also looks good and smells okay for a polyester top. Air permeability is almost too good, though, and on a cooler weather trip (temperatures often below 50 degrees) less drafty shirts like the **Stoic Alpine Merino Bliss Shirt** ($60, 6 oz) or **Ibex W2 Sport Zip** ($110,

8 oz) would be more appropriate. In the winter, I use the mid-weight **Ibex Hooded Indie** ($120, 9 oz).

In environments that are warm, humid, and shady like the Appalachians, I am more apt to go with a lightweight short-sleeve shirt. I struggle to bear pure polyester in this climate—smelly bacteria does not need any help to grow. But a pure wool shirt is not an ideal solution either because of its warmth and moisture retention. The happy medium is a wool/polyester blend: It smells better than pure poly and manages moisture better than pure wool. Additionally, it is more durable and less expensive. As an example, consider the **Patagonia Daily Merino Polo** ($70, 6 oz).

If these options seem expensive, do not despair. Use these referenced products as a guide to find something similar but less expensive.

For sunny and cooler trips, I wear a relaxed-fit long-sleeve top with a chest zip and collar.

Item 3: Bug shirt

In moderate or heavy bug pressure, the airy hiking shirts detailed in the previous section are unbearable: Mosquitoes, blackflies, and other flying insects will bite through the porous knit fabrics where it is flush against the skin. It can also be dangerous: Disease-carrying ticks will crawl unchecked on these garments.

The solution is to instead wear a bug shirt, which can offer two types of defense:

> Body armor, using a bite-proof fabric made of tightly woven polyester or nylon. These fabrics offer reliable long-term protection against biting insects, but not against ticks.
> Chemistry, using a permethrin-based treatment that repels all insects, including ticks. At-home treatments are available, but the performance of factory-treated fabrics will last longer.

The body armor approach has worked well for me in Alaska and Canada's Yukon, where it's half-joked that the mosquito is the state bird. But it's less appropriate for other locations. First, it does not offer a complete solution in tick-infested areas. Second, the tightly woven fabrics have low airflow, and thus tend to be hot and stuffy. To address this, porous mesh vents can be added under the arms and along the back. But the improvement is marginal and negated by the use of a fabric through which bugs can bite.

Permethrin-treated garments, in contrast, can have airflow and dry times identical to untreated knit hiking shirts and are, therefore, better suited for high-exertion hiking and for warm or muggy climates. I cannot yet attest to the long-term performance of factory-treated fabric, but supposedly it's effective for "the expected lifetime of the product." During a buggy one-week trip in Alaska, clients with new treated garments seemed to have a force field around them.

skurka'spicks
BUG SHIRTS

For the sake of comfort, I would rather my bug shirt be made of permethrin-treated fabric, not body armor. Treated garments are available from ExOfficio, Columbia, RailRiders, and a few others. The treatment is the same but may be branded as Insect Shield, Bugs-Away, or Insect Blocker.

Another option is to send an untreated shirt (or other clothing) directly to Insect Shield, who will treat it for $10. This greatly expands your choice of shirts. You could have your favorite hiking shirt treated, or a new one that you like more than the pretreated models. In addition to the desirable qualities of hiking shirts discussed above, your bug shirt should have long sleeves, a high collar, and the ability to lock off potential entry points like sleeve cuffs and the neck. If these features coincide with what you demand of a hiking shirt, you can eliminate one item from the Core 13, leaving you with 12 pieces that can be mixed and matched for the full range of three-season conditions.

As a last-minute solution, use a spray-on or wash-in treatment. These are more economical in the short run, but the effectiveness is shorter-lived. ▥

Item 4: Running shorts

So long as I'm not bushwhacking, being pestered by biting insects, or needing to protect my legs from intense sun or cold temperatures, I wear shorts. Specifically, I wear lined running shorts, which offer superior freedom of movement, ventilation, and moisture management.

As a lifelong runner, I cannot stand conventional hiking shorts and convertible pants/shorts, which are made of woven nylon. They are heavy, hot, and constrictive; they are slow to dry; and they are usually too loose in the waist, since the nonelasticized waistband cannot make up for intra-trip fabric stretch or weight loss.

Fabric & features

Running shorts have an integrated liner, eliminating the need for underwear. The liner should be made of silk-weight polyester with a small spandex component (about 10 percent) for improved stretch and fit. The shell should be made of silk-weight polyester, perhaps with some nylon for additional durability.

I've never seen high-end running shorts without a liner, designed instead to be used with standalone underwear. But this would be welcome: It would give me a choice of underwear, and it would speed up dry times. For backpacking, I like an inseam of four to six inches; for context, my pant length is 32 or 34. Shorter shorts have the best range of motion and ventilation, but longer shorts are more modest and less chilly in cooler temperatures.

skurka'spicks
RUNNING SHORTS

Every runner has a favorite pair of shorts, but there is no consensus choice. When I'm shopping for a new pair, I visit a specialty running store with a good selection, like San Francisco Running Company, or buy multiple pairs online and keep the one or two that fit best.

The shorts I currently use for backpacking were on closeout at Marshall's a few years ago. I would have preferred a shorter inseam and a brief liner (rather than a boxer-brief liner, which is warmer and absorbs more moisture), but, most important, they don't chafe me or constrict my stride. For my daily runs I use the R-Gear Your Long Run 3-inch short ($40, 3 oz), but most will find them too skimpy. ▥

Items 5 & 6: Pants & underwear

In temperatures too cool for running shorts (less than about 50 degrees), I wear hiking pants and underwear.

Probably more often, however, I wear pants only to protect my legs from brush, sun, and bugs. In these instances, the additional warmth of pants is actually a liability.

Pants

The intended application will dictate the optimal fabric weight, fiber, and treatments. For cooler temperatures and extensive bushwhacking, a heavier stretch woven nylon fabric is preferred. But if the pants are merely for sun, bugs, and mild brush, a lighter and more loosely woven polyester or nylon—perhaps even with mesh vents—would be more comfortable. A permethrin treatment is a must for lighter, loosely woven fabrics during peak bug seasons; otherwise, bugs will bite through where the fabric is flush against the skin.

Pant fabrics with a small spandex content will offer better stretch and fit, but they will be heavier, absorb more water, dry more slowly, and fit worse over time as the spandex loses its elasticity. Pants treated with DWR (durable water repellent) will shed some precipitation when new, but the treatment will quickly degrade due to abrasion, dirt, and body oils. In fact, after a few weeks of use there is no difference between pants with or without a DWR treatment.

Underwear

Personally, I prefer boxer briefs made of lightweight polyester or nylon with a small spandex component. Merino wool underwear would be more odor-resistant, but I prefer synthetics because of their lighter weight and

superior moisture management. I regularly hand wash my underwear (no soap), which helps to keep odors at bay.

To reduce redundancy in the Core 13, I have tried to use tight shorts or compression shorts instead of running shorts (Item 4) and underwear (Item 6). But the optimal fabric weights for these items are simply too different:

> Underwear fabric is too thin and revealing for standalone shorts.
> Tight shorts are thicker and more modest, but too warm for layering underneath pants.

skurka'spicks
PANTS & UNDERWEAR

For cooler temperatures and heavy abrasion, I can recommend the **Sierra Designs Stretch Cargo Pant** ($85, 12 oz), although they are not the only acceptable choice in this category.

It is much more difficult to find pants that are designed for warm and humid conditions. The most promising lead I can offer are the **RailRiders Eco-Mesh Pant** ($86, 10 oz), which feature permethrin-treated lightweight nylon and full-length mesh vents for enhanced airflow.

The **ExOfficio Give-N-Go Sport Mesh 6-inch Boxer Brief** ($30, 2 oz) is the most comfortable underwear I have found. While most men's underwear seems biologically ignorant, the Give-N-Go provides a pouch to support your stuff. Stick with the 6-inch version—with a 3-inch inseam, the legs ride up too easily. But fit varies; like running shorts, you may have to try multiple styles until you find the right pair for you.

I can't speak credibly to women's underwear, but female clients regularly have praised styles from ExOfficio, Lululemon, Patagonia, and Under Armour.

Item 7: Fleece top

When the wind picks up or the skies open up, or before or after the peak daytime temperatures, my Go Suit becomes inadequate on its own to keep me comfortable. So I dig into my second layer, Storm, which consists of a fleece top and rain gear.

A fleece top serves two purposes:

> A second layer for cool conditions, like a windy summit or a crisp morning; and

> A mid-layer, worn between my hiking shirt and rain shell, to increase warmth and buffer moisture in cold-and-wet conditions.

In mild temperatures a fleece can be used as a low-cost insulating layer. But it's less thermally efficient (i.e., warmth per weight) than a down- or synthetic-filled insulated jacket and less compressible, so it's not my preferred choice.

Materials

Fleece fabric—which is a two-sided pile material—can be made of polyester or merino wool. I prefer polyester fleece: It is less expensive and warmer for its weight, it absorbs less water, and it dries faster.

Like polyester and merino hiking shirts, fleece tops are available in multiple weights. They may be labeled "lightweight" or "midweight," or by the fabric weight in grams per square meter, like 300-weight, which translates to 8.8 oz per square yard. Premium fleece fabrics, like Polartec Power Grid, are higher performing, but run-of-the-mill fleece can be satisfactory so long as the garment is well tailored and well constructed.

Windshirts

A silk-like water-resistant windshirt like the Patagonia Houdini ($100, 4 oz) is a popular alternative to fleece as a second layer, since it is lighter and more packable. But a windshirt is ineffective as a mid-layer: It does not buffer moisture or provide any warmth when wet. When developing the Core 13, I felt that a windshirt and fleece top were redundant, and ultimately chose the garment with more functionality.

Please don't interpret my decision as being anti-windshirt, however. In a narrower range of conditions a windshirt can be a very useful garment, at an extremely low weight and size, too. For example, I often pack one when:

> Day-hiking in dry weather, as insurance against temporary cold or windy conditions, or maybe even an unexpected drizzle;

Inexpensive polyester fleece is useful as a second layer in crisp temperatures and as a mid-layer in wet conditions, worn between a hiking shirt and shell.

> Leaving for a short backpacking trip with a reliably dry forecast; and
> Running in the wintertime, to wear while I'm warming up or on a long descent when I generate less heat.

Softshells

Another fleece alternative is a softshell jacket, like the Arc'teryx Gamma MX Hoody ($350, 24 oz), which has decent breathability, stretch, and abrasion resistance, and which offers more protection than fleece against wind and light precipitation.

For winter aerobic activities like backcountry skiing, softshells are fantastic. But for backpacking they are inferior to fleece because they:

> Have less airflow;
> Dry more slowly; and

> Are much heavier and more expensive.

If I really needed softshell performance for a backpacking trip, I would at least consider the combination of a fleece top and a windshirt as an alternative. This system would be lighter, more versatile, and less expensive.

skurka'spicks
FLEECE TOPS

A fleece top should be simple. Avoid features that add weight, absorb water, reduce breathability, slow dry times, and add cost, specifically: high spandex content, wind-blocking membranes (e.g., Windstopper), panels of water- and abrasion-resistant fabric, a full zipper, and lots of pockets.

part (2)

For this application I stick with 100- or 200-weight fleece; 300-weight feels like more of a jacket than a mid-layer. The **Marmot Rocklin 1/2 Zip** ($60, 10 oz) is well executed, and I've never heard regret over the purchase of a premium **Patagonia R1 Pullover** ($130, 12 oz). Personally, I use a prototype pullover made of lightweight Polartec Power Grid that never went into production. ▪

Items 8 & 9: Rain gear

In a few instances I will leave behind my rain gear, notably on short backpacking trips in dry environments, when there is no precipitation in the forecast, and on longer trips in hot and humid environments, when a soaking is actually welcomed. But otherwise I bring something to help keep me dry when it rains.

The fundamental challenge of rain gear is protecting the user from external precipitation while still allowing perspiration and body heat to escape. If rain gear fails in one or both areas, the comfort—and, sometimes, safety—of the user is at risk.

Jargon

To understand rain gear, you must understand the following terms:

Waterproofness is an absolute term, but it can be measured in degrees, specifically with a hydrostatic head test. If a fabric measures 1,500 mm or more, it is considered rainproof. A poncho from a reputable outdoor brand will meet this criteria, as will a metal roof, even though they are not equally waterproof.

Breathability is the layman's term for "moisture vapor transfer rate," or the ability of a fabric to permit the passage of moisture through it. Again, it's an absolute term, but there are major degrees of difference. For example, consider the amount of moisture that will pass through a wispy hiking shirt versus heavy-duty Carhartt pants. Both are "breathable," but one much more than the other.

Ventilation is the exchange of air, which will probably contain some amount of thermal energy (i.e., heat) and moisture. Ventilation is the overlooked aspect of rain gear performance: Manufacturers constantly tout the breathability of their garments, but ventilation is far more effective in keeping the user cool and dry given current fabric technologies.

Durable water repellent (DWR) is a fluorocarbon-based treatment that causes water to bead on a fabric surface (and hopefully roll off), without impairing breathability. Such fabrics will be described as "water-resistant." Think of DWR as "new car smell": When a garment is new, the DWR performs as intended. But it slowly degrades with exposure to abrasion, dirt, and sweat, among other things, and ultimately the fabric is no more water-resistant than an untreated one.

Umbrellas

No, I'm not kidding. Imagine this situation: You're backpacking in Virginia's Blue Ridge Mountains in June, when average daytime temperatures even on the summit ridge are in the low 70s and when high humidity is a constant. It starts to rain. Your buddy pulls out his or her expensive rain jacket, while you grab your umbrella. You are the subject of laughter for the first five minutes, but soon your buddy—who starts to overheat and bathe in sweat—begins to ask you questions about your Gossamer Gear Lightflex umbrella ($45, 8 oz) because you are still dry and relatively cool.

An umbrella thrives in such conditions. It can also be used as portable shade when traveling in the desert.

But it has too many limits and, therefore, was not included in the Core 13. Umbrellas:

> Catch air, so they break in high winds and create drag;
> Offer scant protection in driving rain;
> Require one arm, which can't be used for anything else; and
> Snag on vegetation, like on low-use trails or when off-trail.

Ponchos

During most of the Sea-to-Sea Route, I used a waterproof nylon poncho as my primary rain gear. Because it is worn over the pack and pack straps, and because it has huge vents along its sides and bottom, it worked well in the East's humid climate and

An umbrella offers good rain protection and excellent ventilation, but it restricts trekking pole use and gets caught by brush and wind.

afforded more extensive coverage than an umbrella.

But it was less stellar on brushy trails, the windy Dakota plains, and the high elevations of the Rockies and Pacific Northwest. The misery I endured during one June storm in Idaho's Selkirks is particularly memorable and highlighted a poncho's primary liability: It leaves the lower arms and legs exposed to cold precipitation.

One cottage company has a creative poncho solution. The poncho-esque Packa ($145, 10 oz) is worn over the pack, vents from the bottom, and is made of waterproof nylon shelter fabric. But it has a full-length front zipper and arm sleeves, giving it a more jacket-like fit and functionality. The tailoring needs work, but I admire the ingenuity and I'm genuinely excited to field-test it; look for a review on my website.

Waterproof/breathable outerwear

The most popular choices for backpacking rain gear are jackets and pants made of waterproof/breathable fabric. Overall, a jacket and pants are more field-friendly than an umbrella or poncho, which is why I included them in the Core 13. They offer full coverage, they don't catch as much wind or trailside vegetation, and the wearer is more agile.

Waterproof/breathable (WP/B) fabric technology is fascinating and the subject of a great deal of research and development, media attention, and marketing. Nevertheless, this technology doesn't work as well as it's touted to.

My experience during hundreds of storms is that WP/B fabrics are not satisfactorily waterproof or breathable, especially during prolonged wet conditions and if the garment is not new. While the relative levels of waterproofness and breathability of different fabrics can be measured in a lab, the ultimate outcome is the same: I will get wet from the outside, the inside, or both. It's really just a question of timing and method.

Problem & solution. The form-fitting silhouettes of jackets and pants create a major problem: near-complete loss of airflow, especially when worn under a backpack. If rain gear were made of the same material as umbrellas or ponchos, the wearer would be protected from external precipitation, but heat and moisture generated inside the garment would be unable to escape.

The supposed solution to this body bag scenario are WP/B fabrics like Gore-Tex, eVent, and NeoShell, plus proprietary fabrics like Marmot's Precip and Patagonia's H2No. That "waterproof-breathable" is an oxymoron is perhaps the first clue that this fabric technology might be over-hyped. A "waterproof" fabric does not allow moisture through, yet a "breathable" fabric does. So how can a material be both?

Construction. WP/B fabrics are laminates, consisting of up to three distinct bonded layers:

> A DWR-treated face fabric, usually made of polyester or nylon;

> A WP/B membrane, which is made of microporous expanded polytetrafluoroethylene (ePTFE, or Teflon), nonporous hydrophilic polyurethane (PU), or both; and

> An internal fabric that improves user comfort by assisting in the passage of moisture through the membrane, or at least the perception of it.

Fabrics following this full construction are described as "three-layer." They are the most waterproof, most durable, heaviest, and least breathable. By replacing the interior fabric with a treatment (e.g., silicone dot matrix) or eliminating it entirely, weight and expense can be reduced, but not without sacrificing waterproofness and durability.

One WP/B laminate deserves specific mention because it is unlike the others. Frogg Toggs and O_2 Rainwear supply inexpensive (less than $50) jackets and pants made of a microporous membrane sandwiched between layers of polypropylene. They are highly breathable but extremely fragile, and will not withstand outright abrasion or long-term wear and tear.

How it works. It's often explained that WP/B membranes contain microscopic pores that are too small for water liquid but large enough for water vapor. This is true in the case of eVent and Frogg Toggs (although not the whole story).

With other laminates, moisture must pass through a water-loving polyurethane (PU) film via solid-state diffusion. That is, the PU film absorbs water vapor, which then moves through the film as water liquid until it reaches the film's exterior, where it can revert to water vapor and evaporate. This PU layer may stand on its own or may be bonded to expanded polytetrafluoroethylene (ePTFE).

Regardless of the fabric construction, the passage of moisture is driven by relative humidity levels. If it's more humid inside the jacket than outside, moisture will want to move outward to establish atmospheric equilibrium. The DWR applied to the exterior face fabric is critical to this process—the face fabric must stay dry (by having water bead up and roll off) to allow the escape of interior moisture.

Testing. The degree of waterproofness and breathability of WP/B fabrics can be measured, but the industry lacks a uniform testing system—like the EN test for sleeping bags, described later—that would generate trustworthy apples-to-apples comparisons. Even if such a system did exist, the results would not necessarily be translatable to a fabric's performance outside the lab because this also depends on personal metabolism, weather conditions, shell-specific features like sizing and ventilation, and the DWR's resistance to dirt, body oils, and abrasion.

The water column test is the most commonly cited measure of water resistance. The result refers to the height of water that can be vertically suspended over a fabric swatch before it leaks and is typically shown in millimeters or in pounds per square inch. A fabric that claims water resistance of 20,000 millimeters (or 29 psi) means that there was a 66-foot column of water above the fabric before it began to leak.

Most tests of breathability measure the amount of water (in grams) that passes through one square meter (m^2) of fabric over a 24-hour period. A fabric rated at 20,000 g/m^2/day, means that about 29 ounces of water pass through a square meter of the fabric per hour. For context, the average adult perspires 25 to 50 ounces per hour while exercising and has an average body surface area of 1.7 square meters.

Failure from the outside. The Achilles heel of conventional WP/B fabrics is the DWR-treated face fabric. As the DWR degrades, the fabric "wets out" and becomes saturated with moisture. At best, this brings breathability to a screeching halt, resulting in interior clamminess. At worst, the moisture can work its way into the WP/B membrane, lured by the relatively less humid interior air, and soak the user.

When you notice that your DWR is failing, restore it with a wash-in or spray-on treatment like ReviveX Durable Waterproofing spray ($15). But do not expect good-as-new results.

Exterior precipitation can penetrate the jacket in other ways, too. Zippers, even those covered by a storm flap

	"water-resistant" shells	"waterproof-breathable" shells
water resistance	Initially good, but ultimately no better than untreated fabric due to degradation of durable water repellent (DWR).	Initially excellent, but fails with moderate use. Face fabric wets out, and moisture seeps in through seams & zippers.
breathability	Decent. Not as good as a knit shirt, but sufficient for moderate exertion like running in cool temperatures. Generally, the more water-resistant, the less breathable.	Limited. If users do not get wet from the outside, they will get wet from inside because of accumulated perspiration. Some fabrics breathe better than others, but marketing claims greatly exceed performance.
best use	As second layer for windy summits, dry snow, light drizzle, or warm rain.	To prolong dryness in wet conditions. Low aerobic activities in cool temps.
cost	Low to moderate	Moderate to high

or described as watertight, can fail in extended wet conditions. So too can the waterproof seam-sealing tape, especially if the garment was poorly constructed or if it's older and is deliminating.

Failure from the inside. Technically, moisture—and with some membranes, hot air—can pass through WP/B fabrics. But the rate of passage is utterly inadequate relative to the normal generation of perspiration and body heat when hiking. This is especially true in muggy and warm conditions, when interior moisture has nowhere to go (because it's already very humid outside) and when the wearing of a jacket will inevitably lead to overheating. Ironically, when you need rain gear most—when it's raining—the humidity is generally highest.

Next-generation rain gear. I'm hopeful that technology and design will continue to improve so that I can remain dry when it's wet. I see three promising opportunities.

Columbia recently introduced Outdry Extreme, the first fabric to place the WP/B membrane on the outside. In doing so, they removed the DWR-treated face fabric, the failure of which they have acknowledged in their marketing. Long-term field-testing has not yet validated the claim of "permanent water repellency," which would indeed be a breakthrough. Gore-Tex has since released a similar fabric, Active.

Sierra Designs has focused on Airflow Rainwear, in an acknowledgement

how 2
restore DWR

1 Launder the garment to remove dirt and body oils;

2 Expose it to heat from a clothes dryer, iron, or even a hair dryer; or

3 Use an aftermarket spray-on or wash-in treatment.

Ultimately I have found maintaining the water resistance of a DWR-coated fabric to be futile, especially on long-distance trips when I have limited access to laundry facilities and it's difficult to find specialized aftermarket treatments.

of the limits of fabric breathability and the importance of garment ventilation. I think there is more opportunity here, specifically by using waterproof/nonbreathable fabrics and by including more vents, like in the forearms and hood.

For cold-and-wet conditions, U.K.-based Páramo has developed a strong following, although not yet in the U.S., where availability is very limited. Páramo consists of a water-resistant windshirt laminated to a hydrophobic mid-weight polyester pile that replicates animal fur, so that moisture moves directionally away from the user. It's reportedly more water-resistant and warmer than a conventional softshell or the combination of a windshirt and conventional fleece.

skurka'spicks
RAIN GEAR

When choosing rain gear for a particular trip, I mostly account for the:

> Likelihood and duration of rain events;
> Relative humidity; and
> Ambient temperature.

On most trips in the Mountain West I expect no or little precipitation, short-lived storms, low humidity, and cool temperatures. For these conditions I pack ultralight and relatively inexpensive rain gear like the **Outdoor Research Helium II Jacket** ($160, 6 oz), and maybe the matching pants for full-body defense against cold and wet conditions. These garments will have minimal features: no pit zips, ankle zips, multiple hood adjustments, hem closure, or pockets.

My rationale for this selection is simple. First, since I may not even need my rain gear, I'd like to keep its weight and volume to a minimum. Second, if I do need it, by the time I'm starting to get wet (from the outside or inside), the storm will have hopefully passed over. That doesn't always happen, but it's a risk I'm willing to take.

After the durable water repellent (DWR) on my WP/B jacket failed in prolonged wet conditions in the Arctic refuge, I had to rely partly on a plastic trash bag to stay dry.

tools & techniques

I size my rain gear so that it fits over a hiking shirt and mid-layer top, or pants and underwear. Unlike a winter shell, it need not be so large to fit over an insulated jacket or pants. For my purposes I avoid "helmet-compatible" hoods, which are excessively large and poor-fitting when I'm only wearing a hat. Finally, if pockets are to be useful, they must be accessible while wearing a backpack. Otherwise, why bother?

WP/B rain gear struggles much more when conditions are at the other end of the spectrum (i.e., reliable and long-lasting rain events, high humidity, or warm temperatures). In these conditions, I think highly waterproof rain gear with generous venting and airflow will be more effective in keeping you dry than rain gear with a best-in-class WP/B fabric. Even so, prepare to get wet—pack a mid-layer and sleeping clothes, learn how to start a fire, and mentally accept it as part of the experience.

If you have given up on WP/B jacket and pants, I would understand. As alternatives, consider the aforementioned Packa and Light-flex Umbrella, and maybe a rain kilt from ULA or ZPacks. ■

The no-frills 6-ounce OR Helium II Jacket

Items 10 & 11: Insulated outerwear

During cool camps, cold nights, and midday rests on crisp days, I preserve my body heat with a high-loft insulated jacket, or "puffy." If I expect nighttime temperatures below about 30°F, or long camps with temperatures below about 40°F, I will add insulated pants to my kit. Only once have I regularly worn insulated clothing while active—during the first two weeks of my Alaska-Yukon Expedition,

tip | Expect the warmth of insulated outerwear and bags to be compromised in the field, mostly by moisture, but also by dirt and body oils.

part 2

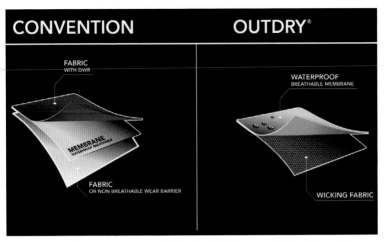

CONVENTION

FABRIC
WITH DWR

MEMBRANE
WATERPROOF BREATHABLE

FABRIC
OR NON BREATHABLE WEAR BARRIER

OUTDRY®

WATERPROOF
BREATHABLE MEMBRANE

WICKING FABRIC

By eliminating the DWR-coated face fabric, Outdry Extreme avoids "wetting out."

while skiing down Alaska's windy Arctic west coast in temperatures as low as minus 25°F.

Insulated outerwear sandwiches down or synthetic-fill insulation between lightweight shell fabrics. These insulations reduce convective heat loss by trapping body heat within tiny chambers formed by the insulation's fibers as it tries to escape into the cooler outside air.

Puffies are much more thermally efficient (i.e., warmth per weight) than synthetic or merino fleece, making them the ultimate "Stop" pieces. Modern high-end synthetic insulations are about three times as warm as 300-weight fleece per weight; high-end down, about five times warmer. The garments are also much more compressible and wind-resistant; the shell fabrics are water-resistant, but that's of dubious value, as discussed above.

While a puffy is warmer for its weight, it should not replace a fleece mid-layer. Puffies are less air permeable and slower to dry, and the warmth of down and synthetic insulation is more adversely affected by moisture.

Down insulation

Upfront cost aside, down is the superior insulation for high-loft insulated outerwear—and sleeping bags, too. Different from a feather, down is the soft and fluffy cluster of filaments that is found underneath the feathers of a goose or duck.

Quality. Down is differentiated only by its "fill power"—technically, the spatial displacement (in cubic inches) for a single ounce of down. Hence, one ounce of 700-fill power down will displace 700 cubic inches. By using a higher fill-power down, the garment or bag will be lighter because less down is needed to fill it. Although 800-fill down is considered premium, some manufacturers

tools & techniques

tout 800-plus-, 850-, and even 1000-fill power. Low-budget puffies and sleeping bags will feature 600- or 650-fill power down.

Construction. To ensure uniform warmth, down is contained within a garment or sleeping bag by smaller baffles, or chambers between the outside and inside shell fabric. Stitch-through baffles are the simplest and least material-intensive, but heat escapes where the shell fabrics are sewn together; these baffles are commonly found on lightweight jackets and parkas. Sleeping bags and winter-worthy parkas feature advanced-construction baffles like box wall, shingle, and wave.

When wet. When trying to sell synthetic insulations over down, it's often claimed that synthetics are "warm when wet," whereas down is not. Unless you take a hot shower in your synthetic-filled gear, this is patently false—if your jacket is soaked with cold water, you will lose heat through conduction. Furthermore, this is a bit of a straw man argument since insulated outerwear should never get "wet." It's not meant to be worn as rain gear or while fording a river, and it can be kept dry inside a pack by using a waterproof pack liner or stuff sack.

Conventional down is, however, more susceptible to ambient humidity or trapped perspiration. When my down feels damp and flat, I take the

Since getting wet in wet conditions is inevitable, I insist that my gear be made of quick-dry materials, and I plan to dry my things out regularly.

part 2

first opportunity I have to dry it, such as in a sunny meadow or at a Laundromat. In the meantime, I don't worry too much. Down is so much more thermally efficient than synthetic insulations—the best of which are on par with 600-fill down—that moisture-degraded down performs about the same as a high-performance synthetic that is perfectly dry.

Though competing technologies have evolved, the original Gore-Tex remains a market dominator.

Water-resistant down. The supposed wet-weather advantage of synthetics became even weaker in 2014 with the introduction of water-resistant down, whereby each down plume has been treated with DWR. The performance of water-resistant downs—which are branded as DownTek, Down Defender, DriDown, Encapsil, and others—is not equal, but it generally retains its loft better when wet and dries faster than conventional down. The long-term performance of DWR-treated down is not yet clear.

Synthetic insulations

There are two popular brands of synthetic insulations: PrimaLoft and Climashield, each of which has a range of products. Some brands have also developed proprietary synthetic insulation, like Thermoball from The North Face and Exceloft from Montbell.

The primary advantage of synthetic insulations over down is their relatively low expense. In really wet conditions, they may offer more reliable warmth, too.

Otherwise, they are less thermally efficient, less compressible, and less

soft. Their performance is also short-lived because they do not recover fully from repeated compression. After just a single long trip, I have to replace my synthetic-filled jackets and sleeping bags because they lose so much warmth. In contrast, I have owned my down-filled gear for years, with no notable decline in performance. If you can afford the upfront expense, this makes a better long-term investment.

Shell fabrics

Down and synthetic insulations are sandwiched by an outer and inner shell fabric usually made of polyester or nylon. Aside from the type and amount of insulation, they are the most important feature of insulated outerwear and sleeping bags. They affect a product in several critical ways:

Weight. Especially when using premium insulations, which fill a lot of volume for little weight, the shell fabric is very influential in the product's overall weight. For example, the weight of a Western Mountaineering sleeping bag drops 15 percent when a 1.0 oz/sq yd shell fabric is used instead of a

	wool	fleece
warmth per weight	Worst. Heavy for warmth.	Fair. Suitable low-cost insulation layer.
wet weather performance	Fair. Absorbs moisture but retains some insulating ability.	Good. Absorbs little moisture & can be nearly wrung dry.
compressibility	Limited	Limited
life span	Fair. Wool fibers not as strong as fleece.	Good. Stays intact, though pills & picks with use.
cost	Moderate to high	Low to moderate, depending on brand

1.7 oz/sq yd fabric. The lightest fabrics commonly used are just below 1.0 oz/sq yd.

Warmth. A shell fabric affects the warmth of insulated layers and sleeping bags due to its weight, air permeability, and down-proof-ness. If the fabric is too heavy, it will compress the insulation, thereby reducing the size and number of air-trapping chambers. Given that lightweight shell fabrics are found even on entry-level bags today, this is not the concern that it once was; heavy cotton fabrics are now found only on cheap bags that are not suitable for backpacking anyway.

A shell fabric must have some air permeability so that water vapor can pass through it and evaporate into the atmosphere. Otherwise, condensation would form, creating an uncomfortable user experience and wetting the insulation. However, if the shell fabric has too much air permeability, body heat will escape too easily. As an extreme scenario, imagine how drafty a jacket

or sleeping bag would be if its shell fabric were made of fishnet stockings.

The source of a fabric's air permeability—specifically, the density of its weave (the space between adjacent fibers)—is also responsible for whether it is "down-proof," or resistant to losing down plumes. Today's shell fabrics are excellent in retaining down, but they are not as effective in withholding quill-bearing plumes, or feathers. Because the technology used to separate feathers and down has improved, there are fewer quills in today's high-loft down, and the down-proof-ness of a shell fabric is not as critical as it once was, particularly when using premium down fills. If your garment or bag occasionally loses feathers or even down, you do not need to be concerned—a few missing plumes will not noticeably affect its warmth.

Water resistance. Last, the shell fabric can improve the water resistance of an insulated layer or sleeping bag against light precipitation or

synthetic fill	down
Good. When new, premium fills equal to 550-ish down.	Best. Unsurpassed thermal efficiency.
Fair. Less affected by moisture than down, but absolutely not warm when wet.	Depends. Known to absorb moisture & lose loft. Water-resistant down an improvement.
Good	Best
Fair. Loses loft with repeated compression.	Excellent. Reliable warmth for years of use.
Moderate	Moderate to high, depending on fill quality

condensation on shelter walls. However, even a highly water-resistant shell fabric will not keep the insulation dry in wet conditions—it will still absorb ambient humidity and perspiration.

Measuring warmth

Unlike sleeping bags, no standardized lab test yet exists to measure the warmth of insulated outerwear. To gauge the warmth of a down garment, I consider the fill power of the down, fill weight, loft height, baffle construction, and shell fabric air permeability. Of this list, fill power and fill weight are the only specs regularly provided. In the Mountain West I have found that a hooded jacket with 3.0 to 3.5 ounces of 800-fill down is about perfect for three-season conditions; in the East, a hoodless jacket with 2.5 ounces might get more use.

The warmth of synthetic insulations is determined by the insulation's warmth per weight and weight per area. Unfortunately, comparing the warmth per weight of various insulations is difficult because the data is rarely published. It can be measured in clo, where one clo is equal to the amount of clothing required by a resting person to remain comfortable indefinitely in an ambient temperature of 70°F, humidity of less than 50 percent, and a 0.5-mile-an-hour wind.

At least most manufacturers will specify the weight of the insulation. For example, Montbell uses a 50 g/sq m version of Exceloft in its lightest garments, but an 80 g/sq m version in warmer ones. The warmer garment would not be exactly 60 percent warmer because the shell fabrics also trap heat.

skurka'spicks
INSULATED OUTERWEAR

My sole consideration in insulated outerwear is its thermal efficiency. It need not be capable of

When I expect my hiking clothes to get wet, I bring dedicated sleeping clothes, like light underwear (left), thermals (middle), or a fleece suit (right).

part 2

much—basically, I just want to be able to stand around or sleep in these pieces without getting cold.

I prefer a slightly oversize cut so that my outerwear fits comfortably when worn over a hiking shirt and mid-layer, or underwear and hiking pants. It doesn't happen often, but there's room for a rain jacket and pants too, for when I'm desperately cold. The jacket and pants should seal off drafts in the torso area, so the jacket should be mid-butt (requiring a ladylike hourglass cut so it doesn't bunch up at the waist), and the pants should rise nearly to the belly button. Thumb loops in the sleeves help keep wrists and hands warm.

I avoid features that add weight without warmth like fleece-lined pockets, unnecessarily heavy zippers, stretchy underarm panels or arm cuffs, and hood and waist cinch cords and locks that are no substitute for good design.

Wispy 10- or 20-denier shell fabrics are ideal. Heavier fabrics are more durable, but little durability is actually needed for this application. WP/B fabrics are much heavier, and, ironically, their poor breathability leads to the insulation getting wet from trapped perspiration.

A handful of outdoor brands produce beautiful insulated jackets, including but not limited to Montbell, Patagonia, Rab, and Western Mountaineering. You will be satisfied with your purchase, but it is an investment—the current benchmark, the **Mountain Hardwear Hooded Ghost Whisperer** (8 oz), costs $350. I won't offer a specific recommendation, since many of these garments use essentially the same shell fabrics, insulations, and Asian sewing factories.

Lower-priced alternatives exist. Check closeouts and house brands, big-box department stores

 **To keep insulated outerwear and bags dry, use a waterproof pack liner, dry them in the sun every few days, and use a shelter with good ventilation.**

like Costco and Target, and fast-fashion houses like Uniqlo. More reliably, consider minimalist synthetic-insulated garments.

There are fewer worthy options for insulated pants. For pure three-season backpacking, the **Montbell Superior Down Pants ($145, 8 oz)** leave little room for improvement. But if you plan to use your insulated pants in the winter too, it's worth investing in full-length or three-quarter-length leg zippers, so that the pants can be easily pulled over big winter boots. Such models are available from Arc'teryx, Montbell, and Western Mountaineering.

A budget solution is the "long" version of the military's M-65 insulated pant, available on eBay and at military surplus stores. For less than $20 with shipping, it is the hands-down best value. ▮

Items 12 & 13: Sleeping clothes

Even with proper gear and technique, being damp, wet, or even soaked is a likely and sometimes guaranteed experience when backpacking in wet climates like the eastern woodlands, Pacific Northwest, or Alaska. If you want to be dry, sometimes there is no other choice but to find a motel.

If that's not an option, you should at least have the opportunity for a night of quality rest. A separate top and bottom layer used exclusively in camp and while sleeping go a long way in making this possible. During the day these layers should be kept dry inside your pack. If your hiking clothes did not dry overnight—either naturally or with the help of a fire—you should change into them before starting your day or risk getting your sleeping clothes wet, too.

I do not carry sleeping clothes to keep my sleeping bag cleaner or to keep food smells away from my shelter. Frequent backcountry laundering and good personal hygiene address the first concern, and I'm dubious of the effectiveness of the second (though if such a policy were required, like at Philmont Scout Ranch, I'd abide by it).

skurka'spicks
SLEEPING CLOTHES

On my trips in the semiarid West, I don't carry sleeping clothes. It's true that I've been soaked on multiple occasions, but it's uncommon and there's an easy solution: When the sun next emerges, I dry my wet clothing and gear in 20 minutes by spreading it out on the ground.

In wetter climates, however, my opinion is that leaving behind sleeping clothes falls into the category of "stupid light," especially if it's a wet forecast or a long-term trip. Sure, it can be a one-pound weight-savings, but what is the cost—to your body and your morale—of a crappy night of sleep?

My exact choice of sleeping clothes is driven by the expected nighttime low temperatures. On mild nights, I need only a short-sleeve shirt and underwear made of lightweight fabric. Whereas for colder temperatures I will bring "expedition-weight" base layers or even 100-weight fleece pile. The threshold for sleeping clothes is low: Are they comfortable to sleep in? It's unlikely a deal breaker if they don't fit well, are last decade's colors, or have holes in the elbows. ▓

Vapor barrier liners

In three-season conditions, fabric breathability is a desirable quality in clothing. But in the winter it can be a liability. First, heat is lost through evaporation. Second, outer layers get wet from perspiration because perspiration vapor will turn into perspiration water when it reaches the dew point, which is within the layers. (This is not an issue in three-season conditions because the dew point is outside of the layering system.)

To remedy these two problems, I use vapor barrier liners (VBLs) on some winter trips—especially colder and longer

A VBL jacket will reduce evaporative heat loss and prevent moisture from accumulating in outer layers.

ones—and in a more limited capacity during cold shoulder seasons. When used properly, VBLs can be beneficial to all outdoor winter enthusiasts.

What are VBLs?

VBLs can be made of any nonbreathable material, like polyurethane-coated nylon. Waterproof-breathable fabrics are fundamentally different from VBL fabrics. While the breathability of WP/B fabrics is limited, they at least allow the transmission of some moisture, whereas VBLs do not.

VBL clothing and sleeping bag liners are available from Integral Designs, RBH Designs, Stephenson's Warmlite, and Western Mountaineering; Luke's Ultralight sells waterproof/nonbreathable rainwear

part 2

that functionally will be the same. No major manufacturer offers VBL products—it's too niche and counterintuitive, and would necessitate too much consumer education.

It is redundant and unnecessary to use both VBL clothing and a VBL bag liner. A liner is simpler, lighter, and less expensive, but VBL clothing has three key advantages:

> I can sleep with all of my clothes on, layering as follows: skin, base layer, VBL, other clothes, sleeping bag. If I wore all of my clothes inside a VBL liner, my clothes would become soaked by my own perspiration.

> During the day, VBL clothing keeps dry my outer layers, like my down-insulated parka. A sleeping bag liner cannot be used during the day.

> VBL clothing is more form-fitting than a sleeping bag liner, so I notice quickly if moisture is beginning to accumulate inside the VBL. By contrast, a bag liner could have roomy chambers where excessive moisture can build.

Personal history

In the winter of 2004–2005, I snowshoed 1,400 miles of the North Country Trail through both peninsulas of Michigan, northern Wisconsin, and northern Minnesota as part of my 7,800-mile, 11-month Sea-to-Sea Route trek. This was my first real winter trip, and a problem that became immediately clear was that my clothing and sleeping system failed to adequately manage perspiration.

If I perspired and then stopped, for example, I would become chilled by the evaporation of my perspiration. A more serious problem was that my outer layers and sleeping bag were getting wet from my perspiration. In the minus 20°F nighttime temperatures, water vapor emanating from my body would turn into water droplets before it reached the outside and could evaporate. My down-filled sleeping bag and puffy clothing became wetter—and less warm—every single day; my footwear was frozen stiff each morning by trapped perspiration from the days before. Also, it was difficult for me to sense my rate of perspiration; I recall one morning that steam emerged from my sleeping bag when I zipped it open.

If I did not have numerous opportunities to dry my gear—usually one or two times a week, either in homes or motels—I am certain that I would have shivered through more nights than I did. The total failure of my most critical equipment was unpreventable with the clothing and sleep system that I had.

Effects & benefits

In January 2007, I returned to Minnesota for a 380-mile, 16-day snowshoe trip I named "Ultralight in the Nation's Icebox." Among my objectives was perfecting my deep-winter gear list; VBLs were a core part of my strategy. I brought a VBL jacket, pants, socks, gloves, and balaclava. My VBL system had four effects:

> I became keenly aware of my perspiration rate. If I started to

overheat, I immediately noticed the increasing humidity between my skin and the VBL layer, and I would have to reduce my effort or remove a layer.

> Because I was not perspiring as much, I stayed better hydrated, which led to improved circulation and respiratory efficiency. I also didn't need to spend as much time or fuel melting snow for water.

> My clothes did not become sweat-soaked, and my VBL layers prevented evaporation of heat-holding perspiration.

> The warmth of my outer layers and sleeping bag was not degraded by my perspiration. Instead, my perspiration stayed within the vapor barrier liner, so my outer layers remained dry and warm.

When to use VBLs

As with a conventional three-season layering system, there are no set rules about when to use VBLs. It mostly depends on personal experience and preferences. I consider three factors:

Weather conditions. I can use VBLs below about 40°F, but at these temperatures I can only wear items that are easily removable, like gloves. As temperatures drop into the 20s, I can add a jacket; and below 10, it's cold enough to start wearing socks and pants, which can't be easily removed or adjusted.

Accumulation period. How often will I have an opportunity to dry insulated layers and my sleeping bag? As this period grows longer, VBLs

VBLs are suitable only for very cold conditions, like those I experienced in Alaska's Arctic in March, when daytime high temperatures were regularly below ten degrees.

become more critical in preserving warmth. If I went on a one-week ski trip, for example, seven days of moisture inside my gear would definitely have noticeable effects. Whereas on a weekend trip, the loss of warmth would be less worrisome.

This is not to say that VBLs cannot be valuable during short-term efforts. For example, toward the end of a full day of alpine skiing, when the sun disappears and the temperatures begin to drop, many skiers feel chilled because their boot liners, gloves, and clothing have absorbed sweat during the day. This problem could be solved with VBLs, and these skiers might be warm enough at 4 p.m. to catch a last run.

Insulation type. Down is more susceptible than synthetics to loft loss when exposed to moisture. Synthetics are vulnerable in the long-term too, but the rate of degradation is lower. Therefore, using VBLs is more important when using down insulations than when using synthetics. On trips with long accumulation periods, however, the warmth of both insulation types will benefit from the use of VBLs.

Layering

A VBL can be worn next to the skin or as a second layer, over a lightweight base layer made of polyester or merino wool. I prefer this latter approach because it:

> Creates a small buffer that eliminates any sensation of clamminess, but without significantly reducing my sensitivity to perspiration, which dictates the adjustments I make to my physical output and my layering system.
> Protects my skin from direct contact with frigid winter air if/when I need to ventilate. For example, if my hands are getting too warm, I can remove my VBL mitts without exposing my bare hands to sub-zero temperatures.
> Prevents moisture from building up on my skin, which can lead to moisture-related skin issues like maceration.

VBL clothing should be versatile and easily adjustable so it can be fine-tuned according to the conditions and the user's level of exertion. As an example, the combination of Luke's Ultralight SilNylon Rain Shell ($85, 5 oz) with a 200-weight fleece is lighter and more versatile than the RBH Designs VaprThrm NTS Jacket ($225, 14 oz).

Headwear

A brimmed hat has many benefits, and I wear one nearly all the time. It:

> Protects my face from the sun;
> Keeps rain, snow, and sweat out of my eyes;
> Holds jacket hoods (e.g., from my rain jacket or parka) above my face;
> Prevents bug netting from a head net or bivy sack from contacting my skin, in which case bugs could bite me through it; and

> Makes for a convenient place to clip an LED-powered light.

Low sunlight

In areas where there is minimal sun exposure, like the thickly forested Appalachians, my go-to headwear since 2003 has been the Headsweats Supervisor ($21, 2 oz), which is made of quick-drying materials and has excellent ventilation. For those who are thinner up top and can burn even in low-light conditions, the Headsweats Race Cap ($20, 2 oz) would be a better choice.

Intense sun

Cowboy-style hats from Tilly, Outdoor Research, and Sunday Afternoons offer good protection in sun-blessed locations. They don't fit well under hoods, however, and can be kite-like in moderate winds. For these conditions, I instead prefer a lower-profile ball cap with an integrated drape that covers my neck and ears, such as the Headsweats Protech ($26, 3 oz). In a pinch, an alternative solution is to wear a bandanna underneath a Supervisor or Race Cap, but a dedicated sun hat is less fussy.

Insect protection

It's a mistake I only had to make once: leaving behind a 0.5-ounce head net to "save weight" during the High Sierra's peak mosquito season. Dumb, dumb, dumb. While I was able to minimize bites by lathering insect repellent on my face (at the time, poisoning myself was most definitely worth it), I was

unable to stop them from pelting my skin and flying into my eyes, nose, and mouth.

Head nets made of fine no-see-um mesh are too suffocating for an aerobic activity like hiking. Plus, no-see-ums don't fly very fast. Larger-pored mosquito netting (which also blocks flies) has much better airflow; you can also see better through it. I've used the Coghlans Mosquito Head Net ($5, 1 oz), but it's too short to create a secure seal around the neck even with a high-collared shirt. Instead, go with the longer Sea to Summit Mosquito Head Net ($10, 1 oz). Since bugs can bite through netting, a head net should be worn over a ball cap so that no netting is flush with skin.

Cold temperatures

My first insulating headwear layer is a Buff ($20, 2 oz), which is a long polyester tube that can be worn as a headband, beanie, or neck gaiter, among other variations. In temperatures below about freezing, I transition

Headsweats Race Cap, which offers more sun protection than a visor for sunburn-prone heads

I successfully combated the Arctic's fierce mosquitoes with a visor, a bandanna, and a head net, in addition to biteproof nylon clothing and DEET.

to a lightweight balaclava, which better insulates my head, jaw, and neck.

My Arctic headwear system, which I've tested to about minus 25°F with a 20-mile-an-hour wind, includes the following: balaclava, visor, wool knit hat, sunglasses or goggles, and up to three hoods, from my base layer shirt, shell jacket, and insulated parka, the last of which has a coyote-fur ruff sewn to its perimeter.

The biggest challenge of an Arctic-worthy headwear system is finding a way to manage the moisture from respiration. When I cover my mouth and nose with material, moisture builds up on the inside; but if I leave skin exposed, it becomes prone to frostbite. My solution is a merino wool neck gaiter: When a patch of it gets uncomfortably wet, I rotate to a dry patch. Wet patches eventually get rotated to

the back of my neck inside my hoods, where they can dry out.

Handwear

When hiking in temperatures below about 50°F, my hands won't stay warm on their own, especially if it's also raining or windy. Like my clothing system, I have a few handwear layers that I can mix and match to the desired effect. All-in-one gloves and mittens work well for throwing snowballs and scraping frost off a windshield, but they are not versatile enough for the range of conditions and exertion levels encountered on a long trip or throughout a backpacking season.

Liners

An effective liner will do several things well: provide warmth, retain dexterity, and stand up to abrasion, especially from pole grips. My favorite is the DeFeet DuraGlove ET Wool ($25, 3 oz), which scores highly in each of these regards.

As standalone gloves, I can run in them in temperatures down to about 30 degrees; I generate less body heat when hiking, so the cutoff is more like 40 degrees. (Based on what I see other people wear in comparable conditions, my hands run cold.) Dexterity is sufficient to tie shoelaces, operate a stove, and adjust a zipper. And the durability is better than any other liner I've used, thanks to the 52 percent nylon content and the rubber logos throughout the palm, finger, and thumb areas that increase grip and abrasion resistance. On a backpacking trip, the DuraGloves last 4 to 6 weeks when I use them daily for 10 to 14 hours per day; I burn through pure polyester, fleece, and merino wool gloves in half that time.

Shells

For added insulation and for protection from cold precipitation, I add a shell mitt to my handwear system. Fully waterproof options (i.e., featuring waterproof fabric and taped seams) are available from Luke's Ultralight, Outdoor Research, and ZPacks. Costs vary from $60 to $80 and weights from 1 to 3 ounces per pair.

For backpacking shells I'd try to avoid waterproof/breathable

or ultralight fabrics, the long-term waterproofness of which is greatly compromised by pole grip abrasion. A waterproof/nonbreathable fabric will trap hand perspiration, but they can be fully vented by simply taking them off. Plus, you'll never hear me complain about having hot hands when it's 40 degrees and raining.

Winter gloves

When daytime temperatures are reliably below freezing, and precipitation will almost certainly be snow, I trade out my shells for vapor barrier liner mitts. (Because the seams of my VBL mitts are not taped, they can't be trusted in wet precipitation.) I continue to use the DuraGloves as liners.

Mittens may not provide the same dexterity as gloves, but they are much warmer, and sufficient for holding trekking poles or zipping up a jacket. I adore the RBH Designs Vapor Mitts ($145, 9 oz) for their reliable warmth and have tested them in temperatures

The silicone pads and high nylon content improve the durability of these wool liner gloves.

down to minus 25°F. The shells are überdurable, lasting several hundred days; the liners must be replaced more often, because the fleece and synthetic insulation flattens out.

Eyewear

Sunglasses and goggles help protect my eyes from bright sunlight, glare, cold wind, and blowing particles like snow and sand. Eyewear is not necessary on every trip—little sunlight penetrates the East's thick forests, for example; and in northern Alaska, the sun is very weak and the skies are often cloudy.

Sunglasses and goggles seem outrageously expensive, but you do pay for what you get: High-end models generally offer better optics, improved durability, greater wearing comfort and stability, and a more advanced design (e.g., peripheral vision and ventilation). Fortunately, the technology is not advancing like that of driverless cars, and often you can find deeply discounted prices on last season's models. I scored my favorite pair for one-third of MSRP.

Lenses

Shopping for sports sunglasses and goggles is a two-step process: Pick your frame, and then select the lens. There are four basic lens options: photochromic ("transition") or not, and polarized or not. Each style has trade-offs:

> Nonphotochromic/nonpolarized lenses are the least expensive, but they have the narrowest usable range (due to a static VLT, or visual light transmission) and offer little protection against glare.

> Nonphotochromic/polarized lenses offer glare protection and are reasonably priced, but they still have a narrow usable range.

> Photochromic/nonpolarized lenses can be used in the widest range of light conditions, but they are expensive and they offer no glare protection.

> Photochromic/polarized lenses would seem like the best type, but the polarization limits the photochromic range, making them less versatile than comparable photochromic/nonpolarized lenses. They are also the most expensive.

Personally, I've been very happy with my Julbo Dirt ($190, 2 oz) sunglasses with polarized/photochromic Falcon lenses (9–20% VLT). However, they wouldn't be dark enough for glacier travel (which I don't do), and they're too dark in shady forests or in heavy overcast (when I don't need sunglasses anyway). I prefer photochromic lenses over interchangeable lenses, which are a hassle in the field.

Goggles

Only on one trip, when daytime high temperatures were below minus 10°F and there was a fierce Arctic wind, have I needed goggles. In warmer conditions, goggles are too good at protecting my face: They fog up because my skin starts perspiring.

footwear

Our mistake was textbook. A few miles before our first camp, Gerry mentioned to me that he might have some blisters coming on. We should have known to address them immediately, especially since we'd identified foot health as being vital to this project, but we decided instead to deal with them later. Indeed, that's exactly what happened.

When I saw Gerry's feet in camp, I instantly regretted our decision and felt that I'd let him down. He was an experienced endurance athlete but was relying on my backpacking know-how to complete an ambitious seven-day thru-hike of the 224-mile John Muir Trail. With Gerry now having nickel-size blisters on the ball of each foot that I rightly feared would become the size of quarters and eventually half-dollars, with pain to match, our goal suddenly seemed less viable.

In trying to manage the blisters, we tried every trick in the book. At least once per day, we applied fresh dressings of Leukotape and moleskin donuts, and sometimes duct tape and Bonnie's Balm Healing Salve. Gerry aired out his feet at every rest stop and kept them warm and dry each night. I once carried him across a river so he could keep his shoes dry. We tried multiple pairs of socks and cut holes in his insoles to relieve pressure. Alas, the genie was out of the bottle, and recovery would not begin until we reached Mount Whitney or quit. Gerry, being

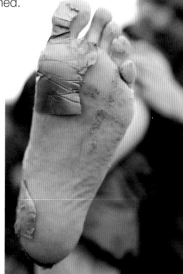

Feet are like car tires: Without good ones, a muscular engine and a full tank of gas are useless. You must take care of them.

exceptionally tough, refused to stop short of the lower 48's high point, reaching it on schedule, remarkably.

The goal of this chapter is to help you avoid Gerry's experience. That starts with the selection and testing of footwear and continues in the field with diligent foot care. With both, you're more likely to have happy feet, which makes for a happy hiker.

Boots & shoes

What to eat and what to wear on your feet are the two most personal choices that backpackers make. For every backpacker who swears by a particular product, I could find another for which it does not work at all. Rather than engage in this debate, I will offer some parameters to help you find an appropriate footwear system for you.

Considerations

When buying boots or shoes for three-season conditions, or deciding which pair to use on a particular trip, what characteristics are most important?

Fit. Your boots and shoes need to fit your foot, period. Online reviews, "gear of the year" accolades, and a discounted price may lead you to them, but are no guarantee of a good fit. Well-fitting boots and shoes will:

> Match the length, width, volume, and general shape of your foot;
> Securely cradle your foot, especially your heel, but without causing uncomfortable pressure points or irritating bones or tendons; and
> Allow for a natural walking gait, including foot strike and push-off.

Your shoe of choice may—but need not—have a wide toe box, barefoot-inspired design, rockered geometry, zero drop, medial post, maximalist cushion, or any other yet-to-be-invented feature that is touted to cure podiatric ills. Such design specifics are just means to the larger goal: a good fit.

how2

shop for new shoes

1 Wear your preferred hiking sock to ensure an accurate fit.

2 Jam your toes into the front of the shoe and try to squeeze your index finger between your heel and the back of the shoe. If you cannot, the shoe is too short and your toenails will get battered and blistered during downhills.

3 After lacing the shoes, try moving your heel up and down, forward and backward, and side to side. A good heel cup and lacing system should lock your heel securely in place and limit this movement.

4 Wiggle your toes. The toe box should be roomy enough to do so, but not so roomy that your foot slides side to side, which will become a problem when side-hilling.

5 Take a short walk to ensure that the shoe allows for a natural stride, foot-plant, and heel-to-toe rotation.

tools & techniques

67

Durability. Footwear with an unsatisfactory life span is problematic. First, the cost of replacement adds up. Second, such shoes can't be trusted on longer trips with infrequent resupply opportunities. If they blow out, you're out of luck—most repairs merely buy time and must be babied.

Shoe uppers made extensively of mesh particularly worry me, and I will not even consider them for backpacking if they lack a reinforcing exoskeleton and a sturdy toe bumper. Mesh offers unrivaled airflow and is more supple than leather or heavy-duty nylon, but it tends to prematurely rip and fray. To extend the life span of mesh uppers with subpar durability, I will preemptively apply Aquaseal glue where blowouts are known to occur.

I expect my shoes to last about 500 miles before needing replacement, plus or minus depending on the conditions to which they are exposed (e.g., wet or dry, on-trail or off-trail).

I swap out my shoes about every 500 miles.

Normally there is not a definitive moment at which shoes must be replaced. Rather, with continued use the upper will show increasing signs of stress, the cushioning will become thinner, and the outsole will wear flatter. When I'm no longer confident that they will hold up or remain comfortable through the end of a trip (or until my next resupply), I will swap them out. For an important trip, I'm more willing to use a new pair than to risk more miles in an older one.

Protection & sensitivity. Fortuitously, durable uppers—which will have a toe bumper and be made of either real or synthetic leather, or nylon mesh with a rigid exoskeleton— also better protect the sides and top of the foot. This is more than a nice-to-have quality when bushwhacking, talus-hopping, scrambling, or kicking steps into hard snow.

For more manicured trails, a protective upper is less important. However, all-mesh uppers tend to have some stretch, and thus struggle to firmly secure the foot, laterally and fore/aft, resulting in sloppy control.

To protect the foot from hard and uneven surfaces, shoes may feature a soft foam midsole, midsole rock plate, or rigid outsole. Midsole foam absorbs impact and is normally made of ethylene vinyl acetate, or EVA. Polyurethane (PU) foam is more resilient, but heavier and more expensive. A stiff outsole or midsole helps to blunt pressure but does not cushion it. Stiffness has additional value when kicking steps into snow or trying

part (2)

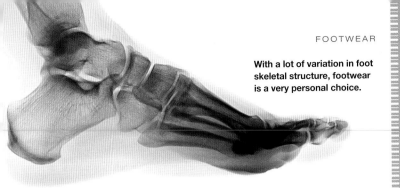

With a lot of variation in foot skeletal structure, footwear is a very personal choice.

to hold an edge on steep terrain or rocky scrambles.

Underfoot protection, however, comes at the expense of another essential quality of footwear: sensitivity. When wearing shoes lacking ground feel, I feel less agile and less confident in my foot placements.

What is the optimal balance of underfoot protection and sensitivity? For well-maintained surfaces, I gravitate toward a plusher, more cushioned ride. But for precision handling when on technical trails or off-trail, I opt for stiffness over cushion, and a low center of gravity. This way, my feet can better feel the surface with which they are in contact, while still having some underfoot protection.

Grippy outsole. Secure purchase, especially on wet or uneven ground, is largely a function of the outsole's compound, design, and durability. A branded outsole, such as from Vibram or Michelin, is an encouraging sign; but some manufacturers, particularly those with a climbing history like La Sportiva, have proprietary

rubber compounds that are equally grippy. There is a general trade-off between stickiness and durability, but some rubbers are better than others.

An aggressively lugged outsole is appropriate for mud or snow. But a moderate design is usually best: It will be lighter and offer better overall traction on a wider range of surfaces since more rubber is in contact with the ground and since big lugs wobble under pressure. Outsoles with minimal tread are slick and short-lived, but light.

Weight. Six times more energy is required to move weight on the feet versus weight in a backpack. I'm not making up the ratio—read "Energy Cost of Backpacking in Heavy Boots," by S. J. Legg and A. Mahanty, published in *Ergonomics,* Volume 29, Issue 3, 1986, pages 433–438. So wearing two-pound shoes instead of four-pound shoes is equivalent to lightening up your pack by 12 pounds!

Heavy footwear causes premature fatigue and general clumsiness. I would propose that this increases the likelihood of an accident, such as

To improve the life span of my shoes, I use Gear Aid's Aquaseal urethane repair adhesive and sealant to fortify known blowout points before I take them outdoors.

tools & techniques

rolling an ankle, badly stubbing a toe, or tumbling on talus.

Air permeability. In warmer weather, footwear with high air permeability (i.e., a mesh upper) is overwhelmingly preferable to waterproofness. Your feet will stay cooler, foot sweat will more easily evaporate, and your shoes and socks will dry faster after getting wet. Overall, this will best prevent the risk of blisters, maceration, and fungal infection.

In prolonged wet conditions, "waterproof" footwear—which is made of waterproof/breathable fabric, treated leather, or polyurethane-coated nylon—is ineffective at keeping your feet dry. Seriously, someone needs to file a false advertising lawsuit. The breathability of waterproof/breathable fabrics is inadequate to keep up with normal rates of perspiration, and, with moderate use, the fabric's waterproofness will be compromised by overstressed seams and exposure to dirt and sweat. The sealant on

full-grain leather wears down, and restoration is not factory-level quality. And a waterproof/nonbreathable fabric will trap all perspiration.

Even if the uppers were effective in keeping feet dry, boots and shoes still have a giant opening at the top, into which water will flow if you accidentally step into a deep puddle or must ford a swollen creek. Also, water will run down your legs and into the shoes while hiking in heavy rain or through tall dew-covered grass.

Options

Boots and shoes for backpacking are not easily sorted into well-defined categories. Instead, they fall along a rough spectrum. On one end is the classic "backpacking boot," featuring a full-grain leather upper, thick rubber outsole, and highly constructed midsole with PU foam, rock plates, and thermoplastic polyurethane (TPU) shanks that increase torsional rigidity.

At the other end of this spectrum is the "trail-running shoe." This

Are high-top boots helpful?

By design, feet and ankles adapt to surface abnormalities—they are incredibly nimble and dexterous. In contrast, knees and hips have a more limited range of motion, as anyone who has seen me dance will confirm. By constricting an ankle in a high-top boot, a less capable part of the body (e.g., knees and hips) is forced to absorb unevenness in the terrain. Moreover, a high-top boot does not guarantee a sprain-less trip: Weak ankles will still roll under pressure. However, high-tops can offer some assistance.

Not really.

part (2)

Hikers' footwear options fall along a spectrum.

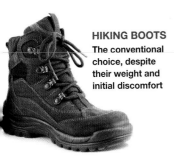

HIKING BOOTS
The conventional choice, despite their weight and initial discomfort

TRAIL RUNNERS
Lightweight and comfortable, but generally not as durable or supportive

HIKING SHOES
A happy medium—lighter than boots, more supportive than running shoes

category has been heavily influenced by the barefoot movement, and I personally feel that many of the newer models are too flimsy for backpacking (though lovely for running.) Thankfully, many models still feature a nylon mesh upper with a reinforcing exoskeleton, and a midsole and outsole with some underfoot protection and stiffness.

In between the stereotypical backpacking boot and trail-running shoe are "hiking boots" and "hiking shoes." Hiking boots could be described as scaled-down backpacking boots, and hiking shoes as ruggedized trail-running shoes, or maybe low-cut hiking boots.

It is not difficult to find exceptions to these generalities, however, and these product categories quickly get messy. For example, the midsole construction of low-end backpacking boots can be as simple as the average trail-running shoe, and some of the most popular trail-running shoes have waterproof and high-top versions.

Boots or shoes?

Backpackers are expected to wear boots. But for three-season trips, *most* will have better results with low-cut, nonwaterproof trail-running shoes. Here's why:

> They are comfortable right out of the box. Unlike boots, they do not need to be "broken in," which is a kind description for a boot's earliest miles, characterized by foot soreness and blisters.

> They keep the foot cooler and drier because heat and moisture easily escape through the mesh upper. If they get damp or soaked by external moisture, they are quick to dry.

> They absorb less moisture than boots because they are made of fewer materials.

Continued on p. 74

tools & techniques

tried&true

how to take care of your feet

part (2)

Because my itineraries are extremely hiking-centric, I need to care for my feet 24/7. If I fail to notice and remedy a problem, I'll have to spend more time in camp than I want to in order to let my paws recover. I also insist that others in my group be equally vigilant—just one person with battered feet can immobilize all of us.

There are four basic themes to my foot care regimen that have served me well over the years:

Preemptive treatment
Spending five to ten minutes now can save hours of lost time (and/or

miles of painful hiking) later on. Before I even leave the trailhead or camp, I protect areas where I get frequent blisters with Leukotape. If I notice an emerging "hot spot" after I begin hiking, I protect this irritated skin immediately before it becomes a blister. I keep my toenails short to prevent blisters from forming underneath them, and I keep them devoid of sharp edges that will cut adjacent toes and/or snag my socks.

Clean, warm, & dry

I wash my socks daily (inside and out; no soap) to prevent grit and organic matter from abrading my skin. At least once a day I take off my shoes and socks to let my feet dry and air out. And at night I put on a clean, dry, and warm pair of socks, which helps my feet recover overnight so they can withstand another day of abuse.

Moisture management

When my feet are kept wet, the outer layer of skin absorbs water and becomes pruned (or macerated). Macerated feet are itchy, sore, and blister prone, and they can crack after drying out. However, I know of no technique to keep my feet dry in prolonged wet conditions—I've experimented with every conceivable solution (including waterproof shoes, waterproof socks, and even rubber boots), and they all fail. Instead, I hope simply to minimize the effects of wet feet:

> At night, after my feet have dried out, I coat the bottoms with Bonnie's Balm. This moisturizes my skin and serves like a water sealant, which will help to reduce maceration the next day. It works best when it has had several hours to absorb into the skin—it will not help much if it's applied immediately before your feet get wet.

> I wear thin socks and non-waterproof shoes made of low-absorption materials, which do not retain as much water as thick socks, conventional boots, or "waterproof" footwear. They also dry much faster.

Miles-proven footwear

Before I trust new shoes and socks on a long trip, I test them during low-risk outings. Generally, I like a small-volume shoe with a secure heel lock, roomy toe box, and generous cushion and forefoot protection but without any "corrective" supports like medial posts. Poor biomechanics and/or a weak muscular system may be partially remedied by orthotics or arch supports. And blisters between toes can be solved with Injinji toe socks.

Got a blister? First, lance it and drain the fluid. Second, try to identify its cause(s): heat, friction, or moisture. Third, address these contributing factors, which sometimes requires creativity.

tools & techniques

> They are less expensive, relative to boots of comparable quality, but generally don't last as long as boots either.
> At 1.5 to 2 pounds per pair (for men's size 9), trail-running shoes are about half the weight of a backpacking boot at 3 to 4 pounds. In terms of energy expenditure, this is equivalent to dropping 9 to 12 pounds from a backpack.

	boots	hiking shoes
best use	Mountaineering, back-packing in dry snow	Backpacking with moderate load and/or on rough terrain
comfort	Uncomfortable until "broken in"	Comfortable out of the box
breathability	Poor; leather prevents escape of moisture	Decent, so long as they have no WP/B liner
dry time	Once wet, very difficult to get dry	Better than boots; not as good as running shoes
durability	1,000+ miles	750-ish miles
underfoot protection	Excellent	Good or fair
sensitivity/ agility	Poor	Fair
weight per pair	3 to 4 lb	2 to 3 lb
ideal temperature range	Cool or cold	Mild or cool
water resistance	Best, but foot will get soaked in prolonged wet conditions	Minimal without WP/B liner, some with
sole stiffness	Very stiff	Moderate
support	Maximum, but overkill for most applications and users	Good
cost	$150+	$100 to $150

I have worn trail-running shoes on all of my long-distance backpacking trips, even on rugged off-trail outings in the High Sierra and Iceland, and on wet and muddy trips in Alaska and the Appalachians. Most of my clients wear trail-running shoes as well, and I have never heard one express regret about their decision. In fact, clients new to trail-running shoes typically say something like, "Where have these shoes been my whole life?"

Stability & ankle support

Admittedly, my footwear recommendation is biased by my personal circumstance. I'm a lifelong runner; I have good biomechanics and no history of foot injuries; my skeletal system is well supported by strong muscles, ligaments, and tendons; and I carry a lightweight backpack and use two trekking poles.

If you can't say the same, you may be a candidate for footwear that provides more stability, support, and motion control through medial posts, TPU shanks, or a high ankle cuff. If you are especially prone to ankle sprains, you might even consider an ankle brace. A limited number of trail-running shoes would fit the bill, but you'll find more options if you expand your search into hiking shoes, hiking boots, or even backpacking boots.

trail-running shoes

Trail running and backpacking with light load

Comfortable out of the box

Good, so long as they have no WP/B liner

Fast

500-ish miles

Fair or poor

Good or excellent

1 to 2 lb

Warm or mild

Minimal without WP/B liner, some with

Minimal

Fair

$100 to $150

skurka'spicks
BOOTS & SHOES

My favorite three-season trips are mostly off-trail. This exposes my shoes to extensive brush, lingering snowfields, unbridged water crossings, and talus, scree, and slickrock. In short, my shoes must

tools & techniques

stand up to abuse and must protect my feet.

Within this context, I'll offer several preferred pairs, with the expectation that at least one or two of these models will remain in production for multiple seasons and will fit you well. Try the **La Sportiva Ultra Raptor** ($130, 12 oz), **Adidas Terrex Fast R** ($115, 12 oz), and **Salewa Ultra Train** ($140, 10 oz).

If you want more shoe, consider these options: the **Salomon X Ultra** ($120, 13 oz), **Merrell Capra Sport** ($130, 13 oz), or **Salewa Multi Sport** ($140, 12 oz). If you instead want a cushioned shoe for easy trails, look at the **Altra Lone Peak 3.0** ($120, 11 oz). ▧

Unconventional footwear

Most backpackers will be best served by boots or shoes. But I'd like to weigh in specifically on the use of multisport sandals, water shoes, and minimalist barefoot shoes.

While I don't think camp shoes are worth it, if you must have them, Crocs are a good option.

Sandals & water shoes

For warm weather and wet conditions, multisport sandals and water shoes are appealing. They vent extremely well, absorb little water, and dry quickly. I have experimented with such footwear: I carried Chaco sandals on my Appalachian Trail thru-hike, and I wore Salomon water shoes for several hundred miles through the Grand Canyon. Ultimately, I concluded that they were ill-suited for backpacking:

> My feet were too vulnerable to rocks, sticks, thorns, and abrasive dirt. I'm still emotionally scarred from the half-dozen cactus needles that impaled my left arch.
> Because the uppers have less surface area, they rarely fit as snugly as conventional shoes, and the pressure is concentrated.
> Few models provide the cushion, underfoot protection, and stability that most backpackers desire.

Barefoot footwear

After *Born to Run* was published in 2009, minimalist footwear exploded in popularity. But models like the Vibram FiveFingers are much less popular now. With scant cushion, underfoot rigidity, or protection in the upper, I find them too minimal for running or day-hiking, never mind backpacking in rugged terrain with a week of food and gear on my back.

part ②

Extra shoes

I understand the motivations for carrying an extra pair of shoes:

> If your primary hiking shoes become uncomfortable or soaked, you have a backup pair;
> If you need to ford a creek or hike through a downpour, you can keep your primary hiking shoes dry; and
> In camp, you can wear something more comfortable (and dry).

While I've carried extra shoes before, I'd generally discourage the practice. Here are my solutions:

Backup shoes

If your primary shoes are appropriately chosen and if you have tested them previously on low-risk outings, backup shoes are unnecessary and not worth the weight. Plus, in prolonged wet conditions, you end up with two pairs of soaked shoes. It's

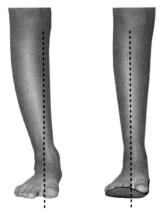

Biomechanical flaws may be solved through conditioning or arch supports, or a combination thereof.

better to learn to manage wet feet, as explained in this chapter's Tried & True feature (pp. 72–73).

River shoes

In particular locations (e.g., Alaska and the canyons of southern Utah), and in particular locations in particular seasons (e.g., the Mountain West in June), dry feet are either an impossibility or an unjustifiable time sink. There is too much water or snow and too little dry ground or bridges. Short of fishing waders, nothing will keep your feet dry from external moisture, and, in the case of fishing waders, your feet will get soaked from perspiration. In this scenario, I wear my hiking shoes full-time and expect them to be constantly soaked by standing water and creeks. A dry pair of sleeping socks awaits me in camp.

In drier conditions, my approach to water crossings depends on the nature of the waterway:

> For a relatively safe crossing, I will remove my shoes, but wear my dirtiest pair of socks. By doing so, I keep my shoes dry, have more protection and traction than bare feet, and incidentally wash my socks.
> For riskier crossings, I wear my hiking shoes. They'll obviously be drenched when I reach the far shore, but I'll be safe. In warm and dry conditions, they will dry out within a few hours or overnight.

Camp shoes

I will carry dedicated camp footwear in one circumstance: If I expect to spend a considerable amount of time in camp *and* if I expect my hiking shoes to be wet. Airline slippers and clog-style sandals work best; bread bags or gallon-size freezer bags (to protect my dry camp socks from my wet shoes) are a lighter solution.

Otherwise, if I want end-of-day relief, I will loosen my shoelaces and remove my insole, and perhaps soak my feet in a cold stream or lake.

Insoles

Shoes and boots come with a non-supportive, generic foam insert that is most accurately described as a "sock liner." To increase support, to accommodate foot particularities, and to improve the fit and comfort of footwear, you may consider custom orthotics or prefabricated arch supports.

Personally, I do not use or feel the need for these products. When I have tried them, I found that they didn't fill the footbed perfectly, that they lifted my heel out of the shoe, or that they were too stiff and corrective.

Sock thickness affects the fit of shoes. I prefer a single pair of liner socks.

how 2

use sock systems for wet and dry climates

1 If I expect that my socks will get wet, then: I hike in my "daytime" socks—which get wet and stay wet. After arriving at camp and letting my feet air-dry, I put on my dry "sleeping" socks, which I never use during the day.

2 If I expect that my socks will not get wet, then: I leave camp wearing Pair A, with Pair B in my pack. Around midday, I rotate Pairs A and B. When convenient, I hand-wash Pair A (no soap) and loop the socks through my pack's compression straps so they can dry. When I pull into camp, I take off the dirty Pair B, let my feet dry, and put on Pair A, which is clean and dry. I leave camp in the morning wearing Pair A. When convenient, I wash Pair B, which will be dry and clean by midday so that they can be rotated again.

However, I know that many others have had the opposite experience: With aftermarket or custom insoles, their shoes were more comfortable and they were no longer hindered by systemic problems, such as a leg length discrepancy, excessive internal rotation, compensation for past injuries, muscle or tendon tightness, and/or a weak muscular or skeletal system.

Prefabricated arch supports from Superfeet, SOLE, and Spenco cost $30 to $50 and last about one year, depending on the intensity of use. If you experience recurring foot problems that you cannot self-remedy, seek the help of a foot health professional, who may recommend custom orthotics. These are based on a mold of your feet and are most helpful for those with very wide or narrow feet, specific biomechanical issues, or high arches, as well as for very heavy or large individuals. Orthotics cost $300 or more and can last years.

If you use arch supports or orthotics, you should take them with you when you go shopping for new footwear.

Socks

In three-season conditions, I wear lightweight socks in order to:

> Prevent blisters by reducing friction between my skin and shoes, and between my skin and debris that has entered my shoes; and

> Prevent maceration by wicking moisture away from my skin.

Darn Tough, DeFeet, Injinji, Smart-Wool, and Wigwam, among other brands, specialize in outdoor socks; many big retailers and athletic apparel companies make socks, too. Socks may seem like a generic item, but they are not—their materials, thickness, and construction greatly affect their performance.

Materials

Most socks are made primarily from polyester or merino wool. But they should also include nylon for improved durability, especially in high-friction areas like the toes and heel, as well as a small amount of spandex for improved fit. For more detailed fiber information, refer to the Clothing chapter (pp. 30–65).

Three-season conditions

The conventional three-season backpacking sock system consists of two

The ever trustworthy Wooleator

pairs. A thin liner sock is worn next to the skin. Its primary purpose is to manage moisture. Between the liner sock and the shoe, a thicker outer sock is worn to provide cushioning and insulation. I've also heard the claim that this two-sock system helps to prevent blisters by reducing friction, one of the three factors in blister formation. However, two socks will also create more heat and absorb more moisture, which are the other two.

Personally, I wear only a liner sock, specifically the DeFeet Wooleator 3-inch ($15, 2 oz per pair), which has been the case since 2007. The Wooleator is thin and unpadded; it's made of 63 percent merino wool, 36 percent nylon, and 1 percent spandex. If I sought more padding, I would look for a more cushioned shoe before I used a more padded sock. I would suggest a different sock only if you tend to get blisters between your toes. In that case, look at toe socks from Injinji.

how 2

make a fashion statement with your gaiters

1 Visit *www.dirtygirl gaiters.com.*

2 Place an order for a pattern like Wild Thang, Fetish, Lime Gaiterade Hurl, or Running with the Rockstars. Dirty Girl gaiters cost $19 and weigh 1.2 ounces per pair.

3 When they arrive, make sure to install the Velcro strip to the back of your shoe. Otherwise they will slip off the hind foot.

Gaiters help to keep dirt, sand, rocks, and sticks from getting into my shoes.

I prefer just a liner sock because they:

> Dry faster;
> Absorb less moisture; and
> Are cooler in three-season conditions.

I prefer the Wooleator over DeFeet's polyester version, the Aireator, because it better resists odor and remains more supple over multiple days. The Wooleators are fantastically durable: I replace them about every 300 miles when on the trail and less often at home when I can better clean them.

Gaiters

Dirt, leaves, sticks, rocks, sand, and snow can enter my shoes, usually through the gap between the ankle and the shoe. The purpose of gaiters is to seal this gap and, ultimately, keep my feet cleaner and happier.

When hiking in shorts, I wear gaiters full-time; when in pants, they are helpful but less critical.

Conventional gaiters are made of waterproof/breathable fabric or coated nylon, and stay positioned with a durable instep strap and with a metal hook that grabs the shoelaces. Prices range from $25 to $90, and weights range from 5 to 12 ounces per pair. Unfortunately, the mountaineering-inspired gaiters from Black Diamond, Mountain Hardwear, and Outdoor Research perform poorly for three-season backpacking:

> Their breathability and ventilation are limited, contributing to the buildup of perspiration and the overheating of the lower legs;
> The gaiters are broadly sized— usually S/M and L/XL—so the fit is often imperfect. The calf cuff can be loose, the body can be baggy, and the hook can be incorrectly aligned with the laces; and

NEOS overboots are versatile, but heavier and bulkier than winter boots.

When hiking in snow (or snowshoeing), I wear a waterproof mid- or high-top boot.

> Since many trail-running shoes and hiking shoes lack an instep, the instep strap prematurely fails due to intense abrasion.

A better option is the Simblissity LevaGaiter ($27, 2 oz per pair). They stay put without an instep strap or cord, and, relative to conventional gaiters, they cost less, breathe better, and are lighter. Unfortunately, the LevaGaiters are rarely available, since Simblissity is not the owner's full-time concern. Even worse, I do not know of a comparable alternative. For on-trail hiking, the Dirty Girl gaiters are a decent solution, but they'd be quickly thrashed on rugged outings.

Beyond three seasons

In the Colorado Rockies, three-season conditions extend from about June through September. In other parts of the world, the season can be longer or shorter. What footwear systems do I use for the remainder of the year?

Boots & shoes

Low-cut, nonwaterproof trail-running shoes are a tough sell for daytime temperatures near or below freezing. For hiking or snow-shoeing in such conditions, I instead use a waterproof back-packing boot like the Salomon X Ultra Mid GTX ($165, 14 oz) to keep my feet warm and dry while pushing through frozen snow. Although, when I purchase boots again, I will look more seriously at full-grain leather models, since their waterproofness can be better restored. For skiing, I own full-grain leather telemark boots and plastic alpine touring boots, which are insulated with Thinsulate and foam, respectively.

Socks

A traditional backpacking sock is better suited for cool and cold

The extra thickness of my cold-weather socks forces me to use a larger shoe.

temperatures, when insulation is needed. I have been a longtime user of the DeFeet Woolie Boolie 6-inch ($16, 3 oz), which has a similar material blend as the Wooleator. I may use it as my only sock on backpacking trips in the fall or in milder temperatures if my feet will be constantly soaked by cold water. Another option for this latter scenario are socks made of neoprene, which is a nonbreathable synthetic rubber that provides good insulation, even when wet; it is used to make fishing waders and diving wet suits.

In frigid temperatures (i.e., daytime highs no higher than about 20°F), I combine the Wooleator 5-inch with the Woolie Boolie. If I'm concerned about the long-term accumulation of moisture in my footwear, I may also add an Integral Designs vapor barrier sock, worn between the Wooleator and the Woolie Boolie.

Gaiters

Since my snowshoeing and telemark ski boots have an instep, I have a wider selection of gaiters from which to choose. My pick is the Outdoor Research Flex-Tex II ($55, 4 oz per gaiter). They are midheight, have a trim fit, and are made of uncoated stretchy nylon with relatively high air permeability.

Overboots

If I expect temperatures to exceed the warmth of my wintertime boots and socks, I may use neoprene overboots for extra insulation. Daytime high temperatures must be

In extreme cold, I wear hiking shoes inside a neoprene overboot.

colder than 10°F to 15°F for me to consider this option. When snowshoeing, I use the Forty Below Light Energy overboots ($130, 16 oz per pair), which are designed to fit low-profile shoes like running shoes or hiking shoes; they are made of 3-mm neoprene and feature an integrated gaiter. Two other cold-weather options are:

> Steger Mukluks, which are made of moosehide and are Native American inspired. They are very warm but not as stiff or supportive as the shoe/overboot combination; they are best for walking around town or on packed trails; and

> NEOS overshoes, which have a rubber outsole and waterproof nylon upper. They are clumsy and heavy, and I would rather wear waterproof boots than a running shoe/NEOS combination.

sleeping bags & pads

"You looked so cold last night that I considered inviting you into my sleeping bag," said Wild Boar, my sheltermate, when I sat up in the morning. Despite her not being my type and despite having met her just ten hours earlier, I responded, "Yeah, I would have liked that."

A cold front had moved into Vermont's Green Mountains the day before, and a clear overnight sky allowed temperatures to plummet into the 40s. It didn't help that the shelter was situated in a deep gorge into which cold air had settled. Six weeks earlier, while farther south on the Appalachian Trail, I had exchanged my three-season mummy bag—which was overkill for the mid-Atlantic's summertime heat—for a 300-weight fleece blanket. And I had gone to bed the night before resigned to nightlong shivering because I thought it was the unavoidable consequence of having an inadequate sleeping bag.

In fact, I could have taken more measures to improve my nighttime

Many factors affect your nighttime warmth, including your shelter and tentmates.

warmth. I could have better insulated myself from the cold shelter floor, like by putting my backpack underneath my feet or sleeping outside the shelter on some uncompacted forest duff; worn my rain jacket and any other extra clothing; reduced the draftiness of my shelter; better hydrated myself and prepared a second dinner before turning in; placed a hot water bottle at my feet; and/or, yes, spooned with Wild Boar. But of the tools that can help keep me warm at night, three are disproportionately important: my sleeping bag, sleeping pad, and shelter, the first two of which I discuss in this chapter.

Sleeping bags

A sleeping bag reduces convective heat loss by trapping body-warmed air in tiny pockets so it does not dissipate freely into the atmosphere. These air pockets are formed by high-loft insulation like goose down or synthetic fill, which is sandwiched between two layers of fabric.

The warmth of a sleeping bag is a function of its insulation (type and amount), shell fabrics, style, and construction. Sleeping bags use the same insulations and shell fabrics used in insulated clothing, and they are covered in that chapter.

Temperature ratings

To help convey the environmental conditions for which a sleeping bag is intended, it is assigned a temperature rating, or several ratings. These ratings can be determined in two ways:

how 2

learn the best uses for your bag

1 Use sleeping bags first on low-risk trips in your backyard or on quick overnights so that you can easily bail and avoid the consequences of prolonged failure.

2 Learn your bag's optimal and extreme uses by testing it in a range of temperatures.

3 Discover how your nighttime warmth is affected by using the bag in conjunction with different sleeping pads, clothing systems, and shelters.

> Field-testing and comparative analysis, or
> European Norm (EN) 13537, a standard laboratory test.

The former system is more likely to produce arbitrary ratings, especially between brands. Unless it's explained otherwise, the rating should be interpreted as the coldest temperature at which an average sleeper will remain comfortably warm. But to gauge their true accuracy, I recommend consulting online reviews, customer service

tools & techniques

reps, and store associates. Some brands have proven to be more trustworthy and to have better quality control than others.

Thankfully, EN 13537 ratings are increasingly common, even in the United States, where published ratings need not be validated through testing. The EN standard uses a sensor-covered mannequin to measure the thermal resistance of a sleep system, of which the sleeping bag is a core part. To generate apples-to-apples results, technicians have standardized all other variables, including the warmth of the sleeping pad and the mannequin's clothing (base layer shirt and pants, and socks), as well as environmental factors like humidity, wind speed, and radiant temperature. Based on the system's resistance, four temperature ratings are assigned:

> Maximum;
> Comfort;
> Limit; and
> Extreme.

The Extreme rating should be ignored—don't buy (or pull from your closet) a sleeping bag based on the temperature at which you're predicted to become hypothermic but survive. The Maximum rating is rarely provided by U.S. manufacturers because it requires another mannequin test. More important, consider whether the bag will allow you to vent easily if you become too warm.

The Comfort rating is technically described as the minimum temperature at which a woman will remain comfortable in a relaxed posture; the Limit rating, the minimum temperature at which a man will remain comfortable in a curled position. But it's more useful to interpret the Comfort and Limit ratings as a range based on the physiological variability among

	mummy	top bag
availability	Most popular style, widespread distribution	Notably Big Agnes, Sierra Designs, Therm-a-Rest
thermal efficiency (i.e., warmth per weight)	Sleeper crushes up to 30% of insulation. Zippers add weight, not warmth.	Attachment system offsets the elimination of underside materials
usable temperature range	Chest zippers offer best venting. Full-length side zippers are heavy but enable quilt-like use.	Fixed girth limits the wearing of additional clothing. Cannot be used as a quilt.
user friendliness	Very draft resistant, but active sleepers may get tangled up inside it	More stable and secure than a detached mummy and pad

people (which is imperfectly correlated with gender).

In the case of exceptional physiologies or dissimilar conditions, the EN ratings remain useful for comparing bags, but will be less reliable in predicting nighttime warmth. For example, the Limit rating may be conservative for Denver Broncos linebacker Von Miller (who is 6 feet 3 inches tall and weighs 249 pounds), whereas the Comfort rating may be optimistic for my wife's petite 94-year-old grandmother. Individual factors besides body type and muscle mass also play a role, like your hydration and nourishment, fatigue, acclimatization to outside temperatures, and backcountry experience.

Styles

My first sleeping bag was an inexpensive, flannel-lined, rectangular bag that refused to be contained by any stuff sack. But I was only ten, and it was perfect for car-camping with my family and the Boy Scouts. In advance of my first real backpacking trip ten years later, I upgraded to a mummy bag.

Mummy bags like the REI Flash ($260, 1 lb 10 oz) fully enclose the body and head in a cocoon-like wrap of insulation. The integrated hood further minimizes drafts, and the tapered design eliminates dead air spaces inside the bag that otherwise would have to be kept warm.

Mummies are all constructed with the same types of insulation, shell fabrics, and construction techniques, often at the same factories in Asia. Multiple brands offer gender-specific bags that mirror the shape of average men and women. Production differentiation is a challenge for manufacturers.

quilt	wearable
A popular cottage product with a growing retail presence due to hammocks	Rare. Will need to search out.
Excellent. No wasted underside materials, no zippers, optional attachment points.	Highly dependent on the design. Insulating separate arms and legs is material-intensive.
Vents well. Variable girth accommodates a range of clothing systems. Struggles in colder temperatures.	Highly dependent on the design
Simple and versatile, but can be drafty. The consensus pick for hammock camping.	In theory, the most versatile bag type, but does it do anything well?

tools & techniques

Especially on clear nights, I avoid open campsites like this one due to extreme radiant heat loss.

Despite being the most popular bag style, the mummy design has drawbacks:

> It is easy to become disoriented inside the bag if you twist and turn, making it hard to stay on your sleeping pad, to locate the side zipper for a midnight pee, or to keep your face aligned with the hood's opening. Wide bags are better in this regard, but they are heavier and less warm (because of dead air pockets).

> Most designs have limited venting features and are therefore not comfortable across a wide range of temperatures. Hoods can be loosened, but the traditional side zipper causes unequal venting. Chest zippers are better, but prohibit the bag from being opened fully and used as a quilt.

> About 30 percent of a mummy's potential warmth is wasted because the insulation is crushed underneath the sleeper, where it cannot loft and trap body-warmed air in its tiny chambers.

> Due to its fixed girth, a wide range of clothing systems cannot be worn without creating dead air space or becoming claustrophobic.

There are three alternative designs to mummy bags:

Top bags like the Therm-a-Rest Antares HD ($500, 1 lb 15 oz) are identical to mummies with one exception: On the underside, you'll find a

Because of their variable girth, quilts can be paired with a range of clothing systems.

single layer of fabric (no insulation or baffles) plus straps or a sleeve so that the bag can be attached to a sleeping pad. The weight, cost, and compressibility of a top bag are about the same as a mummy, all things being equal. Personal preference is the more important consideration. Some appreciate being securely connected to their pad, so that they don't roll off it, while others compare it to being strapped to a gurney.

The most innovative brand in this space has been Sierra Designs, with its Backcountry Beds. These top bags have an integrated comforter that seals an oval-shaped opening in the upper half of the bag. This design retains the security of a conventional top bag while solving some drawbacks of mummy bags, like the claustrophobia and lack of ventilation.

Quilts like the Katabatic Gear Palisade ($470, 18 oz) are similar to those found on household beds. But they are constructed from outdoorworthy fabrics and insulations, and many feature a foot box that extends up to the knees or lower thighs. A quilt should be wide enough to cover a sleeper completely; extra width adds weight but reduces draftiness, especially when adjusting your sleeping position. Most quilts come with a pad attachment system to provide an optional top-bag experience, but I've found that it undermines the reasons for having a quilt and therefore remove it.

how 2

minimize quilt draftiness

The advantages of a quilt can be quickly lost if the sleeper does not address its inherent weaknesses: draftiness and usually no insulation around the head. I try to address these problems by:

1 Wearing hooded clothing at night.

2 Using a full-sided shelter, or complementing an open-ended tarp with a water-resistant bivy sack.

3 Being a calm sleeper. I taught myself to stop twisting and turning at night.

4 Buying an extra wide quilt with a hideaway hood.

Quilts are not widely used despite having many advantages in three-season conditions:

> They are more thermally efficient (i.e., warmth for weight) and more packable than other bag styles because they lack zippers, underside insulation, and material-intensive hoods and draft collars.

tools & techniques

A wearable sleeping bag from MusucBag

which you can stick your legs to walk around camp. And the Nunatak Raku ($545, 32 oz) looks like a winter parka attached to the lower portion of a mummy bag.

The advantage of a wearable bag is its multifunctionality: It serves as both a sleeping bag at night and insulated clothing in camp or during cold midday stops. They sound great in theory, but the extra build will offset some of the weight savings, and sometimes products that strive to be everything are good at nothing. With these particular bags, they must be evaluated on a case-by-case basis.

> They have a broader comfort range because they are more versatile: In warm temperatures, I can loosely drape a quilt over me; in colder temperatures, I can button up the backside and neck collar; and in camp, I can use it as a shawl.

> They dry quickly when laid out in the sun because they open up completely, in comparison to mummies and top bags without full-length zippers.

> They accommodate without compromise a range of clothing systems, due to their variable girth.

> They can be draped over the user, versus having to slide into it. This is a huge convenience when hammock camping.

skurka'spicks
SLEEPING BAGS

When nighttime temperatures are consistently above 30°F, I prefer a quilt due to its wide comfort range and thermal efficiency. My go-to is the Sierra Designs Backcountry

Wearable bags make quilts look normal. Some models, like the Jacks 'R' Better Sierra Sniveller ($270, 1 lb 8 oz), are enhanced quilts that can be configured as a serape or poncho. The Sierra Designs Mobile Mummy 800 2-Season ($350, 1 lb 11 oz) is a mummy with armholes and a long double-slider center zip through

Hiking partner Alan Dixon rocking one of the Jacks 'R' Better Sniveller quilts

part 2

Quilt ($270, 1 lb 8 oz), which has a higher temperature rating than other quilts at similar weights, but which is much less drafty due to its extra girth and length, and hideaway hood. I have used it extensively throughout the West and when hammock camping in the East. I have pushed its 38-degree EN rating into the mid-20s by wearing additional clothing but wouldn't recommend it on a regular basis.

I formerly used the synthetic-insulated Mountain Laurel Designs Spirit quilts in wet climates like the Appalachians and Alaska, where the high humidity compromises the warmth and reliability of conventional down. But with the advent of water-resistant down, wet conditions are no longer such a concern. If you can afford a down bag, go for it: The performance is superior, and its longer life span makes it a much better investment.

When temperatures are consistently below 30°F, I take a mummy bag instead of a quilt, the draftiness of which becomes too much to bear. My **Western Mountaineering VersaLite** ($575, 2 lb) is intentionally oversize in girth and length so that I can push its 10-degree comfort rating well below zero with additional insulated clothing. For big-game hunting and winter backpacking in Colorado, a warmer bag is generally unnecessary; if it is, I'll reschedule the trip, or make a reservation at a 10th Mountain Division hut.

For cold-weather sleeping bags, I again prefer down, because of its superior thermal efficiency and compressibility. To illustrate the difference, consider Montbell's 0-degree mummy bags: The 800-fill down version weighs 2 pounds 14 ounces and compresses to 10 cubic liters, whereas the synthetic-fill version weighs 5 pounds and is 50 percent larger when compressed! With either insulation, moisture management must be addressed on longer-term trips. I use vapor barrier liners, as explained in the chapter on clothing (pp. 30–65). ▧

Sleeping pads

The primary function of a sleeping pad is to minimize conductive heat loss. If I were to lie on the ground without a pad—or similar insulating layer—my body heat would freely transfer into the ground. This heat transfer would be fine if I were napping on warm beach sand, but undesirable if I were on snow or soggy compacted ground.

tip Sleeping pads can double as "virtual frames" in a frameless backpack for added structure, comfort, and capacity. They can also double as splints in emergencies.

CLOSED-CELL FOAM
Reliable and inexpensive, but bulky

AIR
Extremely plush, compactable, and (possibly) warm, but expensive and not as reliable

SELF-INFLATING
More comfortable than foam and less expensive than air pads

The warmth of a sleeping pad—or, more precisely, the pad's ability to resist heat transfer—is indicated by its R-value (R stands for "resistance"). An R-value is a linear measurement, so a pad with an R-value of 4 is four times as warm as a pad with an R-value of 1.

To varying degrees, sleeping pads also increase nighttime comfort with cushioning. If I am free to camp where I please, however, cushioning is never a necessary attribute. A thick layer of pine needles, moss, grass, and leaves can be just as comfortable—if not more so—as plush sleeping pads that weigh two to four pounds, especially if I "landscape" the surface to better match the contours of my body. Moreover, these organic materials are also less thermally conductive than hard-packed ground or rock, so I stay warmer. If I will be forced to camp in established, high-use, hard-packed sites where natural cushioning is long gone, I will be more inclined to take a more cushioned pad. A good night's rest will easily offset the extra weight.

There are three types of sleeping pads: closed-cell foam, self-inflating, and air. As with other product categories, there is no single best pad. To gain some advantages—e.g., warmth, comfort, durability, weight, and cost—trade-offs must have been made, though some less than others.

Closed-cell foam

Foam is any liquid or solid with entrapped gaseous bubbles. Solid foams can be classified as either open-cell or closed-cell, and both are used in sleeping pads. However, only closed-cell can be used as a standalone material.

Open-cell foams—like those found in couch cushions and dish sponges—have interconnected pores that permit passive air convection; these pores can also fill with water. In contrast, the gaseous bubbles in closed-cell foam are isolated in small pockets, so the material is essentially waterproof. Closed-cell foam is also stiffer and more rigid.

Closed-cell foam sleeping pads like the Therm-a-Rest RidgeRest SOLite ($30, 14 oz) are favored by minimalists and those on a budget. They are:

> Inexpensive, with even cheaper options available at big-box stores;
> Very reliable, since they can't leak or puncture; and
> Easily modifiable, like if a custom size is desired (e.g., torso-length), which helps to save weight.

Because of its construction, closed-cell foam is dense and rigid.

Therefore, these pads offer minimal cushioning, and they are not compact. Furthermore, the foam has limited rebound after compression and must be replaced every six to eight weeks of nightly use. As it flattens out, its insulation and cushion are further compromised.

Self-inflating

Therm-a-Rest owned the self-inflating pad market for many years. Like Kleenex and Xerox, the brand name is often used interchangeably with the product category. Self-inflating pads, like the Therm-a-Rest ProLite ($90, 18 oz), consist of open-cell foam that is sandwiched between nonslip polyester or nylon fabric with sealed edges. When the pad's valve is opened, the open-cell foam expands and creates a vacuum, which causes air to rush in.

When skiing in Alaska's Arctic in March, I used a bulky but reliable closed-cell foam pad.

tools & techniques

Almost like home: a comfy air pad, improvised pillow, and e-reader

In truth, these pads are only "partially self-inflating." They must always be topped off with external pressure, from lungs or a pump.

Self-inflating pads were once a luxurious upgrade over closed-cell foam. However, they have been supplanted by air pads in all performance metrics except one: cost.

Air

The most basic air pad, such as the Big Agnes Air Core ($60, 21 oz), is similar to an inflatable pool toy. Its horizontal or vertical baffles lack any internal material or construction to reduce the exchange within the pad of body-warmed air with ground-cooled air, or air displacement due to uneven pressure on the mat.

Most pads, like the Sea-to-Summit Comfort Light Insulated ($170, 21 oz), are more complex. To minimize convective and radiant heat loss, they are filled with down or synthetic insulations, feature mini air chambers within the larger baffles, or use Mylar-coated fabrics. To improve stability, additional structure or materials are used to minimize air displacement.

Air pads are dreamy, with unrivaled thickness, compactness, and (in most cases) warmth. But, of course, they are not perfect. They are the most expensive, especially the insulated versions, and they are prone to leaks and delamination. Air-chamber pads filled with down or synthetic insulations must be inflated with a pump because moisture-filled breaths will adversely affect the insulation's warmth; the life span of synthetic insulations is also relatively short-lived. Finally, in cold conditions, they need to be reinflated after lung-warmed air cools down and condenses.

Pillows

If you use a pillow at home like I do, you will miss one in the field if you cannot replicate your preferred sleeping posture. A few sleeping pads have integrated pillows; if yours does not, pneumatic pillows are widely available.

My preference, however, is to improvise a pillow in the field. First, I'll look for a sleeping area with a natural incline where I can rest my head. Second, I'll create a pillow with stuff sacks, spare clothing, and water bottles; I will also use my food bag, which is a decision that requires more discussion than I will give it here. In addition to

part 2

a headrest, I also like support under my knees to reduce stress on my lower back and to prevent the hyperextension of my knees.

skurka's picks
SLEEPING PADS

For many years I used a torso-length SOLite foam pad in three-season conditions to save weight and give my frameless backpack more structure. I would insulate my lower body with my backpack, maps, and oftentimes my food bag; where permitted, I would seek out low- or no-use camps with soft ground.

But during my guided trips, on which pack weight is a lower priority and established camps are the norm, I became addicted to the comfort of air pads, specifically the **Therm-a-Rest NeoAir XLite** ($160, 12 oz). Now, even on aggressive solo trips, I take one in the belief that the extra weight is offset by the enhanced sleep quality. I also own a less expensive non-insulated air pad for summer weather, when the XLite (with an R-value of 3.2) is too warm.

I've used several pads in the winter. I like the **RidgeRest Solar** ($40, 19 oz) for its reliability and cost. However, the XLite is nearly as warm, and due to its small size it can be conveniently stored inside my pack. It is not as durable, but it has earned my trust. If I need more warmth, I can combine the two, or I could get a warmer pad like the **Therm-a-Rest NeoAir XTherm** ($200, 15 oz). Other air pads are similarly warm, but none are as lightweight. ▮

A slickrock camp in southern Utah, using a down quilt and non-insulated air pad. My pack and extra clothing provided extra insulation and comfort.

tools & techniques

shelters

The forest was dense and the side of the abandoned logging road was filled with brush and slash piles, so I'd wound up pitching my poncho-tarp directly on the road in a lean-to configuration. "That should do," I remember thinking when I anchored the last guyline and skewer stake with a pile of baseball-size rocks—knowing full well that it might not. The barometric pressure had dropped precipitously in the last 24 hours, and the place I was camping, on Washington's Olympic Peninsula, receives about 125 inches of rain per year. Maybe I was also hoping that Mother Nature would show some mercy. I was only three days away from finishing my 11-month Sea-to-Sea Route hike. Of course, it soon began raining hard, with winds to match.

A particularly strong gust at around 5 a.m. yanked a stake from its mooring, and my poncho-tarp fell on top of me like a wet blanket. I briefly considered repitching the shelter but instead got moving. I slithered into my soaking poncho-tarp and started running down the road to generate some body heat.

After about two hours of hiking in the downpour, my situation took a

Mosquitoes in Alaska's Yanert Fork were less bothersome in this wind-prone site.

part 2

180-degree turn. I was inside a home sipping hot cocoa, wearing a fleecy sweat suit while my clothes tumbled in the dryer, and being entertained by Elizabeth Barlow, who grew up beside the mighty Hoh River on property her grandfather had homesteaded in 1892. She passed away in 2010 at the age of 90, but I will never forget her or her treasure chest of Native American artifacts, historical photos, and even a woolly mammoth tooth that she had found while beachcombing the coast. Not to mention her purple sweatshirt, which fittingly read, "Can't complain . . . Nobody listens!"

Considerations

It is commonly assumed that backpackers need a "tent," but I'd encourage you not to limit your options so quickly. By taking a needs-based approach, you may find another type of shelter that checks your boxes and that has more advantages, like less weight or more comfort.

What do you need from your shelter? In approximate order of importance, my top priorities are:

> Environmental resistance
> Campsite compatibility
> Portability
> Adaptability
> Condensation resistance
> Living space
> Ease of use

Unfortunately, many of these attributes are in direct conflict. For example, a shelter with ample living space will not have a small footprint, and one with fantastic ventilation (which helps to minimize condensation) will normally not be as storm-worthy

No shelter is immune from such trade-offs. Ultimately, the right shelter for you to buy or to use on a trip is that which meets your most critical needs while making fewer sacrifices in other areas compared to alternative options. Of course, the cost of the shelter must be acceptable, too.

Environmental resistance

My shelter must protect me from precipitation, wind, and insects. If exposed to precipitation, I will lose heat through conduction; if wind, then convection. And if left vulnerable to insects, I am at greater risk of itchy bites and, more seriously, mosquito- and tick-borne illnesses and diseases. Without adequate environmental protection, I will also struggle to sleep well.

It is not necessary to have full-time protection from all environmental factors—just the expected and unavoidable ones. For example, I'll bring bug protection in the High Sierra in July, but will leave it behind in September; and I'll use a full-sided shelter when camping in the Badlands, but a less robust model in the Colorado Rockies, where I can always find wind-protected camps.

My shelter is not my primary line of defense against cold temperatures, since I can be more efficiently insulated by my clothing and sleeping bag. A few extra ounces of down insulation would provide much more warmth

Condensation is less likely to develop inside shelters with good airflow.

than the same weight in extra shelter fabric or poles. Moreover, to maximize the warmth of a shelter, all airflow must be cut off, which will increase condensation.

Campsite compatibility

With what shelter will I have the most frequent access to high-quality campsites? My sleep quality will undoubtedly suffer if I am relegated to mediocre spots, typified by uneven ground, protruding rocks and roots, standing water atop hard-packed dirt, and fearless mice and other rodents. Moreover, my daily itinerary will be annoyingly impacted by a dearth of good camps—I don't like to pull up early if I have the energy, daylight, and desire, but I also don't enjoy plodding more miles after an already long day in the hopes of finding something better.

Campsite quality and frequency vary by location. On the Appalachian Trail, for example, high-quality ground camps are very rare, while hammock opportunities abound. But on the Wind River High Route, the situation is the exact opposite. If you're not personally familiar with the scene, read trip reports, engage in forums, and call land managers.

Portability

It is sometimes possible to rely on man-made or natural permanent shelters. Personally, I've slept in dozens of shelters on the Appalachian Trail and in the Adirondacks, and have used rock alcoves in the Grand Canyon and in South Africa's Drakensberg Mountains. But usually I need to carry a portable shelter. And to be portable, it must be reasonably lightweight.

The weight of group shelters should be divided by the number of occupants for a per person weight. High-occupancy shelters are more weight-efficient than solo shelters, all things being equal, because an increase in surface area results in an even greater increase in interior volume. For example, a one-person pyramid-shaped tarp with which I have extensive experience weighs 15 ounces, while the two-person weighs 18 ounces. For a 20 percent increase in weight, the interior volume increases by 45 percent.

Comparing shelter weights can be tricky, since apples-to-apples data can be hard to find. Unless you can find more detailed breakdowns in online gear lists, go by the "mini-mum weight" or "trail weight," which includes the inner tent, rain fly, and poles. The realistic weight will be more, since most shelters require stakes and guylines, and you may want to store it in a stuff sack.

Adaptability

A shelter that can be easily optimized for a wide range of conditions is more useful than a static or fixed design, since I backpack in many locations and seasons. This is the case for other avid backpackers and thru-hikers, too.

I look for shelters with versatile pitching configurations and with modular components that can be left behind, mixed and matched, or not employed for every night or on every trip. Such a shelter may be more expensive, heavier as a complete system, and more difficult to pitch than a simpler model. However, it will maintain a high level of performance on all of my trips, and it will be lighter when unnecessary pieces are left behind. Furthermore, it prevents me from having to buy a second shelter or from shipping shelters back and forth as conditions change on a multi-month hike.

Condensation resistance

Why does condensation develop overnight inside a shelter? More important, how can it be prevented so that it does not soak sleeping bags or measurably increase the weight of the shelter when packed away in the morning? Here, I will try to explain.

The amount of moisture that can be absorbed by air is a function of the ambient air temperature. For example, air at 86°F can absorb three times more moisture than air at 50°F. The amount of moisture in the air relative to its maximum vapor content is known as relative humidity. For example, if air at 95°F contains 20 grams of moisture per cubic meter, relative humidity is 50 percent, because it is actually capable of containing 40 grams.

Silicone-impregnated nylon (silnylon) stretches, especially when wet. Guylines should be tightened just before bed or if it begins to rain.

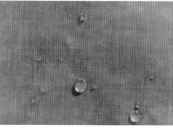

Ripstop nylon with regular reinforcing fibers

Dyneema Composite Fabric (aka Cuben Fiber)

Inside a shelter, the relative humidity is a function of the ambient humidity *plus* additional moisture from occupant respiration, drying gear, steaming cookpots, and (in the case of a floorless shelter) uncovered ground. Exterior air will always be drier (i.e., less moisture per cubic area) even though relative humidity may be the same—inside a shelter, it's usually warmer.

The dew point is the temperature at which the air becomes oversaturated (humidity exceeding 100 percent) and some water vapor condenses into liquid. It forms first on the coldest objects, the air around which has the lowest dew point. The coldest part of a shelter is usually the outermost wall, which is not kept warm by the occupants (like sleeping bags are), the earth (like the floor is), or by an outer wall (like an inner wall is).

The single design feature that will discourage condensation is *ventilation,* in the form of open sides (i.e., tarps),

vents, or panels of breathable material like bug netting (very breathable) or waterproof/breathable fabric (not so much). Venting will allow the exchange of drier exterior air with wetter interior air. Even with extensive venting, condensation may not be entirely eliminated, especially on calm and humid nights. However, it will always be worse without it.

Campsite selection also influences the development of condensation, as well as dew or frost on exterior surfaces. By finding a relatively warm and dry camp (e.g., not in a deep river valley) with some thermal cover (e.g., leaf canopy) and gentle airflow (e.g., ridgetop), surface temperatures are more likely to stay above the dew point.

Usable space

Do not accept manufacturer claims for sleeping capacity or the number of people for which a shelter is supposedly designed. Instead, look

tip Is your fly or floor leaking? Use McNett's Tent Sure to restore polyurethane-coated fabrics and Atsko Silicone Water Guard to restore silicone-impregnated nylon.

carefully at the shelter's physical specs: length, width, height, sidewall slopes, and gear storage. Because sleep capacity standards do not exist, you will see a scary range of shelter sizes all described as being appropriate for the same number of campers. Be especially skeptical of "ultralight" shelters—that often means "ultra small."

A small shelter can be an acceptable choice. I take one, for instance, when I plan to spend little time in it, when I'm tight with my sheltermate, and/or when I seldom need to be sheltered. Otherwise, I've found that an extra few ounces—or a half-pound with multi-person tents—can be a worthy investment, as it translates into more space for people and gear, and more doors.

Ease of setup

A foolproof pitch is not critical to me, but speed and consistency are. In general, I prefer shelters with right-angle footprints, as is the case with squares and rectangles but not with pentagons and hexagons, and shelters with fewer critical stakeout points

(e.g., six instead of eight). I tend to avoid freestanding shelters due to their weight, except when camping on loose sand or unconsolidated snow. In those conditions, the extra weight can be offset by the difficult and time-consuming task of building secure anchor points.

Fabrics

A shelter's weight, durability, breathability, and water resistance are greatly affected by the fabrics from which it's made.

Uncoated wovens

Polyester and nylon are synthetic fibers with a few subtle differences. Nylon is lighter and more abrasion-resistant than polyester, but polyester absorbs less water and is more resistant to UV degradation.

In shelter design, the more important detail is the fabric coating, or lack thereof. Uncoated fabrics are breathable (i.e., they allow transmission of moisture, some better than others), and thus are appropriate for hammocks, the interior canopy

Dome tents protect occupants from precipitation, wind, and bugs. But they are heavy and have limited airflow.

tools & techniques

of double-wall tents, and the top of water-resistant bivy sacks.

The weight of an uncoated woven polyester or nylon fabric is driven by the weight of its individual fibers, which is measured in denier, or the weight (in grams) of 9,000 meters of the fiber. That seems arbitrary, I know. The lightest fibers regularly used are 10 denier (or 10D), but 20 to 40D fibers are more common because of their increased strength and abrasion resistance. A 10D nylon fabric weighs about 0.8 oz per square yard; a 40D fabric, about 1.5 ounces.

Coated wovens

Nylon and polyester fabrics can be waterproofed with coatings or applications of polyurethane (PU), polyethylene (PE), or silicone (sil). "Waterproof" is an absolute term, but in fact there are degrees of waterproofness, usually measured with a hydrostatic head test. Over time, hydrostatic head will decrease due to use, UV exposure, and abrasion. DIY restoration treatments help, but the fabric will never be as good as new. Waterproof wovens are used for rain flies, floors, and tarps.

Per weight, silicone-impregnated nylon is the strongest and most

	double-wall	single-wall	mountaineering single-wall
Environmental resistance	Complete protection	Complete protection	May not have bug netting
Campsite compatibility	Need quality ground site	Need quality ground site	Need quality ground site
Portability/ weight	2–3 lb for practical shelter	Lighter than double-wall	Robust for extreme conditions
Adaptability	Possible independent use of fly & interior tent	Single-piece design; some pitching flexibility	Limited to opening & closing doors & vents
Condensation resistance	Occupants shielded from exterior wall	No protection from exterior wall	Stuffy due to semi-breathable top
Living space	Depends on size; often cramped	Depends on size; often cramped	Depends on size; often cramped
Ease of use	Intuitive & user-friendly	Even simpler than double-wall	Freestanding; pitches from inside

part 2

Waterproof/breathable walls allow single-wall mountaineering shelters to be sealed shut.

tarp systems	mountaineering bivies	hammocks
Optimizable for precise needs	Scant but complete protection	Optimizable for precise needs
Can have very small footprint	Very small footprint	Ideal for forest & high-use areas
Can be equal to double-wall tents, but usually lighter	Oddly heavy for space	Heavier materials needed to support body weight
Versatile tarp pitches & modular components	Minimal. Hood can be opened or closed.	Multiple tarp pitches. Swap underquilts based on temps.
A+ ventilation with open-ended pitches	Stuffy due to semi-breathable top	A+ ventilation with open-ended pitches
Depends on tarp & components	None. Terrible in rain or bad bugs.	Tarp can create huge living space
Flats & A-frames require skill & practice	Easiest: Spread it out on the ground	Steep learning curve: angles, heights, tension

tools & techniques

waterproof coated woven fabric. Several brands currently use a 1.5 oz/sq yd version rated to 3,000 millimeters of hydrostatic head, or about twice the minimum to meet the ISO 811 rainproof standard. Meanwhile, other silnylon versions barely reach this threshold. Silnylon is rarely available through conventional retailers:

> Seams cannot be taped, but instead must be sealed with silicone glue, which cannot quickly be done and thus is normally outsourced to the user (or completed for a surcharge).
> Because it does not adhere to CPAI-84, a standard for the flame-resistance of tent fabrics, it cannot be sold in or shipped to several big-market states like California and New York.

PU- and PE-coated nylons are not as strong or waterproof as silnylon, so long as the coatings and applications are of equal quality. Shelters made of PU- and PE-coated nylons meet fire-resistance standards, and their seams can be taped by the factory.

Bug mesh

Fully enclosed three-season backpacking tents must be made partly of nylon no-see-um mesh in order to keep bugs out while still allowing for some ventilation. The holes are smaller than Ceratopogonidae, also known as no-see-ums, midges, and sand flies. Because these holes are visible to the naked eye, you might

The poncho/tarp is multifunctional, but best used as just-in-case shelter or rain gear.

expect no-see-um mesh to have excellent airflow. It generally does, but on calm nights it will stifle airflow and increase condensation. In this regard, nothing is better than nothing.

Mosquito-grade mesh is more porous, and thus is lighter and more breathable. But it would be a risky choice for shelters; it is more commonly used for head nets.

Waterproof/breathable membranes

Two types of shelters employ waterproof/breathable fabrics: single-wall mountaineering tents and mountaineering bivy sacks. Because the fabric is somewhat breathable, moisture can escape even when the shelter is completely sealed off from the elements. It is never used in three-season backpacking tents: It is heavier, more expensive, and less breathable than the combination of coated fabrics and bug mesh.

Cuben Fiber

The premier shelter fabric is CTF3, commonly known as Cuben Fiber, and technically now called Dyneema Composite Fabric. In layman's terms, Cuben is a grid of Dyneema fibers embedded in flexible polyester film. Per weight, Dyneema is the world's toughest fiber, at 15 times the strength of steel. Cuben is a remarkable shelter fabric:

> Rainproof tarps and canopies can be reasonably made with 0.5 oz/sq yd of fabric, with a heavier 0.75-ounce version offering even more strength and durability.
> The 0.5 oz/sq yd version has been tested to 3,500+ millimeter hydrostatic head, in excess of the best silnylons at one-third the weight, and does not absorb any water.
> It does not stretch, even when wet, lending to picture-perfect pitches.

Cuben is used almost exclusively by cottage brands. First, it requires specialized labor. Second, its cost is too outrageous for the average retail customer—and for the traditional retail price structure. For example, the 13.5-ounce Mountain Laurel Designs

how 2
maximize tarp system performance

1 I must be able to accurately predict the environmental conditions. If the wind blows from a different direction than I expected, my pitch might leave me vulnerable. If I carry a bug nest and bugs never materialize, then I will have carried an unnecessary component.

2 I must know how to quickly and effectively pitch my tarp, which is not nearly as intuitive as a freestanding tent. Before I go out with a new shelter, I will practice in a low-risk environment (e.g., my backyard)—pitch, tweak, disassemble, and repeat. I'll read the written directions, watch videos, and learn the nuances of pitching my shelter, specifically the best order of steps, the optimal pole lengths, and the necessary corner angles.

3 I carefully select my campsites because tarps often lack the bathtub floors and 360-degree protection found on conventional tents.

tools & techniques

Cricket Tarp in premium silnylon costs $185; in Cuben Fiber, $335. Is it worth $150 to drop 6 ounces and gain extra (but no more functional) waterproofness? I can't answer that for you. Extensive use would help to justify the cost, but personally I'd probably look for lower-hanging fruit first and avoid ice cream for a week.

Like coated wovens, the long-term performance of Cuben decreases with use. Repeated folding, normal abrasion, UV exposure, and wet storage will cause the polyester film to thin and soften, decreasing its waterproofness and causing it to absorb water (but not leak). That said, Cuben shelters have been used successfully by many thru-hikers, who in one or two seasons put more wear on their equipment than average backpackers do in a decade. For 0.75-ounce Cuben, the life span is estimated at about 250 hard thru-hiker nights. In comparison, silnylon will last 300 to 500 depending on the quality.

Tents

Neat definitions do not exist for tents or tarps. For every proposal at establishing them, I could point to exceptions, often several. With that disclaimer, I will identify the most common categories and discuss their strengths and weaknesses.

Double-wall

The MSR Hubba Hubba NX 2 ($400, 3 lb 7 oz) is a classic double-wall tent. The main body features a waterproof floor and a canopy made of uncoated fabric and/or bug mesh. For protection from precipitation, a waterproof rain fly is secured over it. (Some models offer the option of pitching the main body without the rain fly, or the rain fly without the main body, to optimize the tent for the conditions and to reduce weight.) Most double-wall tents are freestanding and require a custom pole set; a small number are nonfreestanding and/or are supported with trekking poles, helping to save weight (and cost).

The popularity of double-wall tents stems from their environmental protections (precipitation, wind, and bugs) and their generous protected living spaces. Freestanding designs have the added advantage of a foolproof pitch. Finally, occupants inside a double-wall tent are less likely to be soaked by condensation because it collects first on the rain fly, not inside the tent. However, double-wall tents should not be touted for their condensation management—most designs resemble a sweat lodge.

Double-wall tents are heavier than all other types of shelters. While some models are in the 24-ounce range, their dimensions are wickedly cramped and their materials are of dubious long-term durability. More practical models weigh two to three pounds.

Single-wall

One opportunity to cut weight from a double-wall tent is obvious: Eliminate one wall. The execution is not quite that simple, as it requires strategic balancing of ventilation (via bug mesh) and precipitation protection

Single-wall tents are lighter than double-walls and simpler than tarp systems. But condensation can be problematic, and they are not versatile.

(via coated nylon). Innovation in this category has historically been driven by cottage companies, notably Six Moon Designs, Tarptent, and ZPacks; more recently, wholesalers like Big Agnes, MSR, and Sierra Designs have entered the space.

In addition to being lighter, single-wall tents are also simpler and faster to set up. However, occupants are less protected from condensation, since they are not separated from the exterior canopy by a breathable wall. Especially in humid conditions, bring a pack towel to wipe down the interior if necessary.

Single-wall tents are also minimally adaptable: Their components are permanently attached, and their pitching configurations are limited. As a result, single-wall tents cannot be optimized for a range of conditions and can actually be heavier than a double-wall tent in a fly/footprint-only pitch.

Single-wall mountaineering

For horrible weather in cold environments, single-wall mountaineering tents like the two-person Black Diamond Firstlight ($370, 2 lb 13 oz) are an excellent choice. Because their canopy is made from waterproof/breathable (WP/B) material, they can be completely sealed off (i.e., no open vents or doors) while still allowing moisture to escape. Also, they are designed to be pitched from the inside.

For three-season backpacking, single-wall mountaineering tents are mostly an impractical choice. Due to the WP/B canopy, they will be hot and stuffy in normal conditions. Without bug netting, occupants will be vulnerable to mosquitoes and other biting insects. And, overall, it is overbuilt for less extreme applications.

Tarp systems

With some humility, I'll define a tarp as a sheet of waterproof fabric, or several sheets sewn together in a more pre-defined shape. On its own, a tarp is not a complete shelter system. Instead, it should be used in conjunction with other components—like a bug nest, bivy sack, or ground cloth—to create a tarp system. The end result can offer the same environmental protections as a tent, but it's often more adaptable, less prone to condensation, roomier, and lighter (one to two pounds for the system).

The most common hang-up with tarps is the concern over being or feeling too exposed. The availability of full-sided tarp canopies and fully enclosed interior components should mute this worry. A more legitimate draw-back is that tarp systems are not as user-friendly as tents. It requires more knowledge and skill to make them functional and to use them optimally.

Modular components like this bug nest can be used to create a tarp system.

Flats

Flat tarps like the eight-by-ten-foot Rab Guides Siltarp 2 ($135, 16 oz) are the simplest and least expensive type of tarp. Because they have no hardware like zippers and buckles, they are also the lightest per coverage area. In skilled hands, a flat tarp is like a sheet of flat paper to an origami genius—the possibilities are endless. Basic pitch configurations include the A-frame and lean-to. But if it is storm-ing from all directions, the tarp can be pitched to the ground on all sides; if the wind is blowing from just one direction, more selective protection can be arranged; and if the conditions are mild and humid, the pitch can be maximized for ventilation. The func-tionality of a flat tarp is limited only by imagination—and skill.

On group trips in wet environments like the Appalachians and Olympics, I often pack a flat tarp for group use, in addition to or as part of a personal shelter. For just an extra pound of pack weight, a flat tarp can create a large and comfortable space for cooking and socializing. Without one, heavy rain forces group members into their respective shelters, which are relatively cramped and stuffy.

A poncho-tarp like the Sea to Summit Ultra-Sil Nano Tarp Poncho ($100, 8 oz) is a special type of flat tarp, designed to be used as a shelter, rain gear, and a pack cover. I have extensive experience with poncho-tarps, having used one for about 5,000 miles of the Sea-to-Sea Route

Flat and A-frame tarps are most difficult to pitch. Practice in your backyard first.

and for a thru-hike of the Colorado Trail. Its multifunctionality appealed to me, and, at the time, it represented a significant weight savings over dedicated shelter, rain gear, and pack protection. Eventually, however, I concluded that a poncho-tarp was not a high-performance solution. When used as a shelter, its weather resistance was scant. When used as rain gear, it blew around in the wind and snagged vegetation. And when it came time to make camp in a rainstorm, I inevitably got soaked. A poncho-tarp is best used in dry conditions, when insurance against—but not regular protection from—precipitation is needed.

A-frames

A flat tarp can be pitched as an A-frame, but an A-frame tarp like the two-person Gossamer Gear Twinn Tarp ($230, 8 oz) cannot be pitched in any other way because its center ridgeline features a "catenary curve," which accounts for gravity-caused sagging. The catenary curve eliminates this sag (but not the curve), resulting in a more taut pitch, smoother panels, and less wind-driven flapping. A-frames are often tapered, with more width at the head than the foot.

The storm-worthiness of an A-frame is limited by its two open ends. Beaks or awnings over these openings will reduce this vulnerability,

tip Open-ended tarps leave vulnerable the occupant in storms. Supplement its protection with natural windbreaks like boulders, bushes, and tree clusters.

Continued on p. 112

tools & techniques

tried&true

how to find a good campsite

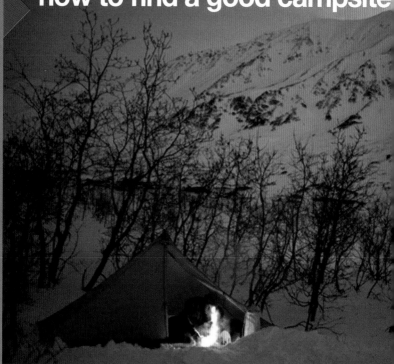

part (2)

Even with a suitable shelter and sleep system, it's difficult to sleep well at a low-quality campsite. You may struggle to get comfortable on hard-packed ground, to tune out a chronic snorer 15 feet away, or to relax if high winds are knocking your shelter around. I am very deliberate and selective about where I camp—a good campsite is a prerequisite for a night of quality rest.

Select a general area

Halfway through my day, I begin to consider where I might camp that night. On my maps, I identify general locations that are:

> Flat, where my odds of finding a level campsite are best, though as a soloist I can often find suitable ground on suboptimal gradients, where there would not be enough spots for a group;
> Within convenient proximity of firewood and water;
> Off-trail, so that I do not disrupt another backpacker's wilderness experience;
> Not in the bottom of a valley or canyon, where the air will be coldest and most humid;
> Not near animal trails or prime habitat, which might lead to an unwanted midnight visitor;
> Not in danger of natural hazards like avalanches, flash floods, and incoming weather; and
> Far from insect breeding grounds like waterlogged meadows and stagnant lakes.

Identify a specific location

Once I select a general area, I try finding a specific campsite that is:

> Covered in natural materials like pine needles, leaves, moss, or sand, which will be more comfortable and which will be less thermally conductive than hard-packed dirt;
> Under and next to something— like trees, bushes, or large rocks—that will block wind and reduce radiant heat loss;
> Dry, because wet ground is more thermally conductive;
> Not at risk of being flooded by groundwater if it rains, as moisture can easily seep through a lightweight floor or a used heavy-duty floor; and
> Naturally contoured for my preferred sleeping position. I'm a back-sleeper, so I like a raised area for my head, a slight depression for my butt, and a short knoll for the backs of my knees.

Once I have identified a potential spot, I lie down to make sure that it is comfortable. If it is, I mark the location of my feet and head with small rocks so that I can pitch my shelter over this exact location. If it's not, I will try different positions or a different spot. Given the importance of my campsite to my sleep, it's worth being fussy.

tools & techniques

tip Before setting up a multi-person shelter, I have everyone lie down in their proposed spots. If anyone is not comfortable, we adjust until they are.

For their weight, pyramid-shaped shelters are more storm-worthy than other designs.

but they restrict pitching options and the ease of entry and exit. I've heard of hikers using umbrellas or rain gear to block off the openings, but this seems unsustainable and desperate. The best solution is to use a bigger tarp. A few extra square yards of fabric—which adds just a few ounces—turns a normal tarp into a palatial hideout.

Mids

The most storm-worthy tarps are mids. Some models like the Mountain Laurel Designs SoloMid ($255, 15 oz) have one apex and are shaped like a pyramid, while others like the Black Diamond Beta Light ($200, 19 oz) have two apexes and look like a two-pole circus tent. Mids are excellent for lightweight winter travel and for harsh three-season conditions. Rain and snow slide down their slanted walls, and wind struggles to grab their symmetric profiles. Also, they can be used as a roof over a cavernous snow pit.

Short and small mids are supported with trekking poles. Taller and bigger mids can be pitched by strapping two trekking poles together, but for heavy snow loads or high winds I would feel more comfortable with a single stout shaft.

When a mid tarp is combined with a matching bug nest, it's functionally the same as a tent. This was my shelter system of choice during the Alaska-Yukon Expedition, during which I was caught by blizzards in the Alaska Range, hordes of mosquitoes in the Canadian Arctic, and multiday rain events in the Brooks Range.

Mids have several drawbacks:

> Relative to flat and A-frame tarps, they are heavier per person.

> Since their shapes are fixed, pitching variations are limited to leaving their doors open and to changing their height off the ground.
> Poles are located in awkward spots, blocking doors and splitting up the sleeping area.
> Single-apex mids typically have low-angle sidewalls, which reduce the usefulness of interior space.
> Doors must be closed when it's raining or snowing, which reduces ventilation. Unfortunately, humidity is highest and ventilation is needed most in these conditions.

Modular components

The tarp is the most important component in a tarp system. But additional components greatly enhance their appeal and livability.

Ground cloths protect the sleeper against moist ground, snow, and dirt. My pick is Gossamer Gear Polycryo Ground Cloths ($5, 2 oz), which are ultralight, inexpensive, and shockingly durable and waterproof. I have also experimented with coated nylon, Tyvek, heavy-duty trash compactor bags, and Mylar emergency blankets. If I expect to regularly camp on wet ground, I bring a Polycryo sheet to supplement the waterproofness of another Polycryo sheet or a used shelter floor.

Footprints are ground cloths that have been custom-cut to be used in conjunction with a specific shelter, usually made of heavy-duty coated nylon. Footprints are heavier and more expensive than generic ground cloths—which, I'll point out, can be cut to a specific shape with scissors. Some footprints feature bathtub floors, which have uplifted edges for more protection against groundwater. This can be a helpful feature, but the need for it may suggest a poorly selected campsite.

Head nets, which cover the head and neck completely with bug mesh, provide excellent daytime protection against swarms of bugs, but they are a bit minimalist for nighttime use. If mosquitoes are your only worry, then use a head net made of larger pored mosquito netting, which is less stuffy than the small-pored no-see-um netting.

Polycryo ground sheets are light, cheap, and tough.

tools & techniques

Alpine bivy sacks are ill-sui as backpacking shelters.

Keep the netting off your skin by wearing a brimmed hat.

A bug skirt is a strip of mesh netting connected to the tarp's bottom perimeter. When it lies flush on the ground, it seals out bugs. The seal can be compromised by wind or a rough ground surface (e.g., high grass) that prevents a snug closure. They are a DIY feature, never offered as a stock option on commercial shelters.

Bug nests, like the Six Moon Designs Serenity NetTent ($120, 11 oz), are identical to the interior body of many double-wall tents, featuring a waterproof floor and a canopy made entirely of bug netting. The only difference is that a bug nest is designed as a standalone and modular component, not just for use with a specific shelter. Bug nests offer more protected living area than other tarp components, making them ideal for peak bug seasons.

Bug bivies, like the Outdoor Research Bug Bivy ($80, 16 oz), are tube-shaped covers for sleeping bags made of bug netting and a waterproof floor. They are lighter and less model-specific than a bug nest, but they do not have as much interior room. Because bugs can bite through the mesh, you'll need to keep the bivy off your face. The OR bivy includes a loop pole; a lighter option is to connect the top of the bivy to your tarp with a shock cord.

Water-resistant bivy sacks are similar to bug bivies, except the bug netting is replaced with breathable DWR-coated nylon; a small no-see-um mesh panel near the head improves ventilation. Water-resistant bivies are very popular among flat tarp and A-frame tarp users. They:

> Eliminate the need for a ground cloth;
> Prevent spindrift and rain splatter from wetting the sleeping bag;
> Add warmth to the sleep system by reducing convective heat loss;
> Protect the occupant against flying and crawling insects; and
> Can be used alone on dry nights to "cowboy camp" (no shelter) without sacrificing bug protection or a ground cloth. This simple camp also reduces setup and breakdown time.

Mountaineering bivy sacks

The aforementioned water-resistant bivy sacks favored by tarp users are offshoots of mountaineering bivies like the Rab Alpine Bivi ($264, 17 oz), commonly used by alpinists who need a lightweight, low-bulk shelter that they can lay down almost anywhere to make an emergency camp—or an intentional camp that would appear like an emergency camp to most people. These bivies feature a waterproof bottom made of coated fabric and a top shell made of waterproof/breathable fabric. Some models have a short pole to suspend the material above the head, and some feature a removable bug screen.

Three weeks into my first thru-hike, I swapped my double-wall tent for a mountaineering bivy, saving 2.5 pounds. So long as nights stayed cool and dry, bugs were minimal, and the skies didn't pour, it was an excellent shelter. Of course, in those conditions, I didn't actually need a shelter.

If the conditions were even slightly suboptimal, however, the bivy was

miserable. I have never used this type of shelter again:

> During stifling summer nights in the mid-Atlantic states, it was unbearably stuffy.
> Because of the bivy's limited breathability and the high humidity, I got soaked from the inside by my own sweat.
> Mosquitoes whined and raindrops splattered just inches from my ears, making it impossible to sleep well.
> It was large enough to sleep in, but otherwise offered no usable living space. If it was raining or if the bugs were terrible, I had no escape.

Hammocks

In rolling mountainous topography, high-use zones, and heavily forested areas with lush understories, ground campsites are typically low quality: neither flat nor level, hard-packed from extensive use, conducive to pooling water, and inhabited by fearless rodents and visited by Snickers-loving black bears. I'm looking at you, Appalachian Trail and areas of similar ilk.

Yet, most backpackers in such locations continue to sleep on the ground. I'm increasingly convinced that this approach is wrongheaded and that a better option is a hammock, such as those from Clark Outdoor, ENO, Hennessy, and Warbonnet. A complete backpacking hammock system consists of five components:

> Waterproof tarp;
> Top quilt (or, less ideally, a mummy bag);
> Hammock with integrated or detached bug netting;
> Underquilt (or, with some models, a sleeping pad); and
> Suspension.

Pros & cons

With a hammock, you can camp nearly anywhere. Find two sturdy trees about five stride lengths apart that bookend an open patch of ground about two stride lengths wide. With so many camps available, you are free to hike as short or far as you wish before stopping, and you can more easily find great campsites—private, quiet, scenic, and relatively dry, warm, and bug-free.

Backpacking hammocks are also extraordinarily comfortable. They support body weight more evenly than the average sleeping pad, which results in fewer pressure points. They are designed and patterned to create a fairly flat lying position. Finally, on hot nights, hammocks can provide 360 degrees of convective cooling.

Since most hammocks employ a tarp for rain protection, hammocks tend to be very resistant to condensation, which coincidentally is a constant concern in areas best suited for hammock camping. The tarp also creates a substantial space to cook and lounge, especially if the sides are "porched" to create more headroom. On trips in New Hampshire, West Virginia, and Colorado, I have sheltered up to ten people under my giant hammock tarp so we could make dinner together out of the rain.

Besides inertia, hammocks have not been widely embraced for a few

Especially when ground camps are sloped, lumpy, wet, and/or overgrown, hammocks are an unconventional but excellent choice.

part 2

other reasons, too. One obstacle is cost. For most backpackers, their first shelter and sleep system is designed for ground camping. Unfortunately, traditional ground equipment like double-wall tents and mummy bags are not compatible with or optimized for hammock systems. Other barriers include:

> A steep learning curve. I recommend reading *The Ultimate Hang,* by Derek Hansen.
> A weight penalty. All things being equal, a hammock system will be heavier because it must support body weight. A ground shelter can get away with lighter materials.
> A need for trees. Some hammocks can be pitched on the ground, but this versatility requires considerable trade-offs relative to dedicated hammock and ground systems.
> A lack of multi-person options. Hammocks are best for solo use. I know of only one model, the Clark Jungle Vertex, that sleeps two.

Hammock types

As you would expect, all hammocks are not created equal. They fall into three categories, with additional differences from there.

Gathered-end hammocks are the simplest, lightest, and least expensive variety. They are made of a rectangular sheet of fabric with sewn channels on the short ends, through which a cord is run and pulled tight, creating a gathered end.

The hammock hangs in a banana shape, but it is wide enough so that the occupant can sleep on a diagonal to the ridgeline, which is a flatter position. Personally, I've found a perfect pitch to be frustratingly elusive in a gathered-end hammock.

Bridge hammocks provide a flatter lying position than gathered-end hammocks, but at the expense of simplicity, weight, and cost. Furthermore, the system is considerably wider due to the spreader bars, which require a larger or lower-angled tarp. As a consistent back-sleeper, I find bridge hammocks to be more comfortable; wider-bodied individuals can struggle with shoulder squeeze depending on the width and patterning of the hammock body.

Platform hammocks look fun and awesomely futuristic, but they're a stretch for backpacking. The lightest model from Tentsile, the Flite ($350, 7.4 lb), would equate to 3.7 pounds per person.

skurka'spicks
SHELTERS

Since writing the first edition of this book in 2011, the most notable addition to my gear closet is the **Warbonnet Outdoors Ridgerunner** ($190, 1.5 lb without spreader bars), a bridge hammock that I pair with a down underquilt and an A-frame tarp. I now use a hammock exclusively for

tools & techniques

three-season backpacking in the eastern woodlands and in select locations in the West, notably national parks with designated backcountry campsites like Rocky Mountain and Glacier.

If I were planning a thru-hike in the East, I would most definitely modify the bridge hammock so that I could use trekking poles instead of the dedicated 10-ounce spreader bars. But I would hesitate in switching to a gathered-end hammock to save a few ounces more.

For mild three-season conditions in the West, I use an A-frame tarp in conjunction with a water-resistant bivy sack, specifically the **Mountain Laurel Designs Grace Tarp** ($130, 10 oz) with the **Mountain Laurel Designs Superlight Bivy** ($175, 8 oz). During the West's arid summers, I rarely pitch the tarp, which saves time and which creates a more enjoyable experience: sleeping under the stars. I always use the bivy, however, so that I stay out of the dirt and have protection from insects.

My final shelter is the **Sierra Designs High Route 1 FL** ($290, 2 lb 3 oz), a double-wall tent that I designed from scratch with technical help from Sierra Designs. It is intended for challenging three-season and moderate winter conditions, but it is entirely appropriate for those who want a single versatile three-season shelter and/or more living space than the aforementioned tarp/bivy system.

Because of its offset pole positions and vertical side doors, the High Route tent avoids pitfalls common among other full-sided shelters that are supported with trekking poles:

> Steeper side walls make interior space more usable.
> Poles do not block the doors or split up the sleeping area.
> Ventilation and rain protection are not mutually exclusive.

We gave the High Route generous dimensions: a 36-square-foot rectangular footprint and a 4-foot minimum height. In calmer conditions, both side doors can be extended like canopies for additional space. For context, the award-winning **Big Agnes Copper Spur 2 UL** ($480, 2 lb 14 oz) has just 29 square feet of interior space and a 42-inch peak height.

Tie-outs

A freestanding tent can be pitched without guylines, or even stakes. In contrast, all nonfreestanding shelters require tension to achieve the desired shape and stability.

Pitching system

In three-season conditions, my guyline system works like this:

> I attach three- to eight-foot-long guyline cords to each tie-out point with a bowline knot. The line length depends on the tie-out location and shelter type.

part 2

With the High Route Tent, I strived to design a single shelter that I could use on all my solo trips with few compromises.

> For tie-outs that are near the ground (e.g., the corners of a mid tarp), I run the cord from the tie-out to an anchor (e.g., a stake) and back through the tie-out's bowline loop. Then I pull the cord back toward the anchor until the guyline is taut, securing it with a slippery half hitch.

> For tie-outs that are far from the ground (e.g., the apexes of an A-frame tarp), I use a trucker's hitch, making the bight with a slipknot.

I want to thank Forrest McCarthy and Mike Clelland for teaching me these techniques. It is a fantastic system:

> The knots are very secure, easily adjustable, and quickly learned.

> With a three-to-one mechanical advantage, relatively little force is needed to get tight pitches.

> Unlike a fixed loop, the anchor location is flexible, which can help to mitigate rocky ground. Also, with longer lines, the anchor can be several feet away from the shelter.

> No fixed knots or plastic tensions are involved, which helps to reduce guyline snares.

On winter trips, I install Nite Ize Figure 9 Small ($2.50, 0.2 oz) rope tighteners to the tie-out points. With them, I can quickly and securely pitch my shelter even when wearing bulky mittens. As with my three-season system, I attach a three- or eight-foot-long cord to the tie-out with a bowline, and I tie the Nite Ize into the bowline loop. The Nite Ize takes the place of the slippery half hitch knot.

Cordage types

Satisfactory guyline cord is inexpensive and can be purchased by the foot or in bulk at outdoor retail and climbing stores. I have installed PMI 3mm Utility Cord ($5 for 50 ft, 2.3 g/ft) on many of my demo shelters and have found it durable and easy to work with.

A lighter but more expensive option is the Mountain Laurel Designs LiteLine ($16 for 60 ft, 0.5 g/ft). On a shelter with six four-foot guylines, the net weight savings over the PMI Cord would be 1.5 ounces. It is stiffer and rougher than the PMI Cord and is not as easy to work with. A heavier but more user-friendly alternative is Kelty Triptease ($20 for 50 ft, 0.8 g/ft), which has a Spectra core and a reflective nylon sheath.

Stakes & anchors

The entire pitch of nonfreestanding shelters depends on the holding power of its anchors. Freestanding shelters benefit from being securely tied out, too: They will be roomier, better ventilated, and more storm-worthy. Anchors are not limited to man-made stakes; I've also used sticks, trees, branches buried in snow, downed logs, and exposed roots.

Use aluminum or titanium stakes. Plastic stakes break easily and stainless steel stakes are heavy. Common designs include nails, tubular rods, Y-shaped, and V-shaped; snow stakes

how²

make a deadman anchor

1 Dig a hole in the snow, about 12 inches deep, where you want the anchor to be.

2 Lay the guyline across the bottom of the hole.

3 Put two forearm-size branches perpendicular to and atop the guyline, or combine smaller sticks of comparable cumulative size.

4 Bury the guyline and sticks, except for the guyline's end.

5 Pack down the snow on top of the anchor.

6 Wait five to ten minutes for the snow to bond with the sticks; make other anchors in the meantime.

7 Secure the shelter to the anchor using one of the systems previously described.

are scoop-shaped and have more surface area. A stake's head should have a deep notch or a hook to more securely hold a guyline or stake loop.

A stake's precise holding power is a function of its design, ground conditions (e.g., dry sand, moist sod, forest duff, and snow), the stake angle, and the pull angle. A stake's holding power can be significantly increased by adding weight (e.g., a rock) atop the stake.

skurka'spicks
STAKES & ANCHORS

I use three types of stakes, depending on the climatic conditions and my shelter:

On most three-season trips, I use aluminum Y- or V-stakes, like the 6.5-inch **Kelty Y-Stakes** ($2, 0.5 oz). This design has proven to be tough and to have good holding power. I can pound them into rocky ground without bending them, and they've helped keep my shelter upright in multiple storms, most recently one in sandy southern Utah with 30-mile-an-hour winds.

If I'm counting grams, I may bring titanium skewer stakes, like the six-inch **Gossamer Gear Tite-Lite** ($3, 0.2 oz each). These have only about half the holding power of the Kelty stakes, and they bend more easily. For anything more than occasional use in mild conditions, I will use them only on noncritical tie-outs (e.g., not the apexes on an A-frame tarp or the corners of a mid).

When I am camping on snow, I avoid stakes because they are difficult to retrieve in the morning. Instead, I loop guylines around my skis, snowshoes, and/or ski poles, which I secure by partially burying. I also use deadman anchors made of tree branches that I can leave behind in the morning. ▨

tools & techniques

On winter trips, I install Nite Ize Figure 9 Small ($2.50, 0.2 oz) rope tighteners to the tie-out points. With them, I can quickly and securely pitch my shelter even when wearing bulky mittens.

navigation

Once you step away from the trailhead, what resources and tools are needed to navigate successfully and proficiently? On my first thru-hike, the Appalachian Trail (AT), I managed to hike 2,175 miles from Georgia to Maine using just a watch and datasheet, which is a bare-bones list of key landmarks and distances between them. I had no maps, route description, compass, or GPS unit. Remarkably, I never got lost since the AT is well worn and marked with white two-by-six-inch blazes to avoid any possibility of confusion at trail and road intersections. If I had been incapable of following the AT, I would have needed to find a different hobby.

The Appalachian Trail is exceptional in how simple it is to navigate, especially given its length. Most backpacking trips will require more navigational skill, even a long weekend in a high-use national park on the trail system. And at the complete opposite end of the spectrum would be an undertaking like the Alaska-Yukon Expedition, which featured 2,110 miles of off-trail hiking and skiing, plus another 1,270 miles in my packraft on rivers and across ocean bays. There were no off-the-shelf resources like guidebooks or GPX files for the route.

In this chapter I detail my preferred navigation system. It can be traced to some of my earliest trips, when I linked together existing long-distance trails and needed custom resources to bridge separate bodies of information. More recently, it has been refined to near perfection by ambitious off-trail thru-hikes of the Kings Canyon High Basin Route and Wind River High Route, for which I later published guides.

My go-to resources include two sets of maps (small-scale and large-scale), a datasheet, and route description. Oft-used tools include a watch, altimeter, and magnetic compass; as a measure of last resort, I also carry a GPS unit.

This system can serve as a template for your own kit. For simple, casual, and familiar itineraries, every component may not be necessary. And for popular trips like the John Muir Trail, the resources probably already exist, and you'll simply need to research and acquire them.

Topographic maps

The single most useful resource for navigation is usually a topographic

I keep my maps accessible and refer to them constantly to "stay found."

map. It depicts terrain ("relief"), watercourses, vegetation cover, and man-made features like roads, buildings, and hiking trails.

Once I became an intermediate-level map-reader, I was able to:

> Orient the map;
> Match topographical features on the map with the terrain around me;
> Pinpoint my location based on those features and on dead-reckoning calculations; and
> Determine the distance and direction between landmarks.

I also learned to stop "bending the map," or convincing myself that nearby features matched my map when clearly they did not, or even that the map was incorrectly drawn. My map-reading skills improved dramatically when I began to hike off-trail.

Now, I use maps to:

> Identify adventurous routes;
> Find unmarked water sources, good campsites, and safe passages over steep ridgelines;
> Select relatively safe locations to ford rivers;
> Predict vegetation types and the location of game trails; and
> Avoid avalanche-prone slopes, ankle-twisting tussocks, and treacherous talus and boulder fields.

The most comprehensive set of topographical maps available for the United States was produced by the United States Geological Survey (USGS). Other countries have comparable government agencies: For example, Canada has the Centre for Topographical Information, and Iceland the National Land Survey.

tools & techniques

Small-scale maps

For precise navigation, which is required when off-trail or when on very low-use trails, the gold standard in the lower 48 are the USGS 7.5-minute quadrangles (aka "quads"), which depict a square area measuring 7.5 minutes of latitude by 7.5 minutes of longitude. (The Earth's surface is divided into 360 degrees of latitude and longitude. Each degree is divided into 60 minutes, and each minute into 60 seconds.) The coverage area of each quad ranges from about 50 to 65 square miles depending on the latitude, since degrees of longitude are widest at the Equator and narrow as they approach the poles.

The quads normally have contour intervals of 40 feet and are at a scale of 1:24,000. This means that 1 unit on the map (e.g., inch, centimeter, or the length of your index finger) corresponds to 24,000 of those units in the field. At this scale, one inch on the map represents 0.38 mile. There are about 57,000 7.5-minute quads covering the contiguous U.S. states, Hawaii, and U.S. territories. Many have not been updated since the 1960s, but since then trails have been abandoned, glaciers have receded, and subdivisions were built.

The 7.5-minute quads are not available for Alaska. Instead, the most detailed maps available are 15-minute quads. They have 100-foot contour lines and are at a scale of 1:63,360, or one inch to the mile.

When following well-established trails, the 7.5-minute quads are excessively detailed and unnecessary. (However, if you want map-reading practice, there is no friendlier map series.) On a long-distance trail, trail-specific map sets will normally be at an appropriate scale for the route and local topography.

Large-scale maps

When deliberating macro route decisions—for example, where

Large-scale recreation maps are useful for route planning and for hiking on maintained trails. But for off-trail travel and low-use trails, USGS 7.5-minute quads like these are best.

A few other useful maps

In addition to topographical maps, I may consult other types of maps when planning or when on a trip: 1) Climatic maps reveal weather patterns and are good indicators of vegetation cover. 2) Political maps show boundaries (federal, state, county) and towns; when combined with a road map, they help me figure out where to "get away" and where to resupply. 3) Land ownership maps help me avoid private property (or get permission to cross it), obtain backcountry permits, and contact local land owners/managers, who usually know the most about an area. 4) U.S. Forest Service maps show official trails, recreation sites, campgrounds, and other national forest attractions. 5) Nautical maps are helpful in predicting the strength of tides and the walkability of coastlines. 6) Aeronautical maps, used by pilots, can be helpful overview maps in very remote areas.

to camp two nights from now, or how to circumvent a pass that is dangerously guarded by an icy snowfield—it is useful to have a large-scale overview map. The USGS 30-minute by 60-minute quads are one option; they have a scale of 1:100,000. In Alaska, use the 1:250,000-scale series.

When available, however, I normally use a recreation map from a private-sector organization, such as Beartooth Publishing, DeLorme, McKenzie Maps, National Geographic, or Tom Harrison. Unlike the large-scale USGS maps, these maps:

> Are revised regularly, and thus have more current information, like recent trail relocations;

> Depict a specific area, like an entire national park, rather than just a checkerboard-like panel of it; and

> Show locations of services, parking areas, designated campsites,

land management boundaries, game units, and more.

The topographic information presented by these recreation maps is very reliable. USGS topo data is in the public domain, unrestricted by copyright and intellectual property law. Private organizations are permitted to improve the data and sell their own maps in printed or electronic form.

Landsat imagery

When planning my routes, I often refer to digital photographs of the Earth's surface taken by the Landsat Program, a joint effort of the USGS and the National Aeronautics and Space Administration (NASA).

Landsat images can reveal detail that is not depicted on topographic maps, including vegetation density, use trails, and recent topographical changes like landslides and shifted

how 2

make a map set in CalTopo

1 Add route notes and other annotations to your map.

2 Create a multipage 11-by-17-inch PDF with CalTopo's print function.

3 Upload the PDF to a local printer or FedEx Office (my pick). Specify full color, double-sided, 24-pound paper. With a corporate discount my price is currently $1.18 per print before tax.

The print quality will not be as good as original USGS quads. It's a function of the scan quality, not the printing.

river channels. It's rare that I take printed Landsat imagery into the field. Instead, I'll annotate my topographic maps with key details and download the imagery onto my smartphone using an app like Gaia GPS.

Sources

Printed USGS maps are available from the USGS online store and from a decreasing number of local vendors. Free digital scans can be downloaded from the USGS website, which historically has not been user-friendly.

The aforementioned recreation maps are available online and from local outdoor retailers, which normally carry maps for local areas as well as popular national and international destinations.

The most definitive maps for long-distance trails are normally produced by the trail association that oversees it, if there is one. In some cases there are multiple competing products, including from private organizations. Smartphone apps, like Guthook's Appalachian Trail Guide, are increasingly popular and available for more trails. With a quick Internet search, you can normally find what's available for the trail in which you are interested.

For several years now, my favorite map source has been CalTopo, a powerful online platform with which I can:

> Pan seamlessly across and toggle between multiple map and imagery layers, including USGS quads, Landsat, and Google Terrain;

> Measure the distance of and create an elevation profile for my route;

> Add annotations, such as the location of a critical canyon exit;

> Import and export GPX and KML files; and

> Export multipage PDF files for printing.

A similar platform is Hillmap, though I'm less familiar with its capabilities or its strengths and weaknesses compared with CalTopo.

tip

My daily pace picks up throughout a trip as my food bag gets lighter and my body hardens. If I am patient early on, I can make up lots of time in the second half.

Datasheets

As defined earlier, a datasheet is a list of key landmarks (e.g., intersections, passes, creek crossings, shelters), usually at least with the incremental and cumulative distance between them. Other information may include elevation, latitude/longitude, vertical change, and average travel times.

A datasheet has no value for a spontaneous itinerary, but it's extremely convenient for a prescribed trip, like a thru-hike or a specific custom route. With it I can quickly:

> Dead reckon to future landmarks;

> Identify realistic camping areas for the night or future nights; and

> Determine if I'm ahead or behind pace, and thus whether I should add a side trip or ration my calories.

Most datasheet information is derived from a topographic map, and thus could be calculated or noted once in the field. However, the data will be more accurate if it's generated with digital measuring tools like those in CalTopo, and a printed document can contain information for many more points than I could ever memorize.

Discussing alternative route options with Roman Dial while persistent headwinds raged outside the Chitina Café in Alaska. Large-scale maps are critical for such unexpected detours.

Continued on p. 130

tools & techniques

tried&true

how to packraft

part (2)

A packraft is a one-person inflatable boat that weighs four to six pounds and rolls up small enough to be carried in or on a backpack. I consider a packraft a critical tool for wilderness travel: I've used one to ferry across glacier-fed rivers in the Alaska Range, to paddle across fjords in Kenai Fjords National Park and open ocean bays on Alaska's Lost Coast, and to float rivers like the Yukon and Copper that were flowing in my desired direction of travel. Packrafts also increase the "fun factor" of conventional backcountry trips. Read *Packrafting!* by Roman Dial and check out the forums at *www.packrafting.org* for more in-depth information.

Equipment

Here's the basic equipment you'll need for an effective packraft system:

Raft. Alpacka Raft makes the most reliable and most white-water-worthy packrafts. Other manufacturers include Feathercraft, NRS, and Sevylor. I get the smallest (and lightest) boat I can squeeze into because my trips are usually centered around hiking and I don't want to carry the extra weight of a larger boat. The eight-ounce spray deck increases the boat's warmth and white-water-worthiness.

Paddle. My 215-centimeter-long Sawyer paddle has four pieces—two blades plus a two-piece carbon-fiber shaft—and weighs 25 ounces. This paddle hits the sweet spot for me. A stiffer paddle would be heavier and unnecessary, and a lighter paddle would be too floppy and weak.

Personal flotation device (PFD). Conventional foam PFDs are heavy and bulky but helpful or necessary if you go swimming. As an ultralight, just-in-case alternative, I use a custom-made double-walled nylon vest that accommodates three two-liter Platy Bottles; the total setup weighs eight ounces.

Basic techniques

Practice these techniques before attempting them in the wilderness:

Secure backpack to boat. Place your backpack horizontally across the bow and anchor it using two 60-inch-long webbing straps with Ladderloc buckles. Lace the straps through the boat's tie-down loops and the pack's compression and shoulder straps. Cinch tightly; the system will loosen up when wet.

Forward ferry. Point the bow upstream at a 45-degree angle to the current and paddle forward. The boat acts like a hydrofoil, and the river will push you toward the other bank.

Backward ferry. When you need to navigate around obstacles in the river, point the stern upstream at a 45-degree angle to the current and backpaddle.

Backpaddle. When floating through splashy rapids, backpaddle so that fewer waves crash over the bow and fill the boat with water.

tip Stay drier by learning how to raft conservatively: Avoid waves, ride the edge of wave trains, backpaddle through rapids, and show the boat's bottom to splashy waves.

tools & techniques

Datasheets can be reconfigured into other quick-reference lists. On desert trips I like to have a water chart, which informs me of each water source's location, reliability, and quality, plus distances to the next source. For a thru-hike it's useful to have a consolidated list of resupply points, with mileage markers, mail drop instructions, and estimated dates of arrival. And for a trip with designated campsites, I could sum distance, vertical change, and estimated hiking time for each day. (I never create this type of list when camping is at-large—within a day or two, it's likely to already be off by a few miles.)

Route description

A small-scale topographic map with a few deliberate annotations is worth a thousand words. I don't need a wordy route description to tell me the distance to an upcoming shelter, the right direction to turn, or the gradient of a climb—such information is more efficiently conveyed by the map.

A route description is useful, however, for providing general information about a section of the route, interesting historical and scientific knowledge, personal anecdotes from the author, and in-depth explanations of tricky sections. The route description can be part of a larger document or book that also includes preparatory information, specifically about backcountry permits, food storage regulations, average weather data, recommended equipment, travel, lodging, and more. (In my guidebooks, I split the route description into two parts: "Before you go" and "As you go.")

When I have attempted routes for which there was no published route description, I have made my own. This custom guidebook served to consolidate bits of information from email and phone conversations, online forums and trip reports, land manager websites, and my travel reservations.

Paper or digital?

While planning a trip, I find it easiest to work with digital maps and files. Plus, normally I am still revising them in the days immediately prior to my departure. But for regular consultation in the field, I much prefer paper materials to the electronic display of a handheld GPS unit, smartphone, or tablet. Paper:

> Is not susceptible to electronic failure;
> Does not require batteries or recharging;
> Will not break if dropped or submerged (nor be expensive to replace afterward);
> Is lighter;
> Has higher resolution, at least compared to most handheld GPS screens; and
> Provides space to jot down notes and thoughts.

Furthermore, a printed page displays significantly more information than a digital screen. For example, an 11-by-17-inch paper sheet with half-inch margins shows about 15 times more information than my 5-inch smartphone screen at the same zoom level.

To protect my paper resources, I store them in two gallon-size plastic freezer bags. In one bag I keep the materials I will need for the current day. So that I can easily access it, I store it in one of my backpack's side pockets. The remaining materials are kept in the other bag, which I store inside my pack, normally inside of a waterproof pack liner.

The freezer bag has two drawbacks. First, the surface becomes scratched with constant use, making it increasingly difficult to see clearly the materials inside. On trips longer than about five days, I solve this by bringing a replacement freezer bag. Second, the bag is not durably waterproof. If you will need to refer to your maps regularly in constant heavy rain, consider a commercial plastic map case. Since summer storms in my home turf are generally short-lived, I don't bother. Plus, a wet map is not catastrophic—I'll be off it in a few hours, and laser toner does not bleed like printer ink.

Tools

In an area such as the High Sierra with good visibility and distinct features, I rarely need more than a topographic map to navigate. Even so, for added accuracy and confirmation, I still take with me a watch, altimeter, compass, and GPS. In more challenging locations, such as the Appalachians, these tools become more helpful, and sometimes critical.

Watch & altimeter

With a simple timepiece, I can:

> Plan breaks and camps, based on intervals and time of day;
> More effectively communicate plans with my group; and
> Dead reckon (i.e., calculate my walking speed, predict my arrival time at future landmarks, and estimate my current location).

When backpacking in mountainous environments, a watch with an altimeter feature like the Suunto Core ($320, 3 oz) helps me to navigate more precisely. By knowing my elevation, I can rule out false summits and passes, double-check uncertain landmarks like an unmarked trail junction, and contour across a slope or around the head of a valley.

Compass

If I occasionally need to roughly find north, a lightweight keychain compass or the digital compass on my watch will suffice. But for more regular use, I like having a magnetic baseplate compass with a declination adjustment and fast needle; a sighting mirror is unnecessary.

I use my compass for five specific operations:

> To orient my map;
> To take a bearing in the field;
> To take a bearing between two points on my map;
> To transpose a bearing in the field; and
> To transpose a bearing onto my map.

When it comes to navigation tools, newer doesn't necessarily mean better.

COMPASS
My preferred navigational aid, along
with good topographical maps

GPS
Offers unmatched precision
and digital map storage

A compass has saved me on multiple occasions, notably during a five-mile bushwhack in Alaska's Kenai Peninsula, a descent from a high pass in Montana's Absaroka Mountains in a whiteout, and canyoneering trips in southern Utah, where it's very easy to get turned around. Seldom have I used my compass to triangulate my position. Instead, I prefer to pay better attention and simply stay found.

GPS units

Many people seem surprised that I can expertly navigate through the wilderness without relying on a GPS (which stands for "global positioning system") unit. These devices can:

> Show my exact location, to an accuracy of a few feet;
> Calculate the distance and direction to key landmarks, like my car, a hot fishing hole, or a trail junction;

> Determine how far, how fast, and in which direction I've hiked; and
> Record a track of my route that I can share or use when I get home.

But these functions do not make a GPS a killer app. I can do exactly the same thing with a topographic map, altimeter watch, magnetic compass, and pen. Furthermore, a GPS cannot replace map-reading skills, especially for off-trail navigation. A GPS can tell me the straight-line distance and direction to a landmark, but it cannot tell me the line of least resistance to get there. That straight line might take me through the thickest brush, into a deep canyon, or across the river at its deepest point.

My stance on GPS units has evolved since I wrote the first edition of this guide. I now consider it an ace in my sleeve for when my standard tools reach their limits. First, on a GPS

I can store maps and imagery of the areas surrounding my intended route, for which I don't have paper maps. Second, a GPS offers unrivaled speed and certainty.

Two particular events sold me on GPS technology. On one of my first guided trips, we had to bail out of the Alaska Range and ended up more than 100 miles away from our intended exit point. Thankfully, a client had a GPS with preloaded maps of the area. Several years later I led a night-time descent of Lucy's Foot West in Sequoia-Kings Canyon National Parks, which drops 1,800 vertical feet in a half mile on sustained Class 2+ terrain. When we reached the bottom, I used the GPS to quickly and precisely lead us to a flat area where we could camp.

skurka'spicks
NAVIGATION

For a timepiece and altimeter, I use a **Suunto Ambit Peak GPS** watch ($500, 3 oz). It shares the features of a normal altimeter watch like a barometer and digital compass, but offers much more, including customizable screens and track recording at 1-, 5-, and 60-second intervals. Plus, I own it already for ultramarathon training, for which it's a game-changing product.

My favorite compass is the **Suunto M-3G Global Pro** ($80, 2 oz), the global needle of which can tilt a forgiving 20 degrees. If you are willing to hold your compass perfectly level, the Suunto M-3D will save you some coin.

My preferred GPS unit is my smartphone, not a conventional handheld device. With a mapping app like **Gaia GPS** (my pick), **BackCountry Navigator TOPO GPS,** or **AllTrails,** my smartphone offers all the features you'd expect of a standalone GPS unit like location identification, waypoint marking, point-to-point navigation, and route tracking. But a smartphone GPS is even better because:

> It adds no extra weight, since I never leave my phone in my car at a trailhead;
> Software is the only additional expense since I already own the phone;
> It has a bright, high-resolution five-inch touchscreen;
> It offers access to map and imagery layers that are far superior to the primitive proprietary layers found on handheld GPS units; and
> It has a huge amount of internal memory to store layer data.

The primary drawback of using a smartphone as a GPS unit is its inferior battery life. If left in airplane mode and used only occasionally, I can do a one-week trip without needing a recharge. But if used more regularly, I bring a portable charger like the Anker PowerCore+ mini for mid-trip charges. A smartphone is also less weather- and impact-resistant, and more difficult to operate with gloved hands. ▮

tools & techniques

trekking poles

Like most college students, I was frugal, erring toward cheap (and, proudly, still am). But when I rolled into the Nantahala Outdoor Center near Bryson City, North Carolina, on Day 8 of my Appalachian Trail thru-hike, I quickly handed over $100 for a pair of trekking poles to replace the stout tree branches that I had been crutching on since Day 4, in an attempt to relieve stress on my worsening shin splints and aching feet. Since then, I've used trekking poles on every one of my overnight trips and on many extended day hikes as well.

Primary benefits

Trekking poles—which are very similar to alpine ski poles—give my arms an opportunity to assist my legs in propelling me forward and upward, and in braking on descents. While they may increase my overall energy expenditure, they reduce the net load on my legs, by as much as 25 percent according to one academic study. This helps to prevent overuse injuries and to delay fatigue.

I find trekking poles to be most useful when hiking in mountainous terrain and/or when carrying a heavy pack—basically, when I am working hardest against gravity. But I have still found a measurable benefit when on extremely flat surfaces, like when I walked across North Dakota. Trekking poles have other benefits, too:

> They provide extra traction on soft and slippery surfaces, like "gumbo" mud in eastern Montana, sandy washes in Grand Staircase–Escalante National Monument, and lingering snowfields in Glacier National Park.
> They offer a third and fourth point of contact when crossing rivers filled with snowmelt or tripping over tree roots in New England or tussocks in Alaska.
> They are useful in probing questionable surfaces like quicksand and rotting snow bridges, and checking the depth of silty puddles.
> They save the weight of bringing dedicated shelter/tent poles since I use them to pitch my shelters.

I have also used trekking poles to defend myself against aggressive

Without trekking poles to help him ford swift creeks and power up climbs, my Alaska Mountain Wilderness Classic teammate Chris used stout willow branches instead.

Doberman pinschers in Maine, wild javelinas in Arizona, and even a grizzly bear in Alaska's Arctic National Wildlife Refuge.

Drawbacks & solutions

Trekking poles are not without drawbacks or limitations. They obstruct hand function. Metal tips offer unreliable purchase on hard rock and pavement. They get tangled in brush. They are a liability on unstable terrain like talus and steep slopes covered in loose rocks. And, per TSA regulations, they are a prohibited carry-on item.

These problems are thankfully solvable. When eating on the go or taking a photo, I hold both poles under one arm. When they are in the way, I stow them away or hold them both in one hand. And I fly Southwest Airlines so that my poles fly free.

Weight considerations

As with footwear, the weight of trekking poles is disproportionately important compared with other items in my pack. Much more energy is required to swing a six-ounce pole thousands of times per day than to carry in my pack an item of the same weight.

With a lightweight pole (less than 8 ounces), proper poling technique—i.e., matching every step with a pole plant—is achievable on good trails; I can also catch myself quickly if I stumble or lose balance. Heavy poles are more difficult to swing. I often see backpackers drag or stow away their poles because their arms have tired; or they walk in irregular sequence (e.g., three pole plants for every four steps) even on friendly terrain because their arms cannot match the speed of their legs.

It's important to invest in poles that you can use correctly. If they feel awkward or if they are always lashed to your pack as dead weight, you'd be better off without them.

Shaft materials

Trekking pole shafts are made of either aluminum or carbon fiber. All things being equal, poles with carbon fiber shafts cost more (by up to $60) but are superior: They are lighter (up to 4 oz per pair) and stiffer; they aren't cold to the touch in cool temperatures; and they have better shock absorption, which translates into a less jolty ride for hands and elbows.

When overleveraged, an aluminum shaft will bend, but normally remain partially functional. In contrast, a carbon shaft will snap; in the short term, try fixing it with splints, duct tape, glue, and/or guyline cord. I have broken both carbon fiber and aluminum shafts, and I've concluded that durability is more a function of product care than material. During my Great Western Loop hike in 2007, I used a carbon fiber model for 5,000 miles before breaking one of the shafts when it jammed in a root as I was falling down a creek bank. And during the tough-on-gear Alaska-Yukon Expedition, I successfully used a pair for 2,000 miles before losing one during a river ford.

Design

Most trekking poles can be collapsed (via telescoping or foldable shafts), and the lengths of most—but not all—collapsible models can be fine-tuned.

Fixed-length vs. collapsible

Relative to their adjustable counterparts, fixed-length poles are stiffer, lighter, quieter, and less expensive. Sadly, no mass manufacturer offers a fixed-length model, which is frustrating because these same manufacturers already sell fixed-length ski poles. I suspect it is a market demand issue, since their ski shafts would be compatible with their trekking grips, tips, and straps.

The lack of demand is understandable. Fixed-length poles can be damaged during delivery or air travel, even when stored in a stiff cardboard

how 2

size trekking poles

1 When you hold the grip, your elbow should be at a 90-degree angle and your forearm should be parallel to the ground.

2 For open terrain and mild grades, lengthen the pole to improve forward propulsion.

3 For steep climbs or sidehills, shorten the pole (or choke up on it) to maintain proper posture.

Trekking poles can be collapsed in two ways.

FOLDABLE

Sections are connected with a durable cord.

TELESCOPING

Narrower shaft segments nest into wider ones, secured with twist or lever locks.

tools & techniques

tubular box covered in "Fragile" labels. When lashed to a backpack, they protrude awkwardly into the air, snagging branches and hindering scrambles. They may not be the right size for your shelter if it is designed to be pitched with a trekking pole of a particular height. Finally, they are generally only applicable for one user and one activity.

Collapsible poles are much more convenient. I have two pairs: One telescopes from a maximum height of 51 inches to a minimum of 25 inches; the other folds from a fixed 47.2 inches to 16 inches. Collapsible poles are more travel-friendly and can even be packed in a carry-on bag (at your own risk). And during prolonged sections of semi-technical terrain (e.g., scrambling through talus or on steep slickrock), they can be conveniently stowed away so that I have both hands free.

Telescoping

The classic trekking pole consists of three telescoping shafts, the extension of which is controlled with internal expansion nuts, levering clamps, or springed ferrules. I would strongly advise against twist-style expansion nuts, which tend to slip, especially when cold and/or wet. The other two designs are more reliable, though I can only attest to the long-term performance of the lever locks, which unfortunately are probably the heaviest system.

Some telescoping poles have an internal spring to damper vibration ("antishock"). This feature sounds appealing, but I'd avoid it. It adds weight and cost (up to 4 oz and $20 per pair), results in squishy and insecure pole plants, and becomes prone to rattling and squeaking.

Telescoping poles offer an unmatched usable length. They can be fine-tuned for an extended uphill or for a small adjustment in the pitch of your shelter; or they can be dramatically resized for an entirely different user or application, like if your spouse wants to use them on a backcountry ski trip. Two-shaft poles are less adjustable than the more common three-shaft poles.

Foldable

Foldable poles are made of three independent shafts connected and tightened with a durable inner cord. They have one advantage: They collapse up to one-half the length that telescoping poles do. For ultra running, I like foldable poles—I can quickly extend them for uphills and stash them away for flats and downhills. But I don't use them for backpacking. The design is inherently heavier; to mask this fact, manufacturers are using thinner and weaker shafts. The joints wiggle noticeably. And most models have a fixed extended length (e.g., 120 cm), and thus have some of the same problems as fixed-length poles mentioned earlier. A micro-adjust feature (e.g., 120 cm to 140 cm) will solve these issues but at a cost of up to $50 and 2 ounces per pole.

Grips & straps

Premium grips are made of cork; high-density foam is an acceptable runner-up. Cork and foam grips glide smoothly in my hand and reduce perspiration buildup. They are also lightweight and thermo-neutral. Rubber and plastic grips should be avoided for three-season use: They are heavy and abrasive, and get slimy when wet. Rubber is okay for winter.

Pole grips are slightly longer than the width of your palm. For a more secure hold, they're knobbed and thicker than the pole shaft. Most grips are parallel to the shaft, which is my preference. But some backpackers swear by angled grips, which they claim to be more ergonomic. The grips on cross-country ski poles are notably different—they are tubular and thinner. I've been told that they work well for backpacking too, but I've been unable to confirm this since no commercial model features them.

Grip extensions, which offer several more inches of nonslip material below the primary grip, are highly recommended. They allow for quick choke-ups on uneven terrain (e.g., off-trail, snowfields, steep trails).

Adjustable and integrated straps are attached to the tops of nearly all trekking poles. I speculate that they are relics from Nordic skiing, in which straps help in pushing off. For backpacking, though, I recommend removing them.

Without straps, my poles are lighter by one to two ounces. My hand movement is less restricted, like when I want to take a photo, look at my map, or grab my water bottle; this is especially the case when wearing large mittens, which do not easily squeeze through strap loops. And, finally, I'm less likely to break my pole if it gets wedged or stuck. If my hands are not tangled in my straps, I can easily let go of the pole before my momentum torques it too far.

Tips & baskets

Trekking poles are equipped with small carbide tips. Carbide is extremely durable and almost as hard as a diamond, though thankfully much less

part 2

expensive. These tips get great purchase on soft and broad surfaces (e.g., a dirt trail) but they are less reliable on hard and small surfaces (e.g., a concavity on a granite boulder). For extensive walking on paved roads, consider rubber caps or walking tips for improved traction.

Eventually the tips need replacement, about every 1,500 to 2,000 miles, depending on the terrain (rocky, more often; soft dirt and snow, less often). The failure is not the carbide tips, but the softer plastic and metals to which the tip is attached. Replacement tips retail for about $15. To remove your old ones, dunk them in boiling water and rotate them off with pliers. Do not glue new tips onto your poles. After a few firm plants, they will stay put.

Two-inch-wide "trekking baskets" are normally included with trekking poles. Unless you plan to hike on beach sand or Arctic sponga (soft, squishy tundra), remove them— they slow the swing speed of my poles and constantly tangle with trailside vegetation and between rocks.

I have a different opinion about wider snow baskets, which

If you want and can afford the best, buy the Black Diamond Alpine Carbon Cork Poles. They are durable, stiff, reliable, and reasonably lightweight.

increase float on soft, winter snow. When snowshoeing or backcountry skiing, they are a must. By around June, however, any remaining snow is sufficiently consolidated to leave them at home.

skurka'spicks
TREKKING POLES

If I were to attempt another multi-month on-trail thru-hike, I would want fixed-length poles. But since the only commercial model I know of, the **Gossamer Gear LT3C** ($130, 6 oz per pair), has worrisomely thin shafts, I would probably make a pair out of golf driver shafts (Extra Stiff flex) or alpine ski poles, aftermarket cork grips, and replacement tips.

If not, I will stick with the telescoping **Black Diamond Alpine Carbon Cork Poles** ($160, 17 oz), which I've used for hundreds of days and thousands of miles. They are durable, stiff, and acceptably lightweight; the lock mechanism has never failed. If you want and can pay for the best, buy these.

An excellent and more budget-friendly alternative comes from Cascade Mountain Tech. On some very rugged trips last summer, I used the **Quick Lock Carbon Fiber trekking poles** ($45, 16 oz), which are available online and at Costco. I found some long-term but solvable flaws, and I'd highly recommend them. On my website you can find long-term reviews of both models. ▓

tools & techniques

food

I found my treasure on a gravel bar near the Kongakut River in northeastern Alaska: a 25-gallon drum containing all my food for the next two weeks, along with maps, stove fuel, and new shoes. Kirk Sweetsir of Yukon Air Service had dropped it there for me two weeks earlier and had sent me the waypoints via email. Because I didn't have a GPS, and because I only had 1:250,000-scale maps (an inch of which depicts four miles) for this area, I was both ecstatic and relieved to find it. I yelled into my camera, "Do you know how nerve-racking it is trying to find a barrel of food in the Brooks Range when you're 300 miles from the closest town in that direction and 300 miles from the closest town in the other direction?"

The cache was a good place to lay over for the night. It was raining; I had not rested since my last resupply, in Fort McPherson, Northwest Territories (NWT), 11 days earlier; and there was a nearby cluster of wind-buffering willows. I pitched my canary yellow mid tarp and started counting out my meals, Scrooge-like. Day 1: breakfast, five snacks, dessert, dinner; Day 2: breakfast, five snacks, dessert, dinner; and so on, until I had 14 days of food parceled out. I started consuming the leftovers, which were not as satisfying as a burger, but I wasn't going to be fussy.

A dietitian might have screamed in horror to see my fuel for the next two weeks—many more bags of Reese's Pieces, cookies, and Fritos than dried vegetables, cheese, and foil packets of salmon. Meanwhile, some thru-hikers may have thought I needed more standard hiking fare, such as ramen noodles and Pop-Tarts.

Like footwear, food is a very personal subject. In both cases, you will find a huge range of preferences and opinions. There is no "right" way, but there is a right way for you, discoverable only through personal trial and error. In this chapter I will share what has and has not worked for me and for others with whom I've backpacked. My own style is based mostly on experimentation, with consideration for some research I have done about nutrition.

Challenges

My history with backpacking food is riddled with mistakes, and so too for many others. Lacking extensive first- or secondhand experience, you should not expect to immediately get it right—in our civilian lives, we have no opportunity to develop instructive knowledge. With regular

Cereal with powdered milk is a fast and yummy breakfast, good cold or hot.

access to grocery stores and restaurants, we can shop and eat as needed. Leftovers and surplus supplies can be stored in our refrigerators and pantries. And we have fully equipped kitchens to prepare, cook, and clean.

It's different in the backcountry. Without refrigeration, our food must be shelf-stable. Since we need to carry it in our backpacks, we have an interest in carrying no more than necessary and in maximizing its caloric and spatial density. And our kitchens are relatively minimal, which further limits our culinary options.

Amounts

How much food should you carry?

By calories

My standard recommendation is to pack 2,500 calories per day per person, plus/minus 250 calories, for a range of 2,250 to 2,750. If you are younger, more muscular, fuller-bodied, and/or regularly active, aim for the high end of this range. If you are older, less muscular, more petite, and/or generally inactive, stay at the low end.

My clients learn to trust this recommendation. I've watched many skeptical clients arrive back at the trailhead with several days of food still in their backpacks because they didn't believe me. Backpackers pack their fears and—understandably—you fear starving; your natural instinct is to pack too much. Not surprisingly, I cannot recall a single client who did not bring enough food.

By weight

Calorie-counting is tedious, especially for trips longer than a day or two. Weighing your food is a more efficient process: Drop your rations on the scale and either add or remove items.

However, this approach works only if you account for the caloric density of your food. Caloric density is equal to a food item's net calories divided by its weight. For example, a Snickers bar contains 250 calories and weighs 2.07 ounces (52 g). Its caloric density is 120 calories/ounce (4.8 calories/g).

tools & techniques

There are three main nutrients: fats, carbohydrates, and proteins. A pure fat like olive oil packs 250 calories per ounce, whereas a pure carbohydrate or protein like instant potatoes or whey protein powder only has 100 calories per ounce. There are no calories in water, so foods containing moisture (e.g., fresh fruit, tortillas, packet tuna) will often provide less than 100 calories per ounce.

If your goal is to pack 2,500 calories per day, your food bag will weigh less if you pack more fat. Take your pick: 10 ounces of olive oil or 25 ounces of gummy bears. More realistically, you can achieve an average caloric density of 120–140 calories per ounce. When you exceed this range, it feels like you are having olive oil with some couscous for dinner.

The difference between 140 calories/ounce and 100 calories/ounce may seem minimal on a quick overnight. But as the trip duration increases, the weight savings become very real. For a seven-day trip on which you packed 2,500 calories per day, your food bag would weigh 2.1 pounds less! This would offset the weight of an ultralight tent or a portable bear-resistant food canister.

Assuming an average caloric density of 125 calories/ounce, one day of food providing the recommended caloric punch of between 2,250 and 2,750 calories will weigh 18 to 22 ounces.

Reasons to take less or more

Admittedly, I do not always stick to my recommended range. There are at least three reasons that you may not either.

Personal experience. If you have learned previously how much food you seem to need, go with what you know. On several occasions I was certain that a client would starve on their miniscule food rations. They were usually older, veteran backpackers, and they knew their metabolism. Always, they proved to be spot-on.

Hiking for weight loss?

Weight loss is a fair motive for hiking, but don't intentionally starve yourself of calories. This approach tends to backfire. When I've been chronically undernourished (not intentionally, but as a result of the circumstances), I've become obsessed with food and have overcompensated once the trip ended, gaining over the long term. And it's difficult to be cheery and energetic when rabidly hungry.

This approach tends to backfire.

part 2

Physical intensity. On my most ambitious trips, I will hike for 15 hours per day, cover 30 to 40 miles (or less when off-trail), gain and lose 15,000 vertical feet of altitude, and start with up to ten days of food. For the first few days of such efforts, I can subsist on my recommended intake, but thereafter I need another 500 to 1,000 extra calories per day to quench my hunger, maintain my energy level, and help with muscle recovery.

Trip duration. Even on a low- or moderate-intensity trip, after about 10 to 14 days I notice that my metabolism spikes. It's not that I'm burning more calories on Day 14 than on Day 1, but that my body has realized its fat stores are being depleted unsustainably. Once my appetite kicks in, it's difficult to ever feel satiated. After I emerged from the Smokies on my Appalachian Trail thru-hike, my then girlfriend's father fed me two grilled steaks, two chicken breasts, two baked potatoes, and a half-dozen cookies before I was full; and in Una-lakleet, Alaska, I ate a 20-inch deep-dish supreme pizza in one sitting.

Disposal of extra food

Your goal is to arrive back at the trail-head with an empty food bag and without having wanted more food during your trip. I'd like to discuss best practices if you miscalculate, and either pack too much or prepare a meal that you couldn't eat completely.

Only two options are acceptable: 1) You can pack it out or 2) you can pawn it off on a hungry hiker. This latter scenario is a win-win:

Stockpiling calories in a resupply town

You lighten your food bag and help satisfy someone else's stomach.

Absolutely do not burn or bury your leftovers in the backcountry, or leave them behind at a shelter. Most significantly, this results in habituated bears and "mini-bears"—the mice, rats, squirrels, rabbits, marmots, pikas, raccoons, porcupines, gray jays, and other small animals that seem to take up residence in popular front country and backcountry campsites.

Also, do not leave extra food in a backcountry bear box. This may protect it from wildlife, but someone else (probably a ranger) will have to pack it out. Do not assume that it will be found by a hiker in need of calories.

Pre-hike weight gain

Even on a 2,500-calorie diet (or more) I lose weight during most of my trips, especially on the harder and longer ones. After a relatively short trip, this is a pure win: When I return, I can fit more easily into my jeans and set new personal records on my regular running routes. On a longer trip, however, unchecked weight loss could result in becoming unhealthily thin, and you may wonder if intentional pre-hike weight gain is a reasonable preemptive measure.

I can think of a few trips when this has made sense, but they always have nutty objectives. For example, Roman Dial walked 600 miles in 24 days across northwestern Alaska without a resupply in 2006. At one point, he was 119 miles away from the closest village or road. Roman figured the effort would require about 130,000 calories, and he supplemented his 45 pounds of rations with about 20 pounds of body fat,

which offered about 3,000 calories per pound. Polar explorers take this same approach.

For a more normal hike, however, I would discourage pre-hike weight gain. In fact, I recommend just the opposite. Before you leave, you should try to gain fitness and get leaner. Three reasons:

An unrealistic concern. If you regularly deprive your body of, say, 500 calories per day, it will react by demanding more calories or capping your energy level. On most long-distance hikes, there are ample opportunities to buy food. To balance your caloric burn and consumption, you will learn to carry more calories and to eat more food while in town.

An incorrect perception of health. An elite endurance athlete normally has a body fat percentage between the high single digits (men) and high teens (women). The body fat percentage of an average American is

between the high 20s (for men) and high 30s (for women). If you are as lean as an elite endurance athlete when you return from your trip, your family and friends may think that you are "too skinny." Cosmetically, this may be true, but in fact you probably have never been healthier.

Performance. Excess body fat has the same effect as putting rocks into your backpack. It puts your body under more strain and hinders your ability to move comfortably and quickly. The beginning of a trip is always a tough adjustment, but it will be easier with a leaner physique.

Considerations
Besides caloric density, which was discussed earlier, what other factors do I consider when selecting food items?

Spatial density
Consider a one-week ration consisting entirely of Snickers bars

Nutrition, caloric density, and shelf life are among the considerations when I buy food for a trip.

(270 calories each) versus Thomas' bagels (also 270 calories each). For that load of bagels, you would need a larger (and heavier) backpack, and you would be unable to squeeze them into a single bear-resistant food canister.

Taste
Hunger is the best seasoning, and I tend not to be fussy when I'm calorically deprived or limited. Even so, I have found that I can delay the onset of caloric boredom through a mix of flavors (sweet, salty, spicy), textures (chewy, crunchy, soft), and spices. Also, when everything else fails, chocolate is almost infinitely satisfying.

Nutrients
My preferred foods are notably lacking in vitamins and minerals, yet my performance seems unaffected. Moreover, I don't hear of thru-hikers—whose diets largely consist of Pop-Tarts and ramen noodles—developing scurvy or being overly susceptible to illness. Still, I try to make healthy choices when it's practical, like by having salads and fresh fruit in trail towns instead of just burgers and ice cream.

Shelf life
At the beginning of the backpacking season, I purchase and prepare most of my food. If I have planned a series of shorter trips, I can quickly pull food out of my inventory before I leave. If I'm out on a thru-hike, the food is shipped to me via USPS, which saves me time,

ensures that I eat what I like most, and makes it possible to resupply even with very limited services. Either way, food items must be very shelf-stable—they may not be consumed for months after purchase, and I don't have enough space to keep them refrigerated or frozen in the meantime

In-field prep time

Prosciutto and cheese is a tasty backcountry delight, but this meal requires that I sit down to prepare and eat it. In contrast, I can grab a candy bar from a side pocket and eat it immediately, without taking my pack off or even breaking stride. During a hard-charging trip, I can be seen doing the latter much more often than the former.

Cost

A 4.8-ounce Mountain House meal retails for $8. That's almost $27 per pound! I'm willing to pay for convenience, but profligate spending is not in my budget. My daytime snack foods average about $5 per pound, and ingredients for my breakfast and dinner recipes average about $3 per pound.

Protein recovery

If you were to maximize the caloric density of your food by packing only high-fat foods, you might be short on a crucial nutrient, protein, which is key to muscle recovery. Nutritional science currently recommends that athletes—a term that includes backpackers—consume about 0.5 to 0.75 gram of protein per pound of body weight. On intense trips, aim for

how 2

make some of my favorite dinners

1 Cheesy potatoes. Reconstitute 2.0 oz of instant potatoes. Add 0.5 oz cheese powder, 0.7 oz powdered whole milk, 1.0 oz crumbled bacon, and 0.3 oz green chiles.

2 Beans & Rice. Reconstitute 2.0 oz instant beans and 1.5 oz instant rice. Then add 1.0 oz cheese, 1.0 oz Fritos, and 0.2 oz taco seasoning.

3 Pesto noodles. Cook a full three-ounce package of ramen noodles; do not add its flavor packet. Then add 0.8 oz sun-dried tomatoes and a pesto sauce consisting of 0.8 oz olive oil, 1.0 oz Parmesan, 0.1 oz garlic, and 0.1 oz basil.

4 Polenta & peppers. Cook 2.5 oz polenta with 0.8 oz dried peppers. Add 0.8 oz olive oil, 1.0 oz Parmesan, 0.5 oz tomato powder, and 0.1 oz garlic powder.

tip

In cold weather, add extra water and make all your dinners into soups—instant potato soup, couscous soup, and so on. Soups will help to warm you up and rehydrate you.

the high end of this range; for more casual outings, the low end.

For me, at 160 pounds, this recommendation equates to 80 to 120 grams (2.5 to 4.0 oz) of protein per day, which more tangibly translates to 10 ounces of Jack Links beef jerky, six Clif Builder Bars, or 24 ounces of cashews. Overall, 120 grams of protein would constitute about 15 percent of the total weight of my daily food ration, which weighs about 800 grams (28 oz), assuming total caloric intake of 3,500 calories at an average caloric density of 125 calories per ounce.

Metabolic efficiency

In addition to caloric density, there is another reason to increase the amount of fat calories in your backpacking diet: metabolic efficiency, or the ability of your body to utilize fat as an energy source.

While hiking, our bodies draw energy from two sources: carbohydrates and fat. Carbs can be quickly converted into energy, but they are in limited supply: about 2,000 calories, stored as glycogen in your muscles and liver. Fats are more slowly converted into energy, but they are in near-infinite

In good spirits, even after four beans-and-rice dinners in two weeks

tools & techniques

Four full days of food, plus two half-ish days on either side

supply: tens of thousands of calories, stored as body fat, even on a lean endurance athlete.

Your metabolic efficiency can be improved by consuming foods with healthy fats like nuts, pesto sauce, and even Fritos (which are made of just three ingredients: corn, corn oil, and salt); and by reducing your intake of carb-heavy foods like sports bars, gels, drink mixes, Pop-Tarts, and gummy bears. With an improved metabolic efficiency, you will better utilize your body fat and your food's fat calories, thus allowing you to pack less food and more calorically dense food.

Portion sizing

Every 2 to 2.5 hours throughout the day I eat a small snack of 3 to 3.5 ounces, or 350 to 450 calories. There are many benefits to eating smaller but more meals. My energy level is more sustained, and I am not at risk of post-meal food comas. The small portions cause less gastrointestinal distress. By the time I get hungry again, it's almost time for another meal. And, finally, each serving has a definitive start/stop, which prevents me from dipping into future rations by taking "just one more bite."

I have seen other backpackers have good results with different eating styles. Some prefer to stop for breakfast after 1 to 2 hours of hiking, by which point they have more of an appetite. Some pack dedicated lunch foods, like hummus and pita, a turkey sandwich, or a tortilla shell stuffed with cheese and salami. And others stop for dinner in late afternoon, then hike for a few more hours before camp, where they might have a small snack or dessert before bed.

Seasonal considerations

When it's exceptionally hot or exceptionally cold, it's wise to reconsider

tip

To learn beforehand the temperature sensitivities of food items, put a selection in your freezer or outside in the shade on a hot day.

your food selection. Naturally, I learned this lesson the hard way.

During the winter portion of the Sea-to-Sea Route, when I snowshoed 1,400 miles through Michigan, Wisconsin, and Minnesota during the months of January, February, and March, I quickly realized that I could break my teeth on energy bars with corn syrup and candy bars with caramel. In a pinch, I've thawed them in my armpits and in my underwear, but they are not a practical choice in persistent cold. At the opposite end of the temperature spectrum, like when I hiked the Southern California section of the Pacific Crest Trail in June, I had to squeeze melted Snickers bars and Reese's Peanut Butter Cup sleeves into my mouth like a Popsicle tube.

What I eat

I start and end each day with a breakfast and dinner, and in between I consume a small snack every 2 to 2.5 hours. Breakfasts weigh about 4.5 ounces; dinners, 6.5 ounces; and each snack, 3–3.5 ounces.

Breakfast

For my guided trips I have some good hot breakfast recipes. But on personal outings, my preferred breakfast is a protein bar or some cold cereal with protein powder.

These options allow me to get out of camp much more quickly.

Daytime snacks

I categorize my snacks into four categories: protein, sweet, salty, and real.

Protein. Examples: jerky, protein bars, and whey protein powder.

Sweet. Examples: chocolate candy (e.g. Snickers, Reese's Pieces, chocolate-covered almonds), fruit bars, cookies, and energy bars. Notice that I don't load up on pure sugar (e.g., gummy bears, endurance gels, and blocks).

Salty. Examples: Pringles, Fritos, potato chips, nuts, honey mustard pretzels, and cured meat like salami.

Nuts and seeds are very calorically dense.

Real. On short and/or casual trips, or for the first day or two of a longer trip, I will bring "real" food. Avocados, a turkey sandwich, or a loaf of homemade banana chocolate chip bread—it's all a welcome break from eating processed food out of wrappers and storage bags.

Hot meals

At the end of a long day, I enjoy a hot meal, but I insist that it require minimal prep: Boil water, add carbs, let reconstitute, and then add spices, fat, and cheese in order to improve flavor and caloric density. Instant potatoes, instant rice, instant beans, couscous, and angel-hair pasta cook quickly.

Butter and olive oil are my two preferred fats. In cooler weather, butter can be safely packaged in two freezer bags; in warmer temperatures, use a container. I transport olive oil in a soft-sided Platypus bottle, inside of a gallon-size bag, to prevent the soiling of gear.

Coffee & hot drinks

No, coffee is not food, but I think many of us would give up half our daily rations before we would give up our coffee. I get my caffeine fix in three ways, depending on the circumstance.

On really intense trips when every gram and minute matters, I forgo coffee and stock up on over-the-counter caffeine pills. The experience is definitely not the same, but the functional outcome is, if not better. Otherwise, I bring both ground and instant coffee, specifically Starbucks Via. Because the Via is expensive, I reserve it for spontaneous espresso shots and for quick midday coffee breaks. Otherwise, I prefer the ground coffee, which tastes better and which is less expensive. With an MSR MugMate Coffee and Tea Filter I can make drip coffee, French press-ish coffee, or cowboy coffee.

I pack tea, and sometimes hot cocoa or chai powder, for casual trips and for trips in cool or cold weather. A midday or evening hot drink does wonders for my comfort because I generate little body heat while spotting for elk or hanging out in camp. During the winter, a tea bag improves the taste of drinking water, which I make by melting snow.

The economical and versatile MSR Mug-Mate Filter ($17, 1 oz)

Bulk bins usually have a good selection and reasonable prices.

Shopping & preparation

Food preparation entails a discouragingly significant amount of overhead time. At a minimum, you must plan your meals and then go shopping. Most likely, you should also expect some at-home prep (e.g., assembling recipe ingredients and dividing bulk foods into individual portions), for which there is a time-consuming setup of scales, measuring cups, bowls, and plastic bags; afterward, of course, I must clean up the mess.

During each backpacking season, I try to endure this process just once or twice. Each time, I prepare food for multiple trips, so that when I am packing up I can quickly take what I need from my stockpiles. For example, immediately before a three-day/two-night trip I can grab two breakfasts, two dinners, and ten three-ounce snack portions. To make the affair

go more quickly, I try to rope in family or friends, promising all-you-can-eat M&M's; I also hire Brent, a local Eagle Scout.

If I am buying for an entire backpacking season, I can justify shopping at multiple vendors, which improves variety and reduces costs. I buy core items like instant potatoes, instant rice, noodles, protein bars, and candy from supermarkets or (for better prices) wholesalers like Costco, BJ's, and Sam's Club. I obtain hard-to-find items like dehydrated beans, cheese powder, dried fruit and vegetables, and powdered whole milk from online retailers like Amazon, North Bay Trading Company, and Harmony House. Specialty grocers like Whole Foods, Trader Joe's, and Sprouts offer bulk foods and unique snacks. Before some especially long trips, I also have called manufacturers directly to inquire about wholesale pricing or volume discounts.

tools & techniques

Storage & protection

It is the responsibility of every backpacker to properly store and protect their food. During the day, it's mostly as simple as not leaving food, or a backpack full of food, unattended.

The conversation about overnight food protection is longer and more nuanced. Multiple techniques can be used, regulations vary by location, and misinformation is abundant.

Importance

Failing to properly protect your food has two possible consequences:

At best, it's only an inconvenience for you. Your trip will have to be cut short, or you will be hungry, or both. The incident may adversely affect your backpacking partners too, who probably will share their rations in order to prevent you from becoming a slowpoke or hangry (hunger-driven anger).

At worst, your negligence will result in the death of a wild animal. Bears, in particular, are often killed by land managers after getting too comfortable around and too aggressive with humans. As they say, a fed bear is a dead bear. Even if wildlife safely get away with human food, it's not considered helpful to their health or natural behavior.

Bears & mini-bears

A shocking number of people are fearful of black bears and grizzly bears, but ironically it's much more common to have problems with

"Mini-bears" plague many high-use camps.

"mini-bears": small animals such as mice, rats, and squirrels, but also rabbits, marmots, pikas, raccoons, porcupines, and gray jays that like to reside in popular front country and backcountry campsites.

While I've never had a bear come into my camp and steal my food, on multiple occasions I've had issues with mini-bears. Overnight, they've nibbled on chocolate bars and chewing gum, run off with my Dr. Bronner's liquid soap, and chewed apart clothing and gear that was encrusted with salt, like ball caps, trekking pole grips, waist belts, and even the armpit area of a windshirt.

Bears and mini-bears are naturally fearful of humans and naturally unaware that we are a potential source of food. But especially in high-use backcountry areas (e.g., John Muir Trail, Great Smoky Mountains National Park, and the Boulder Field below Colorado's Longs Peak), they

part (2)

learn to lose their fear and to associate humans with food.

This explains why I worry less about bears in the wilds of Alaska or Canada than I do about bears in popular backcountry areas in the lower 48. In Alaska, bears that get too close to humans get shot, and backcountry traffic is too light for bears to regularly be "fed" by humans, who leave behind crumbs and food packaging, who bury leftovers that they can't eat, and who will even directly feed the animals in order to set up a selfie.

Avoidance

Before discussing specific ways in which food can be protected, I want to share two methods of preventing outright a nighttime problem with bears and mini-bears.

Campsite selection. I believe the most effective technique is to not camp in the same locations or corridors where most other backpackers camp. In some cases, this means camping a half mile and 200 vertical feet away; in others, it means sleeping in an entirely different zone.

This tactic is sometimes described as "stealth camping," but that's never been my motivation. More simply, I just want a night of quality rest. Off-the-beaten-path locations are less likely to be home to a fearless and well-fed population of mini-bears. And they are probably not a nightly stop for bears, which learn to visit popular campsites as they do huckleberry patches and salmon streams in accordance with the seasons.

I often camp in low- and no-use sites even when my food is well protected. It's difficult to sleep well if mice are scurrying over my sleeping bag or through the leaves just outside my tent, or if bears are playing soccer with my canister.

These campsites have other perks, too. The ground is softer and not compacted, so it is more comfortable and warmer. Rainwater absorbs into the ground rather than pools on the surface. And because these campsites are often away from water, they tend to be warmer, drier, and less buggy.

While this strategy has been effective for me, I suggest it with extreme hesitation. When campsites are in designated spots (e.g., many national parks like Rocky Mountain, Glacier, and Yellowstone), the practice is illegal. When there are already many established camps, it's poor form to create another one.

Finally, even when it is legal and even when established sites are not abundant, I'm not confident that most backpackers can avoid leaving a trace, such as fire rings, Charmin blooms, cleared tent sites, and entrenched use trails. I particularly worry about large groups and "backcountry campers," who have more bodies and more time to make an impact; as well as beginner backpackers, who have not yet developed their Leave No Trace (www.lnt.org) skill set.

If you choose to follow my suggestion of using stealth campsites as part of a broader food protection effort, please be very responsible about it.

Odor control. In addition to using less popular campsites, I think you can marginally reduce the odds of having bears and mini-bears in camp by controlling food odors. Specifically:

> Cook dinner at least a mile before reaching camp. Some backpackers cook dinner even earlier so that they are well fueled for several hours of hiking in the evening.

> Use odor-proof food bags from LOKSAK. In one 12-inch-by-20-inch bag, I can fit about five days of food, plus or minus, depending on my planned caloric intake.

> Burn your trash in a very hot fire. In the morning, fish out aluminum wrappers and packaging that did not burn. It will be covered in soot, but that's more preferable than leftover scraps of tuna.

Among all terrestrial mammals, bears reportedly have the best sense of smell. It can be measured in miles and surpasses that of even a bloodhound. I'm extremely doubtful that you can eliminate food odors, at least according to a bear's nose. But maybe you can convince the bear that your food sack isn't worth the effort or that your neighbor's camp is more promising.

Protection methods

Suppose that bears or mini-bears are in your camp. How will you protect your food and other items that could be construed as food, such as toothpaste, sunscreen, and garbage? Let's discuss the options, and pros and cons.

Sleep with it. Due to safety concerns, no land manager or reputable outdoor organization (e.g., NOLS, Boy Scouts of America) recommends that you sleep with your food. I won't either, though I will point out that the safety concerns are completely unfounded in areas where there are no bears, and very marginal in areas with no recent history of aggressive bears.

Admittedly, however, I have slept with my food on hundreds of nights, even in areas inhabited by black and grizzly bears. And I'm not the only one: Among thru-hikers it's standard practice, and dozens of readers on my Facebook page recently confirmed that they do it as well. To be clear, I don't sleep on my food if local regulations demand otherwise, nor in areas with known bear problems, such as along the Appalachian Trail in the Smokies. Consult rangers, online forums, and news outlets to assess the risk.

Often I use my food sack as a pillow, or I tuck it under my knees in order to reduce stress on my lower back. If I have available better props (e.g., an air pillow), I leave my food bag by my side, in contact with my mattress.

Only once has an animal stolen food that I was sleeping next to—a fox, of course, in a remote part of the Grand Canyon. Thankfully I was able to retrieve the bag by following a bread-crumb trail of energy bars

part (2)

Bears have foiled many food hangs.

that had fallen out as the fox sprinted away. The fox's escape was foiled 20 yards out by a low shrub that snagged my bag. As I approached, the fox gave up and ran off.

A bear has never stolen food that I was sleeping on or next to. (Although, I've never had a bear enter my camp either, which I attribute to the avoidance techniques described earlier.) And I can't find a documented case of this happening to another hiker. I'm sure that it has, but overall the odds seem low.

When sleeping on or next to my food, essentially I'm claiming ownership of it. It's a bold statement, but I'm hoping that a bear decides that easier calories are available elsewhere. If instead my food bag were 20 yards away, I think that's more likely to be perceived as fair game.

Bear hangs. We are all familiar with the diagram of the perfect bear hang: 10 feet off the ground, 4 feet away from the tree trunk, and 4 feet below the tree limb. Yeah, good luck with that.

An effective bear hang is extremely difficult to do. I've only seen one person who can do it, Kevin Sawchuk, who crafted his skill in the High Sierra in the 1970s, when hangs were still an approved protection method. But even Kevin has his limits—when "the perfect tree" didn't exist, we went to bed hoping for the best.

Nearly all of the hangs that I see are pathetic and would be an easy score for any bear who is willing to enter a camp. Hangs are easily undone: Bears have learned to chew the rope, break the branch, and lunge off the trunk and grab the bag mid-flight; sows will also send their cubs out onto branches that are too thin and high for them to safely walk on.

Even when hangs are done to textbook standards, a well-trained bear will defeat all techniques. The simple tie-off, counter-balance, two-tree haul, and PCT method are no match. Many land managers have acknowledged this and no longer permit hangs.

Where hangs are still permitted, or even recommended, it suggests to me that the land manager is not concerned about backpackers using an effective food protection method, probably because bear conflicts are minimal or nonexistent. But at that point, why bother hanging the food at all? A bear that isn't willing to chew a cord probably isn't willing to steal a bag of food out from underneath me, either.

In addition to being ineffective, bear hangs are time-consuming and dangerous, especially if attempted in the dark. Budget at least 30 minutes; large groups with heavy food bags will need at least an hour. Watch out for flying rocks and falling branches. I kid you not: A common role-playing scenario in wilderness first aid courses involves a backpacker hit in the forehead by their own throwing rock. If you accidentally step on the rope during the throw, the rock has a wicked tendency to bounce back.

Mini-bear hangs. Hangs are not an effective method of protecting your food from bears, but they will work against mini-bears. A low-hanging branch works great. And in many trail shelters, nails have been hammered into the rafters for this exact purpose. Suspend your food bag a few feet off the ground, a few feet from the tree trunk, and a few feet below the limb.

If mice are a big problem, as in most Appalachian Trail shelters, you should expect that they know how to climb down the cord of a food sack. To address this vulnerability, separate the hook or nail from the cord with heavy-duty fishing line.

Backcountry infrastructure. At some high-use campsites, land managers have built or brought in

A bear box at a trailhead or in your campsite is a good indication that problem bears are around. Use it.

infrastructure to assist with food protection, such as cables, high poles, and steel boxes. If they are in your campsite, use them—it's a strong indication that bears and/or mini-bears are active in the area.

This infrastructure is not without its problems. As an aesthetic issue, the campsite feels much more industrial. More important, if you rely solely on them for food protection, you will be forced to camp in specific areas (which tend to be heavily impacted and not private) and unable to take advantage of dispersed camping regulations.

Portable canisters. These hard-sided cylinders are heavy, cumbersome, and an added expense. But they work! And, increasingly, they are the go-to solution for land managers who want to reduce the number of bear conflicts in the backcountry. They are now required throughout or in specific parts of the Adirondack High Peaks, Canyonlands National Park, Maroon Bells-Snowmass Wilderness,

North Cascades National Park, Olympic National Park, Rocky Mountain National Park, and multiple areas in the Sierra Nevada. There may be other areas, too—check local regulations.

Canisters are made of plastic or carbon fiber, weigh 2 to 3 pounds, cost $75 to $275, and are available in volumes between 300 and 900 cubic inches, the latter of which will hold about 1.5 weeks of food. Manufacturers include Bearikade, BearVault, Counter Assault, Garcia, Lighter1, UDAP, and Wild Ideas.

I carry a canister when I am required to. Overall, I don't enjoy it, but I do appreciate the peace of mind that it affords. It also doubles as a great camp chair. When not required, I protect my food through other means.

Ursack. An Ursack is about the same size as a portable canister, but it's made of Spectra fibers, the same material used to make bulletproof vests. One particular model, the Ursack AllWhite, has passed the Interagency Grizzly Bear Committee test, which is considered the gold standard. The list of land managers who accept the All-White as an approved storage method is slowly growing.

From a user perspective, the Ursack is vastly superior to hard-sided canisters. At 8 ounces, the weight savings are significant and make it a viable food storage option even when portable containers are not required. Its $70 price tag is relatively low. And because the Ursack is flexible, it is much easier to pack, almost no different than a nylon food sack.

skurka'spicks
FOOD PROTECTION

I rely on five food protection methods, depending on the local regulations and on the information that I have gathered from personal experience, guidebooks, conversations with rangers, and online forums and trip reports.

When my campsite has a permanent food storage contraption, I use it.

Where portable containers are required but where the Ursack is not approved, I use a hard-sided canister, specifically the **BearVault BV500,** which offers a good balance of price, volume, and weight. I can fit almost a week of food into the BV500; your mileage may vary. If I were wealthier or if my go-to backpacking destination required a canister, I'd spring for a carbon fiber Bearikade to save some weight.

Where containers are not required but where I'm genuinely concerned about bears and/or mini-bears, I use an **Ursack AllWhite.** This allows me to store my food away from my shelter, without leaving it unprotected.

When mini-bears are problematic but where real bears are not a concern, I use a mini-bear hang. If such a hang will not be possible, like at an alpine camp, I will bring the Ursack AllWhite.

Finally, when portable canisters are not required, when dispersed camping is allowed, and when my concern about bears and mini-bears is relatively low, I sleep on it. ▩

tools & techniques

cooking systems

In an attempt to travel fast and light, Roman Dial and I decided to carry my 1-liter, 4.5-ounce titanium pot instead of his 4-quart, 16-ounce aluminum pot during a three-day, 115-mile trekking and packrafting trip across Gates of the Arctic National Park and Preserve. The travel was phenomenal: We cruised 50 miles down the splashy Class II+ John River, followed caribou trails up Wolverine Creek, and were charged by a grizzly bear in a tributary of the Alatna River.

Our breakfasts and dinners, however, were painfully slow, because we could heat up only one liter of water at a time. I remember watching enviously as Roman sipped his coffee ten minutes before my pot was ready, and as he ate his last spoonful of freeze-dried lasagna before my water was even boiling. (Roman is 25 years older than me, and more accomplished, so out of respect, he got his hot water first. Plus, the pot decision was mostly mine.) On our next trip together, we agreed, we would take a cook system better suited to our needs.

A cook system consists of at least four items: heat source, cookware, ignition, and a utensil. A mug is convenient; in groups, additional eating containers and utensils are necessary. The optimal system is dictated mostly by group size, meal types, frequency of use, fuel availability, and local regulations.

Other considerations like weight, fuel efficiency, and cooking time should be secondary factors.

Heat sources

The cornerstone of a cooking system is the heat source, of which there are many options.

Open fires

I love open fires for their primal comfort, security, and warmth. Even after being pinned down on Alaska's Lost Coast by a gale or being chased all day by ferocious mosquitoes in Yukon's Arctic, a nighttime fire can magically make me believe that, "It's going to be okay." Open fires have the added perks of being free (no stove or fuel expense) and lightweight, since no fuel must be carried. Open fires are excellent for groups, too: They can generate more heat than multiple

Portable stoves are more suitable than open fires in ecologically sensitive areas like the desert.

stoves, and they create an alluring communal gathering spot.

For regular cooking, however, I find open fires to be impractical. They are difficult or impossible to start in high winds, or when fuel is saturated, of poor quality, or in limited supply. Fuel collection is time-consuming, and the fire must be constantly maintained. And cookware becomes covered in soot, which can dirty my other equipment.

Furthermore, open fires are often discouraged if not strictly forbidden. In high-use areas like national parks, the supply of biomass is usually inadequate for the potential demand; in environmentally delicate areas like deserts and alpine areas, decomposition is critical for ecological health. If poorly managed or extinguished, open fires will cause wildfires. And fire rings, ash pits, and scorched rocks are inconsistent with Leave No Trace principles.

With few exceptions, a portable stove is a better choice than an open fire. They are easier and faster to operate, and their use is strongly advocated by land managers.

Woodstoves

A less environmentally destructive alternative to open fires are woodstoves like the Solo Stove Lite ($100, 9 oz) and DIY designs using paint cans and chicken wire. These self-contained units do not require a fire ring and do not scorch the ground. Fuel is fully combusted, and afterward the ashes can be easily scattered.

Woodstoves are still subject to many of the same pitfalls as open fires, however. Fire-starting skills and quality fuels are critical. During droughts or dry seasons, woodstoves are often prohibited. They produce abundant soot and smoke. And fuel must be collected before each use and fed into the stove continually.

tools & techniques

159

Besides ambience and survival, the only compelling use for woodstoves is on long, unsupported trips with available natural fuels. In this case, the weight savings may be worth the hassle.

Liquid-fuel stoves

All liquid-fuel stoves will burn white gas (aka Coleman fuel), but some can also handle gasoline, diesel, kerosene, and other petroleum-based fuels. These fuels are inexpensive, available throughout the world, immune to frigid temperatures, and capable of producing enough heat to melt snow or boil large volumes of water. For these reasons, liquid-fuel stoves are ideal for world travelers, polar explorers, and institutional groups like the National Outdoor Leadership School.

But liquid-fuel stoves have considerable downsides and are generally ill suited for backpacking:

> They are heavy. The lightest setup weighs 16 ounces for the stove, fuel pump, and smallest fuel bottle.
> The fuels have noxious fumes and will contaminate nearby items like clothing and food.

	open fire	wood stove	liquid-fuel stove
best use	Low-use areas, abundant fuel; get warm, dry out, cheer up	Long, unsupported trip in high-use or sensitive areas	Winter expeditions; frugal groups
ease of use	Poor; laborious, dirty, skill-intensive	Marginally better than open fires	Fair; entails assembly, pumping, & priming fireball
fuel availability	Dependent on location	Dependent on location	Widely available around the world
prep and boil time	Slow to start, fast thereafter	Slow to start, fast thereafter	Fast after assembly & priming
cold-weather performance	Excellent, but melts through snowpack	Excellent if placed atop metal platform	Excellent; the standard among polar explorers
expense	Fire-starting supplies	$100–$150, no fuel cost	$90–$200, inexpensive fuel
weight	Zero	9+ oz, no fuel weight	8+ oz plus pump & bottle

> The simmering function is limited.
> The complex construction creates opportunities for failure, like clogged fuel lines and busted rubber gaskets. Extra parts and field maintenance know-how can be a trip-saver.

Also, I find their operation to be downright scary. A foot-high fuel-wasting fireball is common when starting the stove, and I really dislike sitting near a roaring flame that is just several inches away from a pressurized fuel bottle.

Canister stoves

A simpler, cleaner, and lighter alternative to liquid-fuel stoves are canister stoves, which attach to a pre-pressurized nonrefillable fuel bottle.

As measured by boil times and fuel efficiency, the performance of canister and liquid-fuel stoves is about comparable. However, canister stoves are much more user-friendly. Operation is similar to a backyard gas grill: Open the valve, and ignite the fuel with a match, lighter, or auto-igniter. They do not involve

canister stove	alcohol stove	solid-fuel stove
Large groups; small high-use groups; winter camping	Soloists & couples, 3-season conditions	Soloists & couples, 3-season conditions
Excellent; extremely intuitive, fast, & convenient	Generally good but depends on system; Caldera Cones are superb	Very simple assembly & operation
Mostly limited to outdoor retailers; illegal to mail or fly with	Excellent; carried by most hardware stores & gas stations	Not carried by all outdoor stores, but legal to mail & fly with
Fast setup, fast boil	Fast setup, slow boil	Fast setup, slow boil
With liquid feed, excellent; without, a hassle	Works with futz; inadequate for snow-melting	Good, but not suitable for snow-melting
$25–$225 for stove; expensive fuel	Inexpensive stove & fuel	Inexpensive stove, expensive fuel
2–8 oz + canister	<1 oz + 1-oz plastic bottle	<1 oz + 0.5-oz fuel tabs

tools & techniques

pumping, fireballs, or noxious fuels. They rarely break or need maintenance. And heat output can be better controlled.

Canister stoves come in three varieties:

> Upright, such as the Snow Peak LiteMax ($60, 2 oz), are most attractive for their low weights;
> Remote, such as the Kovea Spider ($65, 6 oz), which are heavier but more stable, and usually winter-worthy; and
> Integrated, like the Jetboil Flash ($100, 14 oz), a very fuel-efficient subcategory of upright stoves that combine a pot, wind-protected burner, and heat exchanger.

Integrated canister stoves mop the floor in terms of convenience, speed, and fuel-efficiency. But their higher starting weight pays off only when used extensively on a trip, like by a group or on a more extended outing.

The primary drawback of canister stoves are the fuel canisters, which contain propane plus n-butane or isobutane, pressurized into liquid. The canisters are:

> Illegal to mail or fly with;
> Reliably available only at outdoor retail stores;
> Expensive, at $5 for the smallest canister; and
> Not user-fillable, so you often must take more fuel than you really need, and they must be trashed (or recycled at specialized facilities) once they are empty.

Furthermore, the canister construction hurts the system's overall weight and fuel efficiency. The smallest canister, for example, weighs 3.5 ounces when empty and contains only 3.9 ounces of pressurized fuel.

Canister stoves are lightweight, fuel efficient, and extremely user-friendly.

UPRIGHT CANISTER
The lightest variety, at 2–3 ounces without canister

REMOTE CANISTER
More stable for large pots, and usually suitable for winter use via liquid feed

Hybrid liquid/canister stoves

A limited number of stoves are capable of using liquid fuels *and* canisters. This can be a convenient capability, but the added weight and expense of these models should be compared with the purchase of two single-fuel stoves that are optimized for your expected uses.

Alcohol stoves

Among long-distance and weight-conscious backpackers, alcohol stove use is widespread. But ironically, you're unlikely to find one at a local outdoor retailer—most alcohol stoves are homemade or purchased from an online cottage manufacturer like Trail Designs. Among the hundreds of DIY online instructions (no exaggeration),

INTEGRATED
Superior fuel efficiency pays off only when used extensively.

how2
use a canister stove in the winter

Canister stoves are not customarily recommended for winter use because in cold temperatures the pressurized gas will not boil off as well (or at all). Without adequate boiling, the flame will be weak, or may not even light. These tricks will help to operate a canister stove in cold conditions:

1 **Keep the canister warm: Store it in a parka before using it, insulate it from the snow by keeping it on a foam sleeping pad, and deflect some heat from the stove back to the canister using a windscreen.**

2 **Use a "liquid feed" by turning the canister upside down so that liquid fuel—not gas—comes out of the canister.**

A liquid feed can be done only with remote canister stoves and can be done safely only with stoves featuring a "preheat tube," which will vaporize the liquid fuel into a gas before it emerges from the jets.

tools & techniques

I recommend Jim Wood's Super Cat stove (about $1, 0.3 oz), which can be made in ten minutes from a three-ounce aluminum cat food can using just a paper hole punch (see Tried & True, pp. 166–167).

Alcohol stoves have many advantages over other stove types. First, they are exceptionally lightweight and inexpensive. My entire alcohol cook kit (stove, pot, windscreen, utensil, igniter, fuel bottle, and coffee mug) weighs 8.7 ounces, and I have priced an entire budget system at just $22.

The fuel is widely available and inexpensive. The paint department of any hardware store will have denatured alcohol ($6 per quart, enough for about 45 one-pint dinners), and most gas stations in cooler climates will sell gas-line antifreeze like HEET (get the yellow bottle, not the red one). The fuel can be stored in any plastic bottle, and you can take precisely as much as you need. There are no consequences of spilling it on skin or gear.

Most alcohol stove designs are fail-proof, with nothing to break or clog. Operation is also extremely easy. Pour some fuel into the stove and light it; some models need to "bloom" for about 30 seconds before the pot can be placed atop it.

Naturally, alcohol stoves are not perfect. Their primary limitation is their lack of firepower, due to inefficient combustion and to the fuel's low potential energy. Thus, they are inappropriate for:

> Groups of three or more, or smaller groups who use their

Pouring alcohol fuel into a Super Cat stove

stove extensively for hot meals and coffee stops;
> Melting snow; and
> Long unsupported trips, when fuel weight would really add up.

In addition, alcohol stoves do not have an on/off switch or a fuel valve. They can be smothered or blown out, but it's best to let them burn out. Use a plastic measuring cup to learn how much fuel is needed for a given amount of water. Because the flame is invisible during daylight, confirm that your stove is out by holding your hand high above the stove before disassembling the system or adding more fuel.

Without flame control, it is difficult to "cook" with them. They are best for hot drinks and for dinners that reconstitute in hot water (e.g., instant potatoes, couscous).

Their efficiency is greatly reduced by wind, making a windscreen imperative. DIY designs can be made of heavy-duty aluminum foil or aluminum tooling foil. Alternatively, get a Trail Designs Caldera Cone or Sidewinder, which will improve pot stability as well.

Finally, boil times are relatively slow. Expect six to eight minutes, depending on the model, water temperature and volume, and windscreen. I find other things to do while waiting, like stretching and looking at tomorrow's maps.

Solid-fuel stoves

Like alcohol stoves, solid-fuel stoves (aka Esbit) are mostly unknown beyond the long-distance and light-weight backpacking communities. These ultralight stoves—platforms, really—burn half-ounce cubes of hexamethylenetetramine, which will boil roughly two cups of water in seven minutes. In terms of weight, efficiency, energy output, speed, and wind vulnerability, solid-fuel and alcohol stoves perform similarly. Esbit has a slight edge in overall simplicity, but its fuel is about five times as expensive as alcohol and its availability is only slightly better than fuel canisters. Plus, the cubes leave a sticky residue on cookware.

Cookware

If culinary creativity is important to you, a multipiece cook set, Banks Fry-Bake pan, or even a Dutch oven may be worth the weight, especially on casual outings. If not, a single cook pot will be adequate for preparing freeze-dried meals, dehydrated leftovers from home, and DIY recipes using easy-cook ingredients like oatmeal and instant potatoes.

The fuel efficiency of this solid-fuel stove could be improved with a windscreen.

Continued on p. 168

tools & techniques

tried&true

how to make a Super Cat alcohol stove

Of the hundreds of homemade stove varieties, I prefer Jim Wood's Super Cat stove, which can be made in ten minutes out of a three-ounce aluminum cat food can using just a paper hole punch. It weighs a mere 0.3 ounce, costs less than $1.50, and does not need a separate pot stand.

This stove is suitable for soloists and two-person groups who eat boil-only meals: freeze-dried packages, angel hair pasta, instant beans and rice, hot drinks, etc. It is not suitable for large groups or for small groups that want to cook.

For fuel, use denatured alcohol or HEET (yellow bottle), available from hardware stores and many gas stations. I keep the fuel in an 8- or 12-ounce plastic bottle, and budget about 0.7 ounce of fuel per meal, as measured with a plastic medicine cup.

To maximize the stove's efficiency, use a one-liter pot that is wide and short, not tall and skinny. Also, an aluminum windscreen is mandatory.

Stove assembly & usage

Remove the cat food and wash out the can.

Flatten any sharp edges around the rim with the hole punch.

Just below the can's lip, make a ring of holes with the hole punch. Leave a gap of about one-eighth inch between the holes.

Below the first ring, make another ring of holes. This lower ring should have half the number of holes as the upper ring.

Pour fuel into the stove. Do not pour more than is necessary. The stove does not have an off switch, and it is difficult to blow out.

Light it with a match and wait 20 to 30 seconds for the fuel to start visibly boiling.

Place your water-filled pot on top of the stove and surround the stove/pot with the windscreen (see below). It will boil 1.5 to 2 cups of water in about seven minutes.

Windscreen assembly

Tear off a length of aluminum foil that is about four inches longer than the circumference of your pot.

Fold the sheet of aluminum foil in half lengthwise.

Fold over the outer quarter inch of the windscreen twice to increase the rigidity and tear strength of its edges. Punch holes across the bottom of the windscreen, about one inch apart to improve airflow.

Surround the stove and pot with the windscreen, leaving a quarter-inch gap between the pot edge and the windscreen, on average. The ends of the windscreen should overlap by 1 to 1.5 inches.

To protect the stove and windscreen during transport, I store both inside the pot and fill the remaining space with food to prevent them from bouncing around. I fold the windscreen in eighths and keep it on the bottom of the pot.

tools & techniques

This setup must be used on a flat *and* level surface. Remove combustible natural materials from the area. For beginner users, a pot lifter is very helpful.

My alcohol stove system is ideal for soloists and weighs just 8.4 ounces.

Volume

In three-season conditions, each group member will need 16 to 32 ounces (475–950 mL) of pot capacity. The low end of this range is suitable for small meals or for meals that are "cooked" elsewhere, like a Mylar or freezer bag. If you have a bigger appetite or want a hot drink with your meal, go for the extra volume. Don't be "stupid light" here—the weight difference between a 16-ounce and 32-ounce pot is minor, but the convenience factor is huge.

In winter conditions, when melting snow is necessary and hot drinks are craved, I increase per-person capacity to two quarts.

Most three-season backpacks and lightweight winter packs can fit a one-gallon pot, which can feed one meal to about eight people. If my group needs more volume than this, I take a second pot, not a larger one.

If I have the option between a short and wide pot or a tall and narrow pot with the same volume and features, I pick the squat one. It will be more stable and fuel-efficient.

Handles & bails

The usefulness of integrated handles or bails depends mostly on the specifics of your stove. For example, a bail is helpful when cooking on an open fire because the pot can be lifted out of the fire with a stick. In comparison, side handles are almost useless in an open fire but are convenient when using a liquid or canister stove. If your pot lacks handles, a standalone pot lifter may be a worthy addition to your kit.

Material

Along with volume, the pot's material is the primary driver of its weight and cost.

part 2

> Stainless steel is the least expensive but the heaviest.
> Aluminum is also inexpensive, but much lighter.
> Hard-anodized aluminum costs only slightly more, but it's much more durable than plain aluminum.
> Titanium is the priciest, but also the lightest and the most durable.

For the average backpacker who gets out only a few times a year, an aluminum pot like the Stanco Grease Pot ($10, 4 oz) or a hard-anodized aluminum pot achieves the best balance of weight and value.

More avid users can better justify the added cost of titanium. It is sometimes criticized for its poor thermal conductivity relative to aluminum, but this is offset entirely by its thin walls. Plus, other factors have a much larger influence on stove efficiency, like the windscreen and pot shape.

Matches are light, but too vulnerable to moisture and wind.

Ignition sources

Without a reliable ignition source, your meals will be disappointing. Even if your stove has an integrated igniter, it is wise to have a backup.

Matches

I once carried matches exclusively. They are cheap and ultralight, and they allowed me to keep my fingers farther away from the stove than with a lighter. To keep them dry, I kept them with my toilet paper in a waterproof plastic bag. "Storm proof" matches were never necessary.

Lighters

A lighter produces a longer-lasting and more wind-resistant flame than a match. It is more useful in starting a fire, and it will still throw sparks even if it runs out of fuel. The downside of a lighter is that fingertips get closer to the fuel, so greater care must be taken when igniting stoves.

Fire starters

An old-fashioned magnesium rod and steel fire-starter kit can throw seemingly infinite sparks, but throwing *accurate* sparks requires a stable surface for the rod, and most stoves lack such a surface. This option is better in theory than practice.

Utensils

Most of my breakfasts and daytime snacks require no assembly or cutting—everything is contained in a wrapper or storage bag. When I pack something less utilitarian, like salami or an avocado, I can use my pocketknife.

My dinners require only a spoon. A fork or knife would be of little assistance when consuming noodles, rice, or soup. Given my voracious hunger by day's end, I want a spoon that resembles a shovel, like the GSI Outdoors Pouch Spoon ($1, 0.3 oz). I trim the handle to make it more packable on three-season trips, but leave it full-length for winter trips.

Titanium spoons are popular among the lightweight crowd, but they are expensive and get cold to the touch. "Sporks" are a classic multifunction item, but they can't hold the same liquid volume as a normal spoon.

Extra ware

A separate drinking mug can make for more enjoyable and efficient meals. Have a hot drink with your breakfast or dinner, and avoid an extra round of heating water. The extra few ounces are well worth the time-savings. Lightweight plastic mugs are available for less than $5; double-walled titanium mugs are similar in weight, but more durable and much more expensive.

In a group, consider how food should be packaged at home in light of how it will be prepared and divided in the field. On my guided trips, meals are packaged individually because clients have personal stove systems. Whereas when Amanda and I go out together, we pack a single group meal, plus two mugs, two spoons, and one extra eating container (one person eats from the pot).

For the soloist, an extra bowl or plate is unnecessary. Eating from your pot works well and results in only one dirty dish.

skurka'spicks
COOKING SYSTEMS

When traveling solo in three-season conditions, I rely mostly on an alcohol system I have dubbed "the Cadillac." This premium setup is extremely light, fuel-efficient, and durable. It includes a Zelph Star-Lyte stove, Trail Designs Sidewinder Tri-Ti windscreen, and Evernew Titanium Ultralight 900-milliliter pot. A 400-milliliter titanium mug, Bic lighter, GSI Outdoors Pouch Spoon, medicine measuring cup, and disposable drink bottle (for fuel) round out the system. All in, the Cadillac weighs just 8.4 ounces and costs $192. Refer to my website for a more in-depth explanation.

To make it more packable, I shorten my spoon's handle.

Cleaning up food scraps—

Once I've consumed all the calories in my pot, I add some water and scrub the insides with my fingers. I don't use soap. If there is stubborn fat or cheese stuck to the sides, I will use something more abrasive, like sand or dirt, and double-rinse. In bear country or in arid climates, I usually drink the gray water; if not, I disperse it in a wide arc. I eat all the food in my bowl. If you don't, pack it out, eat it later, or give it to a hungry thru-hiker. Don't bury or burn it.

I don't use soap.

Alternatively, consider "the Dirt-bag," which is not as fuel-efficient or user-friendly, but it's a fraction of the price. It uses a homemade Super Cat stove and aluminum foil wind-screen, Stanco Grease Pot made of aluminum, and plastic reus-able Starbucks mug. It weighs 8.7 ounces and costs just $22.

If I am projecting a fuel shortage and/or if I need a hot flame, either to boost my morale or to dry out, I will build an open fire when and where it is appropriate.

On solo winter trips, I leave behind my beloved alcohol stove in favor of one capable of melting snow for water. I prefer using a remote canister stove like the **MSR Wind-Pro II** ($100, 7 oz) and a liquid feed. However, because the canisters are difficult to get, I have used liquid-fuel stoves for all of my winter thru-hikes, when I've had to find fuel en route. My current pick is the **MSR Whis-perlite International** ($100, 9 oz) because it can burn other fuels besides white gas.

It's worth carrying a larger and heavier pot when melting snow. I like the **Evernew Titanium non-stick 1.9-liter** ($90, 9 oz). When handling a full pot of hot water, a one-ounce pot grip is critical for stability, control, and safety. I also bring a full-length plastic spoon so that I can reach the bottom of the pot without dipping my fingers below the pot's rim.

The core components of my winter kit double in my three-season group cook kit, too. With a 1.9-liter pot, I can feed one meal to four people, or crank out hot food and drinks simul-taneously for just Amanda and me. When preparing meals for groups, each group member needs their own eating container, utensil, and possibly a mug. I recommend that they eat from a metal pot, which, unlike a plastic container, can be put on the stove to rewarm or simmer a meal. In cold temperatures and at high altitudes, this is especially useful if trying to cook items like polenta and angel hair pasta.

tools & techniques

water

At 80 ounces each, the seven bottles cumulatively contained 35 pounds—or 4.4 gallons—of water, also known as transparent gold to someone attempting a two-day, 70-mile hike across Joshua Tree National Park along a route with no natural water sources. Magically, I squeezed them all into my tiny 50-liter pack, along with four pounds of gear and six pounds of food. Fortunately, I knew my crushingly heavy pack would lighten by 0.75 pound per hour, and never again for the remaining six months of the Great Western Loop would I need to carry this much weight.

I waited until the sun dropped below the Pinto Mountains before leaving my final water source, the Colorado River Aqueduct. My plan was to hike through the first night and rest during the following day's peak heat to minimize my water consumption early on. After two miles, the abandoned jeep track I'd been following petered out in a wash, so I took a bearing on a distant star and began walking toward it through sparse creosote bushes. The loose sand offered poor traction, and the short sections of hardpan were no better because I kept punching into the rodent tunnels just below the surface.

Fatigue began to set in around midnight. I had already hiked 25 miles that day to reach my launching point; my body was also not adjusted for nocturnal travel. I lay down on the sand, and got up again when I became too chilled to nap. I brushed myself off and hiked for another hour before rewarding myself with another ten-minute snooze.

Dreams and reality began to mingle; the hours and miles ticked away. To psyche myself up for a final push into dawn, around 4 a.m., I momentarily stopped hiking, assessed my surroundings, considered what I was doing, and let out an inspired "WAHOO!"

Unexpectedly, I received a response from the north, then the west, and then the southeast. "AWOOO!" howled the coyotes. "WAHOO!" I replied. The conversation continued for a few minutes until silence returned to the desert night.

Hydration basics

If the human body could be compared to a combustion engine, then food would be gasoline and water would be motor oil. Water helps to keep everything functioning as designed. It is critical in:

> Regulating body temperature;
> Protecting organs and tissue;

Water is heavy, and I try carrying no more than necessary. Sometimes, a lot is required.

> Converting food into energy;
> Carrying nutrients and oxygen to cells;
> Cushioning joints; and
> Removing waste.

Risks & perils

Because water is so critical to the body's functions, it's important to maintain hydration within an optimal range.

Dehydration. On several occasions I have been uncomfortably short on water, always when I miscalculated my needs or missed a critical source. The worst incident was during a Colorado Trail thru-hike, when I misread the maps, believing there was water where there was not. As an East Coaster, I was unfamiliar with seasonal or intermittent sources that are replenished only by snowmelt or intense rains.

The earliest warning signs of dehydration are obvious. You'll become thirsty and light-headed, and your urine will be dark and strongly odored.

Fatigue and muscle cramps can follow, and eventually heatstroke, which is a life-threatening emergency.

Hyponatremia. In an effort to prevent dehydration, I have also consumed too much water and become hyponatremic (also known as "water intoxication"), whereby the concentration of sodium in my bloodstream was too low to absorb the water that I'd ingested.

On my first real desert trip, I recall feeling tipsy while leaving several water sources, where I'd knocked back several quarts in half an hour. Other symptoms of hyponatremia include muscle cramps, disorientation, strange behavior, and slurred speech; severe cases can lead to seizures, coma, or even death.

Hyponatremia is a serious concern among ultra-endurance athletes, who lose large amounts of sodium through perspiration and urine, especially when it's hot, dry, and sunny. To offset this loss, they ingest electrolyte supplements like SaltStick Caps or Endurolytes. It's less of an issue among backpackers—we tend to eat salty foods like Fritos, beef jerky, and ramen, and our rate of exertion (and thus perspiration) is less.

How much

You will hear and read general guidelines on how much water to drink (e.g., "two gallons per day"). But recognize them for what they are: guidelines. More important, you don't want to feel thirsty, and your urine should be slightly yellow-tinged.

To remain hydrated while backpacking, often it's necessary to carry water between sources. But at two pounds per quart, you don't want to pack extra. To determine how much water to carry between sources, I consider four factors:

> Duration to the next water source;
> Terrain to the next water source;
> Climatic conditions; and
> My current level of hydration.

So long as I observed past water consumption patterns, I can accurately predict future needs. For example, if I needed a half quart per hour yesterday, and today's conditions are identical, I'll need about a half quart per hour today, too. If I'm already well hydrated or if I'm feeling a bit parched, I'll round down or up.

Personally, I always try to stay slightly more hydrated than necessary, evidenced by clear and copious urine. Specifically, I'll consume one to two quarts of water within the first hour of the day; I'll drink heartily at a water source ("cameling") before a long dry stretch; and when water sources are frequent, I'll remain "topped off" by regularly drinking small amounts.

By maintaining a liquid reserve, I can endure long, hot, and/or dry stretches with less effect, or I can temporarily ignore my hydration to focus on a higher priority, like reaching a good camp before dark or helping a group down a dicey pass. Kidneys can process only about one quart of water per hour. If I were to max out this capacity due to the conditions and my exertion, stopping would be the only way to "catch up" after falling behind on my hydration.

Water storage

A multitude of water containers is available, but my needs are met with just four kinds. Three are plastic collapsible bottles, which offer unrivaled water capacity per weight and take up almost no room in my pack when not in use.

On three-season trips when water is abundant, I bring two 34-ounce Platypus SoftBottles ($9, 0.9 oz). On three-season trips when water is

tip Soft-sided water bottles can be used as pillows at night. Fill the bottles three-quarters full with air and/or water, and put them inside a stuff sack with some extra clothing.

MSR Dromedary Bags

scarce, I carry as many 70-ounce Platy Bottles ($13, 1.2 oz) as needed. For both bottles, I prefer the standard Closure Cap, which is less likely to leak and has a faster flow rate than the HyperFlow cap.

On winter trips when I must melt snow for water, I bring two 48-ounce Nalgene canteens ($20, 3 oz), which seem increasingly rare and expensive. With 96 ounces of capacity, they help me avoid having to stop midday for a time-consuming snowmelt session.

Because of the widemouthed design, the canteens are less likely to freeze shut than narrow-mouth Platypus bottles, and there is less spillage when pouring snowmelt into the bottle from my cook pot. Also, the connected cap can be looped into the strap of a ski or trekking pole in order to retrieve water from open sections of rivers or lakes.

I prefer to bring at least two bottles instead of one with the same total capacity. Smaller bottles are easier to hold and fill, and an extra bottle is insurance against losing or puncturing one, which happens. Even when water is abundant, I always carry two

quarts of capacity so that I can dry camp. I use one quart for dinner and drink the other in the morning to begin rehydrating.

On group trips, I often pack an MSR Dromedary bag ($40 for 4-liter bag, 7 oz), which are similarly collapsible but which are reinforced with nylon for added durability. The extra capacity improves the efficiency of meal preparation and camp breakdown.

Bottles vs. reservoirs

A high-volume water reservoir with a remote drinking tube and mouthpiece like the 100-ounce Platypus Hoser ($26, 4 oz) may allow for hands-free drinking, but overall, I think bottles are a better option. Bottles can be quickly pulled out of a side pocket and filled, whereas refilling a reservoir is a drawn-out process: I must take off my pack, unthread the hose, remove the reservoir, refill it (which isn't always easy), slide it back inside my pack, rethread the hose, and put my pack back on.

With a reservoir, it's difficult to determine how much water I have left. They create an uncomfortable bulge against my back. Mouthpieces have a tendency to leak with long-term use. If not sealed correctly, they can disastrously leak. In cold temperatures, tubes freeze, even if insulated with neoprene. Finally, it is difficult to seal zipper-style closures with mittens and/or cold hands.

tools & techniques

how 2

pack water

1 **When temperatures are above freezing and water is abundant, I keep a one-liter bottle in a side pocket, empty or full, where I can easily access it.**

2 **In the desert, I prevent heavy water loads from affecting my center of gravity by counterbalancing bottles in the side pockets or by centering them in the main compartment.**

3 **In subfreezing temperatures, I insulate bottles with extra clothing and/or foam cozies, or keep them next to my belly just outside my base layer shirt.**

Other bottle types

For backpacking, I believe that bottles are better than reservoirs, and that plastic collapsible bottles are better than other bottle types. But my favorites are not perfect.

For everyday use, consider a more durable stainless steel or hard-sided plastic bottle. I'd pick the former, such as from Klean Kanteen, because it won't leach chemicals or absorb flavors. The weight and volume of these bottles adds up, however. The iconic 1-quart Nalgene weighs 5.5 ounces, or about six times more than a 34-ounce Platypus SoftBottle. Two gallons of capacity, which is a good rule of thumb when backpacking in the desert, would weigh 2.5 pounds before you even have water on board!

Especially among thru-hikers, "disposable" bottles are popular, with 1-liter glacéau smartwater bottles being the most coveted. They are lightweight, relatively durable (if not used for hot liquids), easy to fill, and inexpensive—or free if retrieved from a recycling bin.

Vacuum bottles excel in cold temperatures, insulating like no other storage container. However, they're not cheap or light; a 1-quart Hydro Flask costs $35 and weighs 14 ounces. They are convenient, almost luxurious, but they're not critical—I have managed with my aforementioned system in bitterly cold conditions.

Water quality

On occasion, I have had no option but to drink water from an utterly nauseating source. Among the most memorable were a stock pond on Arizona's Coconino Plateau that was surrounded by cow patties and was the color of urine; a scum-filled water tank above the Missouri River in eastern Montana with dead mice floating on the surface; and two canyons in Grand Staircase-Escalante National Monument, Harris Wash and the Gulch, where I have seen half-decomposed cattle lying in the creek.

The quality of these water sources was clearly suspect, but usually it's less obvious. Before discussing methods of treating water, let's first understand why it's important.

Pathogens

Most discussion about water quality focuses on pathogens that can lurk in the water, specifically:

> Protozoa like *Giardia* and *Cryptosporidium;*
> Bacteria like *E. coli, Campylobacter,* and *Salmonella;* and
> Viruses like hepatitis, polio, and norovirus.

Most pathogens are transmitted by the fecal–oral route (i.e., you ingest water or consume food that has been contaminated by the feces of an infected carrier). The carrier does not need to be showing symptoms to be contagious. For example, about half of those infected with *Giardia* are asymptomatic.

Some pathogens are much more worrisome and/or prevalent than others. The protozoa *Naegleria fowleri* lead to primary amoebic meningoencephalitis, or PAM, which has a survival rate of less than one percent. Fortunately, it's also extremely rare, with 133 cases reported in the United States since 1962. Most waterborne illnesses will present with gastrointestinal distress (diarrhea, bloating) and flu-like symptoms (vomiting, nausea, malaise). The onset can be immediate or delayed, and medical treatment may or may not be required to regain full health.

The severity of a pathogenic infection depends on three factors:

> The amount of pathogen consumed;
> The virulence of the pathogen; and
> The strength of the host's immune system.

North American water

In a matter of minutes, I can obtain temperature and precipitation data for a planned route, but there is no comparable resource that contains information about the quality of backcountry water sources. Mostly, we must assume that they are contaminated.

The protozoa *Giardia* and *Cryptosporidium,* which are common worldwide, get the most attention in North America. Neither is the most harmful or the most common pathogen;

Water contaminated by livestock can be unpleasant, but it's better than none.

rather, they are the most common pathogens that can be harmful. *Giardia* is the most commonly diagnosed intestinal parasite on the continent, and every person I know who has contracted it reports an awful experience.

Most outbreaks of *Giardia* and *Cryptosporidium* infections are traced to faulty municipal water treatment plants, contaminated swimming pools and water parks, community cookouts, and other non-backcountry sources. The most notable case occurred in 1993, when 403,000 residents of Milwaukee were infected by *Cryptosporidia* that had passed through the municipal filtration system. The number of infected outdoor recreationists is low by comparison. And the number of infections that can be traced to contaminated water is even lower. Some research has concluded that poor group hygiene is more often the culprit.

Viruses are the second most common pathogen in North American water sources. Bacteria are the least common. But "common" does not necessarily mean "everywhere" or "enough."

Tests of backcountry water sources show that water quality can be surprisingly good. For example, in 2000, only 23 percent of tests conducted on San Francisco's primary water source—the Hetch Hetchy Reservoir, which is fed by the Tuolumne River flowing out of Yosemite—tested positive for *Giardia,* and then presented levels so low that, on average, a person would have to drink eight liters of water just to ingest one cyst, a small fraction of the minimum needed for infection.

Nonpathogen contaminants

Pathogens are not the only contaminants in backcountry water sources. There are organic and inorganic materials, especially after heavy rains or during spring runoff. And there are biological organisms that reside in the water and soil, like larvae and guinea worm.

But the most worrisome nonpathogen contaminants are chemical pollutants from industrial, agricultural, and natural sources. In Colorado, I have skipped springs and creeks that were clearly contaminated with heavy metals, probably from mining activity more than a century ago. In Southern California, the irrigation canals are polluted with pesticides, herbicides, and fertilizers. And in southern Utah, I have been disappointed by springs that were too alkaline (salty) to drink. Most purification methods are ineffective against such contaminants.

Use good hygiene to prevent group contamination: Regularly wash your hands with soap, especially after "bio breaks" and before meals.

Is the water ever clean?

Yes, backcountry water sources often pose no or little risk to your health if untreated. However, you can never be sure, and you should always treat it. Water quality should be best at its source, where it first gurgles out of the ground or drips from a snowfield. As water flows downstream, opportunities for contamination increase: Wildlife, livestock, and humans defecate in backcountry watersheds. And farther downstream, the rivers carry away pollutants from residences, industry, and agriculture. As the water flows downhill, it generally becomes warmer, more turbid, and discolored.

You can never be certain.

Assessing water quality

Besides distance to source and upstream use (see sidebar above), what other factors are suggestive of water quality?

Volume. The solution to pollution is dilution, right? Perhaps not with seven billion people on the planet, but for our purposes it is still applicable. A water source with a low concentration of contaminants poses lower risk.

Turbidity. If microbes can burrow into sediment and other floaties, some purification methods become less effective, notably chemicals and ultraviolet (UV) light.

Vegetation. Some plant life is a good proxy for water quality. A carpet of lush moss is an encouraging sign, for example, whereas an algae bloom is reason for concern.

Flow. Without an outlet, stagnant water sources are a one-way collection site for contaminants. I do not avoid them, but I do try to take water from the top few inches, which receive more UV light, a proven purification method.

Immunity

Regularly I drink water from natural sources without first treating it. Most sources are low risk, like alpine creeks and lakes in remote watersheds of the High Sierra. But some are at least moderate risk, like small streams in Boulder's high-use foothills and seasonal potholes in the Grand Canyon.

Yet I've never been diagnosed with a waterborne illness. How? Perhaps I'm lucky, extremely skilled at identifying clean water sources, or asymptomatic to all pathogens that I have ingested. But given the volume of untreated water that I have swallowed, I think a better explanation is that I have developed resistance through multiple low-dose exposures. The same is probably true of many other backpackers who frequently drink untreated water without consequence.

Demonstrated immunity does not necessarily protect me from extremely high concentrations of pathogens or from foreign pathogens. When I'm suspect of a water source, I purify it; and if I were to backpack in Asia or South America, where there may be pathogens to which I've never been exposed, I would be especially careful.

Water treatment

To rid water of contaminants, there are four basic techniques:

> Boiling;
> Filtration;
> Chemicals; and
> Ultraviolet light.

Boiling kills all biological matter, pathogens included. I rely on this method frequently, but only when heating water anyway for breakfast, dinner, or midday coffee. Otherwise, it's impractical: It's extremely time-consuming and fuel-intensive, and hot water is hardly thirst-quenching.

The three remaining methods are better for routine treatment. Your specific preference will likely be a function of your group size, the frequency and quality of water sources, and the importance of time, long-term reliability, and cost.

Some treatment methods are labeled as a "purifier," a distinction

	boiling	pump filters	gravity filters	inline filters
effectiveness	Kills all biological matter	Extract protozoa, bacteria, large microbes, and sediment; some catch viruses and chemicals		
treatment time	Slow and fuel intensive	1–2.5 qt per tiring minute	1–2 qt per minute, with no effort	1–2 qt per minute, with manual force
system weight	Fuel weight	12–16 oz	10–20 oz	2–5 oz
expense	Fuel cost	$75–$350	$75–$225	$20–$55
aftertaste	Hot water	None	None	None
best for	Cooking meals	Mostly not recom- mended	Groups	Soloists

reserved for those that extract or kill all pathogens (i.e., protozoa, bacteria, and viruses). The same effect can sometimes be achieved by combining two non-purifiers, like chemically treating water after filtering it.

The do-it-all Guardian is labeled a water purifier.

Some filters go above and beyond, by removing chemicals and improving water taste. The MSR Guardian does all of the above, and even removes viruses. But its exceptional performance comes at a high price—it's $350 and 17 oz. Filters have other trade-offs, too. They leak retained water. Their flow rates are slow to begin with and get worse until the filter is backwashed, scrubbed, or replaced. And most cannot be operated on the move. Specific filter types have additional considerations:

Filtration

At a minimum, filters will strain out larger-bodied pathogens like protozoa and bacteria, as well as sediment, larvae, and other floaties. This should be sufficient for most back-country watersheds, where viruses are rare.

Pump filters are my least preferred treatment technique. They are heavy and their operation involves considerable effort. Pumping large

household bleach	iodine	chlorine dioxide	ultraviolet light
Not effective against *Cryptosporidium*	Limited by cold and turbidity; never effective against *Cryptosporidium*	Kills most pathogens in 15–30 minutes	Kills all pathogens
Depends on dosage	30 minutes	5-minute premix, 4-hour wait for *Cryptosporidium*	90 seconds per liter
<1 oz	<1 oz	2 oz or less	3–5 oz
Negligible	$1 per gallon	50 cents per gallon	$50–$100, plus batteries
Swimming pool	Medicine cabinet	Usually none, sometimes bleachy	None
Emergency or backup	Emergency or backup	Soloists and groups	Soloists who are anti-chemical

tools & techniques

volumes of water is downright tire-some—imagine treating a few liters of water for you and several partners at a typical flow rate of about one quart per minute.

The Sawyer Squeeze filters water quickly, but is not ideal for large volumes.

Gravity-fed filters

like the Platypus GravityWorks system ($120, 12 oz for 4 liters) are ideal for groups and extended camps. Suspend a reservoir of untreated water above an empty res-ervoir—using a branch, boulder, or steep slope—and return a few min-utes later to a full reservoir of filtered water that can then be decanted into individual bottles.

Inline filters like the Sawyer Squeeze ($40, 3 oz) share the same filter tech-nology with gravity-fed filters, but rely on a manual force like suction or squeezing. With some inline filters, you can drink directly from creeks, pools, or bottles by using it as a straw. But it's much easier to squeeze untreated water through it from a collapsible bot-tle. This pressure will cause these bot-tles to fail prematurely; a backup bottle may be wise.

Chemicals

Iodine is an outdated treatment method. The classic Potable Aqua tablets ($7, 1 oz) are lightweight, inexpensive, and widely available, but they are not effective against *Cryptosporidium* and their overall effectiveness is impaired by cold and turbidity. Your water will also taste like a medicine cabinet.

Household liquid bleach (sodium hypochlorite) would be a better home remedy than iodine. However, it degrades with age and it's still slow against *Cryptosporidium.* Plus, it's like drinking pool water.

Chlorine dioxide has been used by municipal water treatment plants since the late 1940s and is the supe-rior chemical treatment. The tablet and droplet forms share identical technology, but only tablets like those from Aquamira ($11 for a 20-pack, 1 oz) have been approved by the Environmental Protection Agency as a "purifier." The marketing copy for the drops claims only that they "kill odor-causing bacteria and enhance the taste of potable water."

Fear not. A proper dose of chlorine dioxide (in tablet or droplet form) will kill most pathogens within 15 minutes, or within 30 minutes for very silty and contaminated ("worst case") water. *Cryptosporidium* is more resilient, however: The recommended dwell time is four hours. Unlike iodine and bleach, chlorine dioxide has minimal chemical aftertaste, if any.

If you plan to use chemicals and expect floaties in your water, it is advised to bring a bandanna or coffee filter in order to strain out large particles before treatment.

Ultraviolet light

The SteriPEN Ultra water purifier ($100, 5 oz) and similar products prevent all pathogen types from reproducing by scrambling their DNA. You still ingest the pathogen, but without offspring there should be no effect.

Its speed—at about 90 seconds per quart—is attractive, but the technology has problems. The cost and weight of replacement batteries adds up. It's incompatible with narrow-mouth bottles, which do not allow the light to be sufficiently submerged. Its effectiveness decreases in turbid water (although it must be good enough to have earned the "purifier" label). Finally, there are too many possible points of failure. The unit can break if dropped, stepped on, or stored poorly. The batteries die, and the battery compartment is not necessarily waterproof. And the electronics can be fickle. For such a critical item, its reliability is discomforting. If you go this direction, I recommend having a backup system.

skurka's picks
WATER TREATMENT

For at least a decade my go-to water treatment method has been chlorine dioxide; it is the standard technique on my guided trips, too. The results have been excellent, and now statistically significant. I prefer **Aquamira** **droplets** ($15, 3 oz), but in temperatures below about 15°F I swap to tablets because they don't freeze. Versus tablets, droplets are more economical (at about 50 cents per gallon) and flexible, since I can easily modify dosages with proportional changes to dwell times. Especially when decanted into smaller dropper bottles, it's an ultralight technique.

Chlorine dioxide is transported as a two-part solution and must be mixed for five minutes before it can be dispensed into water. By storing premix in an airtight and opaque dropper bottle, this wait time can be eliminated. McNett, the manufacturer of Aquamira, discourages premixing due to potency concerns, but the practice seems to be safe with some degree of user education.

In recent years I have also warmed to the **Sawyer Squeeze.** Versus other lightweight methods capable of delivering potable water immediately, it has a better flow rate than the Sawyer Mini, and it's less expensive and more reliable than ultraviolet pens.

The combination of chlorine dioxide and the Sawyer Squeeze may make the ultimate purifier combination. Use the Squeeze to quickly filter small amounts, and the Aquamira to purify large quantities that will sit overnight or in your pack for several hours. For highly suspect water, use both methods. For a group, pair chlorine dioxide with a gravity-fed filter, or get some additional hardware in order to use the Squeeze as one.

small essentials

I considered other names for this chapter, like "Miscellaneous," "Stuff," "Odds & Ends," and "Dinky Things." Ultimately, "Small Essentials" won out—these items will round out your kit, and in many ways are critical to your safety and comfort.

Tools & utility

Knives & scissors

If you plan to be chopping your way through the Amazon rain forest, killing and gutting your food, chopping wood, or cutting rope to make a raft, you may want a big knife. But for solo trips I have never needed more than the Victorinox Swiss Army Classic ($20, 0.8 oz), which has a two-inch blade and small scissors. Slicing salami, opening mail-drop boxes, clipping nails, and trimming medical

For normal three-season backpacking trips, I've never needed more than the simple Victorinox Swiss Army Classic Knife.

and foot care supplies represents the extent of my uses.

On group trips I bring the Gerber Ultralight LST ($19, 1 oz), which has a longer and better quality blade, mostly for meal preparation. I also pack Fiskars 5-inch Blunt Tip Scissors ($3, 1 oz) for more efficient foot care sessions.

Fire starter

You are probably most likely to need a fire when it is cold, wet, and windy. Unfortunately, these are also the most difficult conditions in which to start a fire. Do not wait until you *need* to start a fire before *learning* to. Where and when permitted, practice.

In addition to quality fuel and oxygen, my fire starting regimen calls for a Bic lighter and a Mylar-lined food wrapper such as from a Clif Bar, which is made of highly combustible, long-lasting, and relatively clean-burning plastic.

Ignite the wrapper with the lighter. Hold it over your tinder as fiery globs drop off it. When the flame gets too close to your fingers, drape the wrapper over your tinder, and then add larger sticks. Voilà!

Insect protection

Unless I'm certain that my trip will be bug-free, I carry a 0.5-ounce spray tube of Sawyer Picaridin Insect Repellent ($3, 1 oz), which is as effective as DEET-based repellents but does not harm clothing and equipment. I store it in a hipbelt pocket for easy access.

For intense bug pressure, the most effective defense against biting insects is permethrin-treated, full-coverage

I keep this 0.5-ounce spray tube in a hip-belt pocket for quick access.

clothing: a long-sleeve nylon shirt, nylon pants, brimmed hat, and mosquito head net (not a no-see-um head net, which is almost suffocating). When wearing such an outfit, I apply repellent on my ankles, wrists, and neck to discourage insects from finding the openings.

When bug pressure is more modest, I usually trade in my full-coverage clothing for an airy top and shorts. Strategic application of repellent in oft-bitten areas, like the back of my shoulders and knees, keeps the situation tolerable.

Lighting

For hiking at night and for navigating camp in the dark, I carry a flashlight or headlamp. Moonlight is romantic but unreliable. The only scenario in which

I'll leave behind a light is when I have 24-hour daylight, such as in the Arctic in June.

Light-emitting diodes (LEDs) are now standard in portable lighting, even in low-end lights. Compared to traditional bulbs, LEDs are smaller, more shock-resistant, and more energy efficient. Furthermore, they have an effectively limitless lifespan— they really don't "burn out."

When deciding which light to buy or bring, I primarily consider the expected scope of use. Will I need it only for chores around camp, or will I be hiking in the dark for several hours each night?

Low use. Nearly any light with more than about 25 lumens will suffice for camp chores and limited night-hiking. (Lumens are a measure of the total light emitted, in all directions. It is often listed as a product spec and on display packaging.) I prefer a headlamp, so that my hands are free (e.g., to pitch a shelter, cook dinner, start a fire) and models powered by AA or AAA batteries, which are longer lasting than coin cells and more field-friendly than rechargeable battery packs.

My favorite model is the Fenix LD02 ($35, 1 oz), a three-inch flashlight that I attach to my hat brim using its pocket clip. The LD02 uses one AAA battery; I prefer lithiums for longer

runtime and better cold-weather performance. Its light output is regulated, so its brightness remains the same until the battery is nearly depleted. In its weight class, the LD02's firepower is unsurpassed: It can throw a 100-lumen spot beam for 30 minutes with an alkaline battery, or sip the voltage for many more hours at 25- and 8-lumen outputs.

Extended use. Traveling in the dark is not my favorite thing to do, but I have done a lot of it. In a 100-mile ultramarathon last year, for example, I raced for nine hours in the daylight, and the remaining eleven in the dark.

If I'm expecting extended use, I put more thought into my light selection, particularly with respect to:

> Brightness;
> Beam type; and
> Positioning.

On long-distance trips with limited resupply opportunities, a light's power source and efficiency are also important. Finally, if multiple models meet my specifications, I may consider other factors like price, weight, size, and usability while wearing gloves.

A powerful light is worth every gram. My goal is to light up the forest so that I maintain my daytime walking

To avoid carrying extra batteries unnecessarily, look online to see how long batteries last in your light, and then consider how much you'll be using it.

Different beam types disperse their light in different ways.

SPOTLIGHT
Concentrates light and illuminates objects far away like blazes and cairns.

FLOODLIGHT
Scatters light and illuminates more peripheral vision.

speed, navigate without errors, and minimize stumbles and falls. Also, a bright light helps to prevent end-of-day drowsiness. LED technology is rapidly improving, and lightweight lights with 200+ lumens are now common.

A beam can be reflected and focused in two ways:

> Spotlights concentrate their light on a small area. They are excellent for seeing things far off in the distance, like the next blaze or cairn, or cows on the trail.
> Floodlights scatter their light over a wider area. This is desirable when hiking at night because it is visually exhausting to hike in a narrow tunnel of light.

The optimal beam type—spot or flood—changes frequently, according to conditions and tasks. To address this, some models come equipped with spot *and* flood bulbs, but this two-in-one approach seems unnecessarily heavy, complex, and expensive. I prefer a diffuser lens that allows me to adjust a single beam to my needs.

I position my brightest light at waist level, rather than at eye level. An eye-level light does not cast shadows, making the ground look two-dimensional; it also illuminates snow, rain, and brush that is immediately in front of my face, rather than the ground. For when I need eye-level lighting, like to read my maps or adjust a jacket zipper, I have clipped to my hat brim the aforementioned Fenix LD02 as a secondary light.

For the waist-level light, my current choice is the Coast FL70 ($50, 4 oz), which throws a blinding 405 lumens and is powered by three AAA batteries. By twisting the light housing bezel, the beam can be quickly alternated between spot or flood, or something in between. To minimize bouncing, I rethread the

A wise precaution in grizzly habitat

headlamp with a belt of static nylon webbing.

Bear defense

Prior to my first trip to Alaska, I received an email from a gentleman in Denver who had begun following my adventures after attending a slide show. He pleaded with me to take a gun for defense against bears, especially grizzlies. When I told him I didn't know how to shoot a gun and that I was leaving in a few days, he offered to take me shooting if I made it back alive.

Well, I made it back alive, we went shooting, and I still don't take a firearm when traveling in bear country. Firearms are heavy, expensive, difficult to transport, and sometimes not permitted on public lands. Plus, in order to take down an oncoming bear with one shot, you need to be a sharpshooter and to have a big gun.

I'm not the former, and I don't want to carry the latter.

A better alternative is capsaicin-based bear spray from manufacturers like UDAP and Counter Assault. A potent irritant, capsaicin is the same compound that gives chili peppers their heat. Bear spray is lighter, less expensive, and more widely available than a firearm. These glorified aerosol cans have a 30-foot range and will impair a bear for a few hours, rather than permanently.

Extensive research by Thomas Smith of Brigham Young University has shown that spray is more effective than firearms in preventing injuries from bears. In a 2008 study, Smith found that bear spray is effective more than 90 percent of the time in avoiding a bear attack, whereas firearms are only 50 to 70 percent effective. And in a 2012 study, he concluded that the presence of a firearm had no statistical impact on the outcome of human/bear conflicts.

Foot care kit

Many trips have ended—or hikers have painfully soldiered on—because of foot problems, which are often difficult to manage once they start. Prevention is critically important: Test shoes and socks on low-risk trips, and immediately address developing issues rather than waiting until the next break or camp.

In the field, the two most common challenges are maceration and blisters. Maceration is the waterlogging of skin, which causes it to get soft,

part 2

pruney, itchy, and sore. Blisters are more likely to develop, and the skin can crack while drying out. To reduce maceration, I apply Bonnie's Balm to my feet at night just before I retire; I may reapply in the morning, too.

Blisters are caused by heat, friction, and pressure, or a combination thereof. To properly treat blisters, the source must be understood; even so, sometimes "success" is preventing it from getting worse. On feet I most often use Leukotape P; duct tape, Sawyer Blist-O-Bans, benzoin, and Bonnie's Balm round out my supplies. Sometimes, however, I resort to other techniques, like switching or removing socks, cutting insoles and uppers, and trimming calluses.

Repair kit

Equipment failures are inevitable, especially as the trip gets longer and harder. I've had to repair ripped clothing, pack, and shelter fabrics; blown out mesh uppers on multiple pairs of shoes; and busted trekking poles and sunglasses. I've had partners lose small but non-improvisable items. And, needless to say, I've had to replace my fair share of headlamp batteries.

To combat these setbacks, I carry Aquaseal, Krazy Glue, duct tape, Tenacious Tape patches, needle and thread, and a few specific backup items like batteries, water bottle caps, and a spoon. Sometimes I can solve the problem completely, while in other cases it is a Band-Aid solution until I exit.

Crampons & ice axes

Mountaineering is beyond the scope of this book, but crampons and ice axes deserve cursory mention since they can be helpful or even necessary on particular backpacking routes at certain times of the year. I'm specifically thinking of early season conditions in the West, or winter conditions in the Northeast.

For traction, I prefer Kahtoola Microspikes or similar. They are lighter and more packable than full crampons, and they are compatible with flexible-soled footwear. They stick securely to hard snow and ice, and softer surfaces, too.

An ice ax is useful for arresting a fall, chopping steps, balancing, and braking on glissades. (In lower-risk

Extra precautions, in gear and technique, should be taken in bear country.

situations, trekking poles can replicate some of these functions.) A basic ice ax should be adequate; firsthand practice is the more important element.

First aid

What I carry in my backpack is not a substitute for what's between my ears, and this is especially true with first aid kits and emergency communications. These items do not represent a get-out-of-jail-free card, and I'm much better served by having researched beforehand the environmental and route conditions I will likely encounter, and then using common sense in the field: identifying risks, respecting the limits of my group, and making conservative decisions.

On each trip, I hope to never have a medical or emergency situation. In the instances when I have—like when Jane had an intestinal obstruction, when Peter's Achilles tendon was visible through the hole in his heel, and when Vic partially tore his lateral collateral ligament—I've been humbled by how few things I can fully treat in the field:

> Basic cuts, burns, and scrapes;
> Overuse aches and pains; and
> Minor allergic reactions, diarrhea, and acute mountain sickness.

I suppose there are a few other things, too. But for anything more, a self-rescue or an assisted evacuation will be required.

Medical training

A first aid kit and an emergency communication device do not translate into medical know-how. For that, consider some training—at least CPR certification, but ideally Wilderness First Aid or Wilderness First Responder (especially for trip leaders and avid soloists) through organizations like the National Outdoor Leadership School's Wilderness Medical Institute, the Wound Management Association of Ireland, and SOLO.

DIY vs. commercial kits

Commercial first aid kits are convenient, but I recommend assembling your own. A DIY kit will be less expensive for what you get, especially in the long run as items must be replenished, and better tailored to the unique needs of your group, activities, and environment.

Solo vs. group kit

On a group trip, medical situations are more likely and more diverse in nature, simply due to there being more people, each with a unique medical history. Appropriately, then, my group first aid kit is more robust than what I carry when solo—I bring more items and greater quantities. My solo kit is a slimmed-down version of my group kit; it has fewer items, and all are specific to my needs.

Amounts

The amount of each item I carry is a function of the trip duration, group size, and my sense of its importance. My philosophy is this: If I really need an item, I want to have enough to address fully the medical event. For example, if I come down with iliotibial tendonitis ("runner's knee"), I want enough anti-inflammatory meds so that I can take full dosage until I exit or arrive at the next town with a drugstore.

Items

Refer to Part 3 of this book for a complete inventory of my first aid kit. When assembling my kit, I had four guidelines. Items must be:

> Non-improvisable in the field, such as antidiarrheal medication;
> Useful in a wide range of circumstances, such as Leukotape P;
> Relevant to the trip's environment, duration, and activities, such as Diamox on a Himalayan expedition; and
> Within my medical know-how,

which, for example, is not the case with sutures.

Communications

It's romantic to clip the tether of modern communications, but I've never found it very practical, convenient, or safe. Groups split up, plans change, and emergencies happen. For the weight of a few Snickers bars, communications devices can save time, effort, and even a life. Just as important, they can also help to calm the worries of those back home.

Before discussing the options, I want to make two prefacing comments. First, leave your itinerary with at least one person. Personally, I always leave it with my wife and with a hiking partner who knows the area. Second, contact with the outside world is not a panacea. Search and

From anywhere in the world, I can make a call or send a text message using a satellite phone.

tools & techniques

Satellite communication devices (left to right): PLB, SPOT Gen3, inReach SE and Explorer, and SPOT Global Phone

rescue efforts are not fast, and they are not guaranteed.

Short distances

It can be as important to communicate with someone nearby as with the outside world.

A whistle is no louder than a scream—both are about 100 to 120 decibels—but it's possible to blow one for an extended period of time without getting hoarse. Plus, whistles are a universal sign of distress, and they weigh next to nothing.

Two-way radios make it safer and more convenient for groups to split up. Despite rosy estimates under "ideal conditions," expect a realistic range of 0.5 to 2 miles, depending on the terrain and amount of interference, plus the quality of the radio. Before you split up, always establish a contingency plan, a basic part of which is normally marking the map with an "X" and a meet-up time.

Cell phones

Cell service in the backcountry is location-dependent. For details, check your provider's service map and inquire in online forums or with rangers. If service is intermittent, I would not consider a cell phone to be a reliable emergency communication device, as there is at least some risk that the emergency will occur in a dark zone.

Satellite communication

Beyond the reliable range of cell phones, there are three types of satellite communicators that can make or maintain contact with family, friends, and—God forbid—emergency response teams:

> Personal locator beacons (PLBs);
> Satellite phones; and
> Satellite messengers.

The primary reason that I carry satellite-based communication is to call for help if I ever need it. Because I can share additional details about my emergency with these devices (e.g., location, type of injury, patient information), this also improves the efficiency of search and rescue efforts.

These devices have other benefits, too. Namely, they reduce the worries of those back home—like my wife and mother—by regularly checking in, or by simply not signaling for help. Some devices allow for more engagement, via online location updates and two-way texting or voice calls. Given the general reliability, widespread availability, and relative low cost of these devices, I feel that having one is the responsible thing to do.

It should be pointed out that satellite communicators are subject to failure. They can be dropped, lost, and submerged; the batteries can die; and, in areas with limited views of the sky, reception can be spotty or nonexistent.

Personal locator beacons (PLBs) like the ACR Electronics ResQLink 406 ($290, 5 oz) are capable only of sending an emergency signal. A PLB cannot send an "Okay" message, and it cannot receive messages; it also does not confirm receipt of the emergency signal. Due to this limited functionality, PLBs are probably the least popular type of satellite communicator among backcountry users.

Coverage is worldwide, via the COSPAS-SARSAT satellite network. Emergency signals are received by the COSPAS-SARSAT mission control center, which then dispatches local search and rescue teams.

Long term, PLBs are the least expensive option. The upfront cost is hefty, but there is no monthly or annual service fee. I'm unsure if some fraction of the unit cost helps fund the COSPAS-SARSAT system, or if the network is entirely subsidized by world governments.

Satellite phones like the SPOT Global Phone ($500, 7 oz) and Iridium models are the ultimate wilderness communication device. In a phone call, there is an unmatched opportunity to exchange information, versus a single SOS signal or a series of 160-character text messages. There is often additional meaning in the tone and nuance of the conversation, too.

Personally, I have used a satellite phone to request medical assistance from the National Park Service, to receive weather and river updates in Alaska, and to comfort my wife during the 2013 Boulder floods when I was still two days from the closest trailhead.

Once you use a satellite phone, you'll never want to go back to a PLB or satellite messenger. It'd be like downgrading from a telephone to a telegram, or a smartphone to a flip phone. You don't know how you ever survived before without it.

But satellite phones are not a perfect solution, either:

> They are expensive to buy and to use.
> Calls are frequently dropped, since the satellites are orbiting

The SPOT Gen3 is simple and light, but only one-way.

and since a strong connection is needed to support a phone call.
> Few models transmit GPS coordinates or offer a tracking service.

I will also add that a satellite phone is more disruptive to my wilderness experience than other devices. A phone call is relatively intimate and personal, whereas text messages allow me to remain emotionally immersed in my immediate surroundings.

The ability to send and/or receive text messages with a satellite phone can help to offset the device's inherent flaws. Text messages can be exchanged even over a weak signal, for example. And confirmation via text of a location, time, decision, or other information is more definitive and not susceptible to misinterpretation or call quality issues. Unfortunately, the texting feature is limited or clunky on many satellite phones.

Satellite messengers will be the happy-medium option for most backcountry users. They offer more functionality than a PLB, but they are less expensive than a satellite phone to buy and use.

As the name implies, messengers send text messages, which can be preset or customized, and which can be emergency-related ("SOS") or decidedly not ("Wish I'd packed more M&M's. Love you, good night."). Emergency messages are dispatched to local search and rescue teams, while other messages are received by family and friends via email or text (with GPS coordinates included). As a premium service, messengers also offer tracking, in which a geo-tagged signal is sent at predetermined intervals, like every 10 minutes.

Currently there are just two competing messenger units:

> SPOT Gen3
> DeLorme inReach, of which there is a basic and premium version, the SE and Explorer.

The units differ significantly in their capabilities, size, and cost. I would describe each as being best for a particular user, not necessarily best overall.

At 4 ounces and about the size of a bifold wallet, the Gen3 is the smallest and lightest messenger. It's also the simplest, limited to just four messages: "OK," "Help," "SOS," and a customizable message that must be preprogrammed via the user's online profile on SPOT's website. Finally, it's the least expensive to own and operate, with the unit retailing for $150 and service plans starting at $12.50 per month.

The Gen3's biggest shortcoming is that it cannot receive messages. Specifically, no message will confirm the receipt by the satellite network of an outgoing message, and family and friends cannot send messages into the backcountry.

The Gen3's outgoing messages also cannot be nuanced. "Okay" and SOS" are self-explanatory, but "Help" is not. I recommend a pre-trip conversation with emergency contacts to establish protocols. On my website I have shared my own.

The DeLorme inReach SE and Explorer are heavier and less compact than the SPOT Gen3. They both weigh 7 ounces and look like a handheld GPS unit, complete with the protruding antenna. They are also more expensive to own and operate. The SE retails for $300; the Explorer, $380. The units require a monthly or annual service plan, with the most basic starting at $12 per month.

The key advantage of the inReach units is two-way communication. The devices confirm the receipt of outgoing messages and allow for text message conversations with family and friends, similar to text conversations via cell phone.

Outgoing messages can be preset or spontaneously customized with the unit's virtual keypad or via a Bluetooth-paired smartphone with DeLorme's Earthmate app. The former process is slow and tedious. The latter option is recommended for anything beyond very occasional custom texting, though I dislike the added susceptibility to pairing problems and battery power.

Personal items

Items I need regularly during the day are kept in a hipbelt pocket. Everything else is stored in a small stuff sack, which I put inside my pack near the top.

Dental

Yes, I do cut my toothbrush in half, but mostly because at half-length it is more packable. Avoid the temptation to save grams here by using a fingertip toothbrush. They are gross, especially on a backpacking trip.

Sample-size tubes of toothpaste are light and packable, but I use Dr. Bronner's Pure-Castile Peppermint Liquid Soap instead. Only a few drops are needed per brushing, and

Multiuse Dr. Bronner's soap

it can be used to wash hands, sunglasses, wounds, or a stubbornly dirty pot. Its soapiness is an acquired taste. To avoid carrying a retail-size bottle, I decant the soap into a small 0.2-ounce dropper bottle, which is enough for 10 to 14 days.

Flossing picks are reportedly less effective than string floss. But I find that I'm more likely to use them since they don't necessitate putting my dirty hands into my mouth. To its credit, string floss can be used in gear repair—it's a substitute for thread, in the event that I need to fortify my shoes or repair rips in my clothing.

Bathroom kit

I budget four squares of premium Charmin toilet paper per day and use them only to polish the rearview mirror. For the initial heavy cleaning, I use natural materials like leaves, sticks, and rocks, which are effective, in infinite supply, and more environmentally conscious. If snowball snow is available, I use it from start to finish—it's toilet paper and a bidet in one. In the words of Mike Clelland, "It's like being kissed by the wings of an angel."

Especially in a group setting, hand-washing after a bio break is a must. For convenience, I use hand sanitizer. I don't enjoy its smell or its skin-drying effect, but it's an acceptable trade-off to avoid the fuss of soap and water.

If your bladder is overactive, if your shelter is fully enclosed, or if nighttime temperatures are frigid, add a pee bottle to your kit. Do not simply mark your pee bottle—it should be of an entirely different style than your water bottles. For enhanced aim and privacy, women may want a urination aid such as the GoGirl or Shewee.

Feminine hygiene

I cannot speak credibly about female hygiene. Instead, I will leave that to Trinity Ludwig, who contributed a lengthy article to my website on female hygiene best practices, including about menstruation, pee rags, and vaginal cleaning. It is a must-read not only for women but also for men who would like their female hiking partners to be more comfortable in the backcountry.

Keeping your camera safe

Most cameras can tolerate some water, but not submersion or a thorough soaking unless it is a waterproof camera. When backpacking in light rain, I protect my camera with a 6-inch LOKSAK dry bag, which is a heavy-duty plastic bag with a more secure seal. If it starts to rain harder, I'll move it from my hipbelt pocket to a rain-jacket pocket. In torrential rains, or if it's unlikely that I'll be taking photos for a while, I will put my camera inside the waterproof liner inside my backpack.

A small camera is not an "essential," but I always take one to record my experiences.

Skin care

To combat extreme sun exposure, I wear full-coverage clothing and headwear, and protect any exposed skin with Sawyer Stay-Put SPF 30 Sunscreen, which comes in convenient 1- and 2-ounce tubes. Since I don't care to put sunscreen on my lips, I carry a dedicated SPF lip balm.

In cold and windy conditions, I use Dermatone instead of Stay-Put. Since it's a balm, it offers additional protection against wind and frostbite; I can also use it on my lips.

By regularly washing my nether regions, I find that I can mostly avoid chaffing, known in this specific area as "monkey butt" or "swamp butt." More specifically, I try to wash once per day in arid environments, and shortly after each bio break in humid ones. As a backup, I carry a small jar of Bonnie's Balm to protect and heal chapped skin.

Photography

My smartphone goes on most of my trips since I don't like leaving it in the car. If I were to take only occasional photos, it could serve as my camera, since its image quality is equal to most point-and-shoots. But for more extensive use, a dedicated camera is a wiser choice. It will have less screen glare, longer lasting batteries, more user-friendly physical dials, better ergonomics, and (probably) an optical zoom.

My longtime favorite camera has been the Canon PowerShot S-series, most recently the S120 ($350, 8 oz). This collection stood out for its fast wide-angle lens, RAW capture, and manual controls while being acceptably light and conveniently pocketable. But in 2012 Sony shook up the compact camera market when it released the Cyber-shot DSC-RX100 ($450 and up, 9 oz), which was about the same size as the S-series but

tools & techniques

featured a DSLR-worthy sensor that was 2.8 times bigger. A larger sensor improves image resolution, dynamic range, and depth of field, among other things. Canon has since responded, with the PowerShot G7 X ($600, 11 oz).

I offer these Canon and Sony models as a conversation starter. If you want a lighter or less expensive camera, know that you will have to give up image quality. Whereas if you want a richer kit, you will have to accept the extra weight and bulk.

Batteries & memory cards. Over time I have learned the rate at which I burn through batteries and fill memory cards. (To learn your pace, start keeping track.) On a long trip, I have four options to avoid any disruptions to my filming:

> Carry more batteries and memory cards. On a trip lasting a week or two, this is my pick—it's a simple, light, and reliable solution.
> Charge batteries mid-trip using portable power packs or solar

chargers, and download memory cards to data storage units. This is a more sustainable solution, but heavier, slower, and more expensive.

> Depend on my support team. I mail home depleted batteries and full memory cards, which they recharge or download, and send back to me.
> Take care of it in town. I can carry my battery charger and data storage unit, or I can mail these items ahead to myself in a "bounce box."

Tripods. For self-portraits and long-exposure landscapes, tripods are useful, if not essential. Small, inexpensive, lightweight models are available from Pedco and Joby. If photos are important to you, a lightweight tripod is worth the $15 to $30 and two to four ounces—boulders and logs are stable substitutes, but unreliable.

Journaling

Fourteen years after my first thru-hike, I vividly recall few of the shelters I slept in, the thru-hikers and townspeople I met, and the look and feel of a particular section of trail. Photos and video are helpful in jogging my memory, but the 20-ounce spiral-bound journal that I carried from start to finish that summer feels like more of a treasure. For the Sea-to-Sea Route, my system was lighter: high-quality résumé paper cut in half, which I sent to myself in mail drops.

By 2006 I ditched the paper journal and pen entirely, favoring instead the pursuit of going faster, farther, and lighter. At the end of 15-hour, 40-mile days, I was too exhausted to spend

The Canon PowerShot G7 X: the perfect balance of packability and image quality

part 2

Journaling takes time and mental energy, but it's nice having a written record.

another 30 minutes writing. So I used a digital voice recorder (DVR), a product that has since been killed off by smartphones. The DVR worked wonderfully: I was able to record much more material than I would have ever been able to write down. However, the digital files lack the aesthetics of handwritten entries.

I've since returned to writing down my thoughts, in the margins and unimportant spaces of my top-ographical maps. The geographic context adds color to my notations and ramblings. For when I'm particu-larly inspired and prolific, I carry a few blank sheets of paper. As a capstone, I often publish a trip report on my website with notable events, summarizing thoughts, favorite photos, and helpful "notes for next time."

I prefer to write with a basic black or blue medium ballpoint pen. Gel inks are smudge-prone, and pencil lead fades. In frigid temperatures, when ink freezes, I still stick with pens: I keep one in my jacket while I write with the other, then swap them when the ink begins to freeze.

Wallet

If George Costanza's exploding wallet resonates with you, find a better solution for the backcountry. Personally, I use a card holder–type wallet, which is satisfacto-rily light and low profile; a wallet band or money clip would be even lighter, though not as inexpensive as a sandwich bag. If I'm counting grams, I empty my wallet except for my ID, cash, and credit and bank cards.

backpacks

I said goodbye to my generous hosts at the highway maintenance camp and began hiking into Canada's Richardson Mountains via rain-swollen James Creek. Ahead of me was the most challenging section of my entire Alaska-Yukon Expedition: a 657-mile, 24-day stretch without a single road crossing across Yukon's Arctic and the Arctic National Wildlife Refuge.

This section promised to be memorable, but I did not yet know that I wouldn't see another human being the entire time, that I would encounter Porcupine caribou in the midst of their fall migration, that the mosquitoes would live up to the hype, or that I'd be charged by three grizzly bears, with one getting so close before I saw it that I threw my trekking pole at it before reaching for my bear spray. (Famously, the bear left behind a 20-foot-long streak of berry poop as it sprinted away.)

What I did know as I slogged up James Creek, however, was that this was the essence of backpacking. It was liberating—and humbling—to know that my safety, comfort, and success were fully dependent on what I was carrying between my ears and inside my backpack.

Selection process

Despite the importance of the category, I've intentionally not discussed backpacks until now. It was necessary to first address other gear and supplies, the weight and size of which are the two primary drivers in pack selection. Once you have settled on a few models with the necessary load-carrying and volume capacities, you may consider other qualities like pockets, closure systems, and weight.

In a retail store, backpacks are broadly sorted by the trip length for which they are intended, like "overnight," "multiday," and "extended." These classifications are convenient, but are based on assumptions about your backpacking style, environmental and route conditions, and mode(s) of travel. If you are not average, they may lead you astray.

I generally feel that the guidelines overstate what is necessary, especially for backpackers who are deliberate about what they carry. But there is only one surefire way to find out: Bring your complete setup (with food) to a retailer and try out some packs. Or, order a few packs from online-only vendors and keep the one that works best.

Load-carrying

Backpacks come in two basic flavors: frameless and framed.

To increase my hiking efficiency, I organize my pack to minimize how often I take it off.

Frameless packs

With little effort a frameless backpack can be wadded, folded, and twisted. The design is common among schoolbags and day packs, but less so with overnight backpacking packs. Without a rigid structure, most or all of the weight hangs on the shoulders. Even with a modest load, this can become uncomfortable over time.

Framed packs

In contrast, framed packs have a rigid chassis that helps transfer weight from the shoulders to the hips. Weight is best carried by the hips because they are:

> Supported by larger muscles like the glutes, quads, and core;
> Located closer to an adult's center of gravity; and
> Offer more surface area across which to distribute pressure.

When all of the pack weight is carried on the hips, shoulder straps help only in preventing the backpack from falling backward and bobbing side to side.

External frame packs like the Kelty Yukon 48 ($170, 5 lb 1 oz) were the earliest framed pack design. Shoulder straps, a waist belt, and a pack bag are fastened to an exposed frame, usually made of aluminum. They excel in carrying heavy and bulky loads, and allow for excellent airflow through the back area.

Internal frame packs have almost entirely replaced external frame packs. They are more stable, conform better to the body, and are not as bulky. The construction is more complex, and thus prices are higher. Weights are comparable, all things

tools & techniques

being equal. The frame is embedded in the pack like a skeleton.

The rigidity of internal frame packs is typically created using:

> Stays, which are narrow aluminum or carbon fiber rods or battens that run parallel to the spine;
> Framesheets, which are semi-rigid precurved panes, usually made of hard plastic and embedded in the back panel; and
> Peripheral rods, which border the pack's back perimeter and are made of tubular aluminum.

A pack's load-carrying capacity can be enhanced by using more than one support structure. Stays can be attached to or embedded in framesheets, and peripheral rods can be added to packs with framesheets or stays.

Stays and framesheets are sometimes removable, which is convenient for times when the load does not justify the weight of these suspension features. Peripheral rods cannot be removed.

For maximum load transfer, the frame should be ultrastiff and anchored securely into the hipbelt. It should extend at least a few inches above the shoulder straps, and ideally to the top of the pack. If the frame stops at or below the shoulder straps,

load-lifter straps will not be as useful, and the top of the load will not be well supported.

Frameless vs. framed

The primary distinction between frameless and framed packs is the comfort with which weight can be carried. Frameless packs can be exceedingly comfortable so long as the total pack weight remains below 20 to 30 pounds, depending on the pack, the contents, and the user. Beyond that, a framed pack is in order. Personally, as a 30-something with a runner's build, I'm in the middle of this range when wearing a full-featured frameless pack (e.g., with padded shoulder straps and a hipbelt), or at the lower end if I must carry a bear canister.

For lightweight loads, frameless packs are a great choice. Unlike framed packs, they do not lock your back into a fixed position (straight and upright), limit the range of motion of your torso or hips, or affect your center of gravity as severely as by pushing the load away from your back. In terms of agility and wearing comfort, frameless packs are hard to beat.

Furthermore, they are lighter and less expensive because the designs are simpler and use fewer materials. Prices range from $125 to

Buy your backpack last, after you've assembled all of your other gear and supplies, the weight and volume of which will help inform your needs.

part 2

$200, and weights range from 0.5 to 2.0 pounds, compared with $150 to $500 and 2.5 to 8 pounds for framed models.

Beyond the frame

In addition to its frame (or lack thereof), a backpack's load-carrying capacity is affected by several other features.

Compression straps squeeze the load closer to the frame, which prevents load shifting and bouncing, and pulls the load closer to the user's natural center of gravity. Most packs feature two horizontal straps (or four, with two on each side), but it is not uncommon for them to be positioned diagonally.

Compression straps are also useful in securing skis, snowshoes, and trekking poles. For maximum utility, at least one side of the strap should have a side-release buckle.

In the specific case of a frameless pack, compression straps can be used to create a "virtual frame," whereby the load becomes so stiff under compression that some weight can be transferred to the hips from the shoulders. Transfer will not rival a good framed pack, but the effect is noticeable.

When trying to create a virtual frame, stiff foam helps. Most frameless packs already have a foam pack panel, to blunt hard objects inside the pack. Alternatively, line the inside of the pack with a torso-length closed-cell foam sleeping pad, which gives the pack a nice cylindrical shape.

Hipbelts and shoulder straps distribute most of the pressure on the body. To judge from my own experience, they are difficult to design well. Narrow belts uncomfortably concentrate pressure, but wide belts are hot and constrict movement. Firm padding effectively transfers pressure and absorbs less moisture, but softer foam conforms

how 2

determine if a frameless pack is appropriate

1 What is the weight of all your gear and nonconsumable supplies like maps?

2 At most, how much weight in water, food, and fuel will you have to carry at the same time?

3 If the weight of your gear and consumables will normally be less than 25 or 30 pounds, a frameless pack could be a good choice.

Also consider the frequency and duration that this maximum weight will be carried. If it's seldom and short-lived, it may be more tolerable.

tools & techniques

Frameless packs conform best to the body but are uncomfortable when overloaded.

better to the body. Finally, the pack's shape must accommodate a wide range of body types.

Load-lifter straps create a triangle between each shoulder strap and the top of the pack. They help to pull the load forward and to shift shoulder strap pressure.

A sternum strap extends across the chest between the shoulder straps. It improves stability, further distributes pressure, and prevents the shoulder straps from drifting outward.

Volume

To calculate volume, a backpack is stuffed with Whopper candy–size balls. The main pack body is filled first, then the extension collar, top lid, and external pockets. After the pack is full, the balls are removed and their volume is measured.

Pack volume can be listed in cubic inches or liters. Current nomenclature often includes the liter volume, e.g., REI Flash 65 Pack. If the pack is offered in multiple sizes (e.g., S, M, L), the true volume will be immaterially different for each size.

The design of most packs assumes that a big load is heavy and a small load is light. Thus, larger-volume packs tend to offer greater load-carrying capacity; smaller-volume packs, less. But there are instances when this correlation does not hold. For example, my wintertime load is light but big, because I have a 2-liter pot and a wonderfully warm sleeping bag, parka, and insulated pants, whereas my load in the desert is usually heavy but small, because significant amounts of water must be carried.

Breakdown

The volume of the main compartment is most important, because you will want to put most of your gear inside it. Personally, I don't give much consideration to other sources of volume. Extension collars don't carry weight well if the pack frame ends below it or if the pack is frameless. And I prefer to use top lids and pockets for oft-needed items like water bottles and rain gear; I rarely stuff full these spaces.

Distribution

A backpack's shape greatly affects how it carries. A tall, narrow, and shallow pack body that sits above the waist will allow for unhindered arm swing and will have the least effect on the user's center of gravity. If a pack resembles a pear or a turtle shell, I'd be more skeptical.

Adjustment systems

To extend the usable range of a backpack, various volume compression systems can be used, including nylon webbing, bungee cords, hook-and-loop devices, and gussets. An old 70-liter frameless backpack I used for winter camping, for example, could be compressed to an amazing 25 liters, about the volume of an overnight pack.

However, rarely do these compression systems reduce the pack's volume proportionally. Therefore, the main compartment is very restricted in some places and very bulbous in others. Statistically, compressibility is a great marketing story, but the actual usability is more limited.

Fitting

Pack-fitting is like shoe-fitting. Backpacks are sized according to torso length (which is imperfectly correlated with height.) But a backpack of the correct torso length is not guaranteed to be a good fit—it still must fit your body shape.

Torso length

The torso length of most fully-featured framed packs is adjustable, which allows the user to precisely match their own torso. However, this feature adds weight and cost.

Most lightweight framed packs, and all frameless packs, have *fixed* torso lengths. Depending on the manufacturer, most models come in two or three sizes, and each size accommodates spine lengths within a two- to three-inch range. For example, a size small may fit torso lengths between 16 and 19 inches.

When on the cusp between two sizes, I usually downsize. The pack will ride higher on my hips than the larger size, but I'm okay with that: When carrying a lightweight load, the hipbelt seems to float upward to my waist anyway because it's my torso's narrowest point.

Back panel shape

Due to its rigidity, a framed pack will not fit every body type. It's generally best if

Your spine length is measured from the C7 vertebra (the knob at the base of your neck) to the iliac crest (the top of your pelvic bone below the side of your rib cage).

Continued on p. 208

tools & techniques

tried&true

how to pack a backpack

part (2)

On solo trips I aim to be walking down the trail within 15 minutes of waking up. I can't just stuff everything into my backpack randomly, however. It must be packed so as to minimize the load's effect on my center of gravity and maximize organizational efficiency.

Maintain your center of gravity

The location of one's center of gravity depends on gender and body type. For a normal adult male, it's around the sternum; for a normal adult female, it's above the belly button. A backpack of any weight will affect my center of gravity (and a heavy pack much more so), and I will need to compensate for that with an unnatural walking form, hence the forward lean. My goal is simply to minimize the effect, specifically by:

> Placing the heaviest items (e.g., food, water, and stove fuel) against my back, so I don't have to lean forward as far.
> Cinching the pack's compression straps, which help to pull the weight closer to my back. (Removing compression straps is a classic "stupid light" move.)
> Keeping all or most of the weight below or level with my sternum to prevent swaying, which would make me less nimble and could possibly be dangerous on technical terrain.
> Centering the weight along my spine so that the pack does not tilt to the left or right. This can be achieved by packing the heaviest items against the spine or by counterbalancing the weight.

Keep your pack organized

An unorganized backpack is frustrating and inefficient: I can't find what I need, and I waste time looking for it. To organize my pack, I keep:

> Oft-needed items within easy reach. In my hipbelt pockets I keep my water purification, insect repellent, head net, camera, lip balm, and sunscreen. In my side pockets I keep my water bottle(s), maps, and perhaps a beanie, bear spray, and/ or gloves. I attach my insulated overmitts to my shoulder strap with a small carabiner, which is more secure than my side pockets. And I keep my sunglasses atop my visor when I'm not wearing them.
> Occasionally needed items inside my pack, at the very top. These include my accessory pouch (which contains my LED light, fire starter, toiletries, chewing gum, etc.), a quart freezer bag with my day's rations, layers of clothing (e.g., wind shirt, rain gear, and puffy jacket), and additional bottles of water if I'm in a dry stretch.
> Items I won't need until camp or during future days—like my sleeping bag and my food for the rest of the trip—are placed in the bottom.

The exact way in which I pack up changes each day, mostly due to a decreasing food load, but my general approach remains unchanged.

tools & techniques

Backpacks specially designed for a woman's body are now widely available.

the back panel approximately matches the curvature of the user's back. If it does not, the load may not carry well, or the user may notice uncomfortable pressure points. If you don't know how a properly fitting backpack should feel, work with a knowledgeable sales associate at your local retailer.

A frameless pack is more forgiving and will accommodate a wider range of anatomies because it conforms to the user's back, not the other way around.

Hipbelts

A properly sized hipbelt is crucial to carrying comfort. If it cannot be cinched tightly, the load will sway and the hips will be unable to carry the weight. If it's too small, the padding and hipbelt pockets will not be properly positioned.

Framed packs normally have interchangeable hipbelts. Because of extensive padding, each size can accommodate only a narrow range of waist sizes, like 30 to 34 inches. By permanently attaching the hipbelt, manufacturers give up

a custom fit in exchange for weight and cost savings.

Women's packs

Men's or unisex packs do not fit most women well. Women-specific packs share the same features, but are sized differently: narrower shoulder widths, shorter spine lengths, shorter and more differently shaped shoulder straps, and more sharply angled hipbelts.

Fabrics

Most backpacks are made primarily of woven nylon. One side is often coated with polyurethane or silicone, which enhances abrasion resistance and tear strength, and which makes the fabric waterproof, at least until UV and abrasion degrade the coating. Even when new, few packs are waterproof due to unsealed seams and zippers.

For relatively gentle use, a pack made of 100 denier nylon should be adequate. I would discourage the use of lighter nylons—they require too much babying.

Personally, however, I would prefer a slightly heavier pack made of 210 denier fabric, with the abrasion-prone bottom possibly made of something even thicker. When I need to lower my pack down steep slickrock, bushwhack through guard spruce, carry out elk quarters, or carry metal-edged skis, I want my pack to be worry-free. Premium pack fabrics may be branded as Cordura, Dyneema, Robic, or X-Pac.

Stretch mesh

Elasticized nylon stretch mesh is often used for side pockets and hipbelt pockets. I understand why: to keep these pockets low profile when not in use and to keep tension on the contents. But this fabric can rip and abrade if snagged by vegetation or brushed against sharp rocks. Avoid light-duty varieties.

Cuben Fiber

I'm not yet sold on Cuben, which you may recall from the chapter on shelters, as a backpack fabric. It offers mediocre resistance to abrasion and puncture, which are the primary forms of pack abuse. While the lightest Cuben fabrics will perform better than any fabric of comparable weight, they are still delicate. The 1.2 oz/sq yd fabric might suffice for mild use, but I wouldn't trust it for much more.

Cuben is better used in a laminate. The Cuben provides waterproofness and tear strength, and the 50D or 150D polyester face fabric improves abrasion and puncture resistance. These laminates weigh 2.9 oz/sq yd to 5.0 oz/sq yd.

At that fabric weight, however, I see little value added over standard woven nylons. For most of my Alaska-Yukon Expedition, and on dozens of trips afterward, I used a backpack made of 210D nylon that weighed 4.0 oz/sq yd; I waterproofed it with a trash compactor bag. Even if a Cuben laminate is "better," it seems functionally irrelevant even for extreme applications. Moreover, because Cuben is so expensive, expect to pay $50 to $100 more than for a pack made of premium woven nylon.

Back panels

Are you willing to increase the weight and expense of your backpack, and reduce its load-carrying efficiency, to have more ventilation for your back? In back panel design, this is an unavoidable trade-off.

Basic

The frameless backpack with which I hiked most of the Sea-to-Sea Route had a back panel made entirely of pack fabric. In hot and humid conditions, my back got sweaty, but that seemed like an acceptable trade-off for having the load immediately next to my back, where it carries best. This was also the lightest and least expensive design.

Mesh-covered foam

More recently, most of my packs have featured a thin back panel made of rigid foam covered in open-pored mesh. This design does not notably impact the user's center of gravity, but it only gives the appearance of improved moisture management—it provides no airflow, and perspiration is simply absorbed into the mesh, which can eventually get saturated. Annoyingly, the open-pored mesh tends to collect forest debris like pine needles and seeds.

Pods

For about the same increase in weight and expense, three thick foam pods can be situated at the lower back and both scapulas. Ventilation is dramatically better than the aforementioned options, but the load sits at least an inch or two off the back, which starts to affect the user's center of gravity. In addition, because there is less contact, the pack may not feel as secure.

Trampoline

This final design is described as "suspended mesh," but I think the trampoline is a better analogy. The user's back rests against an airy fabric that extends across a peripheral rod frame. Between the fabric and the pack bag, there is a channel of air.

Suspended mesh is probably the most popular back panel style. But it is also the heaviest and most expensive, and it most dramatically affects the user's center of gravity because the load sits several inches away from the back. In addition, some pack bags have a dramatic arc, which make for difficult packing, especially if a bear canister is being carried.

The frameless Exodus backpack from Mountain Laurel Designs

Loading style

Most backpacks are accessed from an opening in the top ("top-loading") while a few offer entry along the main pack body ("panel-loading"). Fully-featured large-volume models often offer both, as well as a separate sleeping bag compartment at the base.

I prefer to load my pack from the top. It's partly what I'm accustomed to, but I also feel that it's easier to balance and organize a pack from that single point; plus, it's the lightest option and avoids extensive use of blowout-prone zippers. Panel-loaders and sleeping bag compartments are convenient, but are generally unnecessary when carrying a light and well-organized pack.

part (2)

Closure systems

Even by efficiently organizing my pack, I can't avoid having to access the main compartment throughout the day. With this regular in and out, the convenience (or lack thereof) of the pack's closure system becomes noticeable.

Top lid

Most packs are capped with a top lid, which is a separate flap that often hosts a pocket, convenient for small odds and ends. It can be sewn on or removable. Aesthetically, top lids tend to fit sloppily, especially when the pack is less than full. More important, opening or closing the pack's main compartment is unnecessarily time-consuming due to an annoying sequence of straps, buckles, and drawstrings.

Roll top

In the cottage pack market, the standard closure system is a roll top, whereby the extension collar is rolled downward and secured with one, two, or sometimes three buckles. It's a clean look; it can improve load compression, and, if the pack fabric is waterproof, the closure is watertight. However, roll tops are also annoyingly time-consuming.

Zippered top

For ease of access, a zippered opening is unrivaled. But this design must be executed well, with an easy-gliding big-toothed zipper (#8 or #10) and a rain flap so that water cannot freely pour inside. The durability and action of watertight zippers is generally worse.

After washing my socks, I loop them through my pack's compression straps to dry.

Pockets

Packs without external pockets are lighter, less expensive, and more streamlined, but they're extremely inconvenient for backpacking. Imagine needing to take off your pack and open up the main compartment each time you want to take a photo, check the map, reapply sunscreen, put on your head net, or reach for your bear spray, among other things. I suppose the pockets on your shirt and pants could substitute, but I doubt that pants would support well a two-pound canteen; plus, the pockets would be inaccessible when wearing other layers.

Hipbelt and side pockets are the most convenient. Their design matters, however. Dimensional pockets with generous volume are easier to operate and more functional than pockets that are made of flat-lying stretch-mesh, that have minimal volume, or that are overlaid by a compression strap. As mentioned earlier, the pockets should be constructed entirely of woven nylon because stretch mesh is easily shredded. Finally, the side pockets should be accessible by a user with moderate dexterity without taking the pack off. If that's not you, consider a shoulder strap pocket. If you need to have access to more than just a small water bottle, confirm that the pack has an internal hydration sleeve for a reservoir and hose system.

As someone who backpacks primarily in dry climates, I'm less attached to a large rear pocket, also known as a shovel pocket. They are convenient for wet rain gear and shelters, but otherwise I prefer that my gear be stored inside the main compartment, where it carries best and where I can protect it inside a pack liner.

Attachment points

It is sometimes necessary to lash items to the exterior of the pack, like trekking poles, snowshoes, and skis, or a foam sleeping pad, ice ax, packraft and paddle, and climbing rope. For when this need arises, the backpack should have built-in compression straps, daisy chains, and loops that can be utilized, perhaps in conjunction with some additional hardware.

skurka'spicks
BACKPACKS

I have a vested interest in one of my top selections, the Sierra Designs Flex Capacitor, because I spent a year and a half co-developing it. Set for release in 2017, it's an attractive package for three-season trips between three and ten days, or shorter winter trips: The main compartment compresses proportionally

Downsize to a frameless pack. The discomfort of loading gear into a frameless pack will force you to become disciplined about your load's weight and volume.

part (2)

from 60 to 40 liters with a unique gusset and swallows a bear canister; it's made entirely of tough woven nylon; its side, hipbelt, and top lid pockets are extraordinarily functional; and its suspension system was tested by carrying 70 pounds of free-range meat out of the Colorado Rockies. It's expected to cost less than $200 and weigh about 2.5 pounds.

If user reviews suggest I have no future as a pack designer, I can vouch for the **ULA Circuit** ($235, 2 lb 9 oz) and the larger Catalyst and Epic (for packrafting). From clients I have heard positive feedback about framed packs from Gossamer Gear, Six Moon Designs, and ZPacks. I know that REI sells Osprey, Deuter, and Gregory packs by the pallet, but their models don't seem to offer any

additional performance or value, and they weigh pounds more.

My experience with frameless packs has been limited since the first edition of this book, since I now often leave the trailhead with a guide-worthy load, a bear canister, and/or ten days of food. The **Mountain Laurel Designs Exodus** ($195, 16 oz) sets the standard. But for quick overnights and multiday FKT (Fastest Known Time) attempts, I'd look closely at the **Ultimate Direction Fastpack** ($180, 1 lb 9 oz), which shares the same harness system as my favorite ultrarunning pack. ▪

Waterproofing

Very few backpacks are truly waterproof. Pack *fabrics* are often waterproof, but moisture can still make its

A plastic trash compactor bag is an effective and inexpensive way to waterproof my pack's contents. I prefer this method over dry sacks or a pack cover.

way inside when the pack is open, and through zippers and seams (which cannot be fully sealed due to complex construction). To protect the pack's contents from precipitation, four methods can be used.

Pack liners

I recommend a pack liner, which is an oversize stuff sack with a wide opening at the top. Avoid coated nylon pack liners, which are expensive and which slowly lose their water-proofness. Instead, use a 50-cent 20-gallon trash compactor bag made of 2-millimeter polyethylene film. They last about one month before developing irreparable holes. In very wet conditions, consider two: one for items you will not need until camp, like your sleeping bag and inner tent body, and the other for everything else.

Pack liners have only one drawback: They lack an engineered watertight closure. But so long as the bag is oversized for its contents, enough material should be leftover that it can be twisted shut.

Dry sacks

These stuff sacks from Granite Gear, Outdoor Research, and Sea to Summit are made of waterproof fabric and feature sealed seams and a watertight roll-top closure. Available volumes range from 1 to 55 liters (which is larger than many light-weight packs); they cost $10 to $40 and weigh 0.5 to 5 ounces.

On a boating trip, when my pack may get soaked or even submerged, I keep my gear inside a heavy-duty

dry sack inside my pack. For back-packing, though, a trash compactor bag is lighter, less expensive, and easier to access and close.

Pack covers

The least effective way to protect the contents of a backpack from mois-ture—yet one of the most commonly seen—is a pack cover, which is like a waterproof turtle shell for your pack. They cost $25 to $40 and weigh 4 to 8 ounces. Pack covers have a number of fatal flaws:

> They do not protect the entire pack, so precipitation seeps inside after dripping down the user's neck and back;
> They block access to the main compartment and exterior pockets;
> They snag on vegetation;
> In a drenching storm, water can pool in the bottom of the cover, adding weight and soaking whatever is at the bottom of the backpack (probably a sleeping bag); and
> They offer minimal protection during a river ford, when the pack might be entirely submerged.

Ponchos

A variant of the pack cover is the poncho, the back of which drapes over the backpack. The poncho's fit and protection can be improved by tying the back's corners in a knot around one's waist. A poncho is not as effective as a pack liner or dry sacks, but it is more effective than a pack

Repackage supplies in smaller containers, jars, and bags to help save weight.

cover, because it at least covers the gap between the user's back and the backpack.

Organization

When my backpack is carefully and deliberately packed, I can more quickly find what I need, and I'm less likely to lose or ruin gear and supplies. I use an assortment of stuff sacks, containers, and plastic bags for organization.

Stuff sacks

My sleeping bag, cook pot, tent stakes, sunglasses, and loose accessories—including my toiletries, compass, flashlight, lighter, first aid kit, and wallet—each have a dedicated stuff sack. For my small items, I prefer a stuff sack with a large opening so that I can rummage through it easily.

My shelter, bug nest or bivy, and extra clothing are not kept in stuff sacks. Instead, I use them to fill empty areas of my pack, so long as they are dry.

Containers & bags

The weight and volume of full-size items really add up, and it's extraneous since I usually only need a little of something. So I decant Bonnie's Balm, Dr. Bronner's soap, and Aquamira into smaller balm jars and dropper bottles. I use travel-size tubes of sunscreen, toothpaste, and insect repellent. I keep first aid medications in plastic pill bags. I reroll smaller rolls of toilet paper and duct tape, and store 12-inch strips of Leukotape on mailing label paper.

sample

gear kits

218 TRIP PLANNING CHECKLIST

220 CLOTHING

224 FOOTWEAR

225 SLEEP SYSTEMS

226 SHELTERS

228 NAVIGATION & TREKKING POLES

229 STOVE SYSTEMS

231 HYDRATION & SMALL ESSENTIALS

233 PACKING

Page for page, this section of the book is the most instructive. Without reading any of the preceding text, you could replicate these lists and be on your way. But I wouldn't necessarily recommend it: They may not be perfectly relevant to your backpacking style or skill set, your environmental and route conditions, or your existing inventory of equipment. For best results, read the text and use these lists as guides, not doctrine.

A gear list is extraordinarily useful. It will help you assemble your kit without commandeering floor space. It calculates pack weight and can create a budget and shopping list. It serves as a checklist during your final pack-up. And it's a reference for future trips, especially if you add post-trip comments after returning home. On my website you can find a downloadable gear list template to get you started.

Taking bearings with a GPS unit, Wyoming

trip planning checklist

I have planned hundreds of backpacking trips. Many have been personal outings, ranging from long weekends in nearby destinations to multimonth thru-hikes in faraway places. The rest have been guided, when I've been accountable to paying clients.

While I'm getting backpacking trips out the door, this planning checklist helps me to stay on task and to prevent oversights. Normally, I incorporate it into a larger spreadsheet with other trip information.

This list represents the outer limit of things that can or must be done before a normal outing. If my trip is local, for example, I need not book airfare or a rental car; or if I'm heading to an area that I know well, it's less critical that I research the conditions and create a gear list. And if I were planning a long-distance or international hike, the list would need to be modified to include resupplies, travel visas, immunizations, and more.

Several of the tasks are quick and easy, but others like food preparation and gear lists can involve substantial time, especially for newer backpackers. Start early to avoid last-minute stress, and know that, at some point, you just have to go.

part 3

logistics

Finalize trip dates.

Finalize and virtually connect group members, like through Google Groups and Google Drive.

Close up the house: Add a vacation message to email and voice mail, back up computer files, auto-pay bills, unplug appliances, water the plants, and forward or put a hold on snail mail.

travel

Coordinate travel plans with group members.

Book airfare.

Book ground transportation.

Book pre-trip lodging.

Book post-trip lodging.

gear

- Research likely environmental and route conditions.
- Create a gear list.
- Acquire all necessary gear.
- Update contact, message, and service settings for satellite phone or messenger.
- Wash, renew, and repair gear, fabrics, and insulations that need it.
- Insert an empty memory card into the camera.

food & supplies

- Calculate food needs.
- Purchase, prepare, and package shelf-stable food.
- Purchase stove fuel.
- Top off batteries for all electronic devices by recharging or replacement; pack spare batteries, if appropriate.
- Assemble first aid, foot care, repair, and fire-starting kits.
- At the last minute, purchase perishable food.

route

- Finalize route.
- Reserve backcountry permit or campsite(s).
- Create and print (or assemble) topographic maps, datasheets, and guidebooks.
- Load digital files (e.g., GPX, topo maps) onto GPS unit or smartphone.
- Leave route and itinerary information with someone.

the final pack-up

- Food
- Gear
- Permits, maps, guidebooks, databooks
- Park pass
- Personal items: clothes, flip-flops, toiletries, and non-backpacking electronics like smartphone and e-reader (with chargers)

sample gear kits

clothing

The Core 13 is my tight collection of backpacking clothing that can be mixed and matched to create applicable systems for all variations of three-season conditions. Only on a long-distance trip through multiple environments would all 13 pieces be necessary; normally six to ten will get the job done.

Core 13 clothing

Read the clothing chapter for more in-depth discussion of the Core 13. Below is a consolidated list.

item	my pick or suggestion	msrp low	msrp high	when to wear & more info
S/S shirt	Knit poly/merino blend or pure, 120 g/sq m weight	$20	$70	Mild temps, low sun exposure, few bugs; keep cool with air-permeability, chest zip, looser fit
L/S shirt	Same as S/S; 120–150 g/sq m weight	$30	$90	Cooler temps and/or strong sunshine; can double as bug shirt by treating with permethrin
Bug shirt	Permethrin-treated knit L/S, not a stuffy woven	$10	$100	Defense against biting insects & disease-carrying ticks, factory treatments last longer than DIY spray-ons & wash-ins
Shorts	Running shorts with silky liner, 4–6-in inseam	$20	$55	When pants are not necessary; okay as occasional underwear under pants
Trekking pants	Lightweight nylon, low spandex content	$40	$90	For protection against bugs, brush, sun, & cool temps; convertibles better in theory than practice
Underwear	Poly or merino, with spandex for fit & stretch	$15	$50	When wearing pants full-time; one pair for men, two for women; wash regularly, soap unnecessary
Fleece top	100- or 200-weight pull-over, minimal features	$25	$130	As second layer in brisk conditions & as mid-layer between hiking shirt & shell when cold and wet
Shell top	Waterproof/breathable jacket with air vents	$30	$250	Delays getting wet, but ultimately fails; alternatives: poncho, umbrella, windshirt
Shell bottoms	Waterproof/breathable pants with leg zips	$50	$175	Cold precipitation; without ventilation, easy to overheat; alternatives: rain skirt, chaps, or wind pants
Insulated jacket	Premium down fill, or synthetic or 300 fleece	$50	$250	Brisk midday stops, long & cool camps, warmth at night; prefer hooded models
Insulated pants	Down-filled with 3/4 zips, or M-65 military surplus	$20	$175	Static in cool or cold temps, notably in camp during short fall & winter days
Sleeping top	Polyester, wool, or fleece	$0	$50	Rainy & humid trips
Sleeping bottoms	Shorts or thermals, low performance threshold	$0	$50	Not for daytime use; store inside pack, protected; unnecessary if daytime clothes usually stay dry
TOTAL		**$310**	**$1,535**	

Mountain West

The Sierra Nevada and the Rocky Mountains, plus several smaller ranges between these major chains, call for a similar clothing setup. The only notable difference is the intensity of the bug season—locations like the High Sierra and Yellowstone approach Alaska levels, while others like Colorado only have intense pockets.

Philmont Scout Ranch fits within this region, too. One important regulation applies: Scouts must have different clothing for sleeping than for cooking.

item	late spring	early summer	late summer & early fall
S/S or L/S shirt	L/S I Cool temps & sunshine	Maybe I L/S if light or no bugs	L/S I Cool temps & sunshine
Bug shirt	No I Before the hatch	Maybe I For bothersome bugs	No I Bugs gone by Sept.
Shorts	Yes I Unless full-time pants	Yes I Pants often too warm	Yes I Bugs gone, less sun
Trekking pants	Yes I Cool temps & strong sun	Maybe I If thick bugs or dry	Yes I Cooler parts of the day
Underwear	No I Unless full-time pants	No I Shorts have built-in liner	No I Unless full-time pants
Fleece top	Yes I Brisk mornings & summits	Yes I Mid-layer for cold rain	Yes I Back to brisk periods
Shell top	Yes I Precip always possible	Yes I Monsoon in full effect	Yes I Snow sticks in Oct.
Shell bottoms	Maybe I If chance of precip	Maybe I If chance of precip	Maybe I If chance of precip
Insulated jacket	Yes I Chilly in camp & shade	Yes I Cool camps & high peaks	Yes I Normal lows 20s-30s
Insulated pants	Maybe I Only for long camps	No I Overkill	Maybe I Only for long camps
Sleeping clothes	No I Clothing should stay dry	No I But required at Philmont	No I Clothing should stay dry

Desert Southwest

Between the soaring ranges of the American West lies vast desert. Some parts are barren and boring, but others are just the opposite, like the Grand Canyon, Big Bend, and Death Valley.

My lists below assume a "high desert" location like Canyonlands or Escalante, both nearly a mile above sea level. For a low desert location like Saguaro, they will need to be seasonally adjusted.

item	spring	summer	fall
S/S or L/S shirt	L/S I Sun protection	L/S I Sun protection	L/S I Sun protection
Bug shirt	No I Light or no bug pressure	No I Light or no bug pressure	No I Light or no bug pressure
Shorts	No I Too sunny & brushy	No I Too sunny & brushy	No I Too sunny & brushy

Trekking pants	Yes I Sun & brush protection	Yes I Sun too intense for shorts	Yes I Sun & brush protection
Underwear	Yes I Wearing pants full-time	Yes I Wearing pants full-time	Yes I Wearing pants full-time
Fleece top	No I Unless chilly forecast	No I But could sub for puffy	No I Unless chilly forecast
Shell top	Yes I Good policy even if dry	Maybe I If rain in forecast	Yes I Good policy even if dry
Shell bottoms	Maybe I If cold precip likely	No I Precip short-lived & warm	Maybe I If cold precip likely
Insulated jacket	Yes I Cools off at night	Yes I Just a light one	Yes I Long & cool nights
Insulated pants	No I Unless cold forecast	No I Nights much too warm	No I Unless cold forecast
Sleeping clothes	No I Clothing should stay dry	No I Clothing should stay dry	No I Clothing should stay dry

Pacific Northwest & Alaska

For consistently cool and wet conditions, plan a trip to Washington's Cascades, Alaska's Brooks Range, or the Canadian Rockies. Pants are usually the norm here, although shorts may be acceptable for warm and bug-free conditions when on well-maintained trails.

item	late spring	early summer	late summer & early fall
S/S or L/S shirt	L/S I Cool temps	No I Bug pressure likely	L/S I Once bugs die off
Bug shirt	No I Before the hatch	Yes I At least moderate bugs	No I Bugs gone by Sept.
Shorts	Maybe I If warm & on trail	No I Too much brush & bugs	Maybe I If warm & on trail
Trekking pants	Yes I Cool temps, sunny snow	Yes I Bug & brush protection	Yes I For cool temps & brush
Underwear	Maybe I If not taking shorts	Yes I Assuming full-time pants	Maybe I If not taking shorts
Fleece top	Yes I Mid-layer & second layer	Yes I Mid-layer for chilly precip	Yes I Mid-layer & second layer
Shell top	Yes I Precip likely	Yes I Still wet in "dry" season	Yes I Precip likely
Shell bottoms	Yes I Cold precip likely	Maybe I If forecast is wet	Yes I Cold precip likely
Insulated jacket	Yes I Cool at night & in shade	Yes I Unless unusually warm	Yes I Cool at night & in shade
Insulated pants	Maybe I For long camps	No I Temps don't warrant	Maybe I For long camps
Sleeping clothes	Yes I Clothing likely to get wet	Yes I Clothing likely to get wet	Yes I Clothing likely to get wet

Northeastern Woodlands

My clothing systems for the northern Appalachians and Great Lakes states are similar to those for the Pacific Northwest and Alaska, where it's also generally wet and forested. However, the backpacking season in the Northeastern Woodlands is a couple of months longer, with warmer and more humid summers; and unfortunately, the region is also the epicenter for Lyme disease.

part 3

item	late spring	early summer	late summer & fall
S/S or L/S shirt	L/S I If unusually warm, S/S	No I Bug pressure likely	S/S I Until temps cool off
Bug shirt	No I Unless after tick hatch	Yes I Peak bug season	No I Unless ticks are a worry
Shorts	Yes I Unless unusually cool	No I Too vulnerable to bugs	Yes I Until temps cool off
Trekking pants	Yes I For cool mornings & elevations	Yes I For bugs & ticks	Maybe I For cool temps or if worried about ticks
Underwear	No I Unless pants full-time	Yes I Assuming full-time pants	No I Unless full-time pants
Fleece top	Yes I Mid-layer & second layer	No I Precip is usually warm	Yes I Mid-layer & second layer
Shell top	Yes I Precip likely	Yes I Precip likely	Yes I Precip likely
Shell bottoms	Yes I Cold precip likely	Maybe I If cold & wet forecast	Maybe I If cold & wet forecast
Insulated jacket	Yes I Cool at night & in shade	Maybe I Just a light one	Yes I Once nights are cool
Insulated pants	Maybe I For long camps	No I Nights too warm	No I Unnecessary until Nov.
Sleeping clothes	Yes I Clothing likely to get wet	Yes I Clothing likely to get wet	Yes I Clothing likely to get wet

Southeastern Woodlands

Three-season conditions exist nearly year-round in the southeast, save for the highest elevations during the worst of the winter. Precipitation and tree cover are near universal; summers are brutally hot and humid. Lyme disease is not as prevalent as in the Northeast, but it is steadily creeping south along the Blue Ridge.

item	early spring	late spring through early fall	late fall
S/S or L/S shirt	L/S I If unusually warm, S/S	No I Bug pressure likely	S/S I Until temps cool off
Bug shirt	No I Unless after tick hatch	Yes I Peak bug season	No I Unless ticks are a worry
Shorts	Yes I Unless unusually cool	Yes I Treat with permethrin	Yes I Until temps cool off
Trekking pants	Yes I Cool mornings/elevations	Maybe I Alt for shorts if bugs & ticks are bad	Maybe I If cool or ticks a worry
Underwear	No I Unless pants full-time	Maybe I If full-time pants	No I Unless full-time pants
Fleece top	Yes I Mid-layer & second layer	No I Precip is usually warm	Yes I Mid-layer & second layer
Shell top	Yes I Precip likely	Yes I Poncho or umbrella	Yes I Precip likely
Shell bottoms	Yes I Precip likely	No I Warm precip	Maybe I If cold & wet forecast
Insulated jacket	Yes I Cool at night	Maybe I Just a light one	Yes I Cool & long nights
Insulated pants	No I Unless cold & long camps	No I Definitely too warm	No I Unless cold & long camps
Sleeping clothes	Yes I Clothing likely to get wet	Yes I Clothing likely to get wet	Yes I Clothing likely to get wet

Other clothing & accessories

Besides the Core 13, a few additional clothing items and accessories may be needed to complete your kit. Some are seasonal, while others are always critical.

item	my pick or suggestion	msrp low	msrp high	when to wear & more info
Headwear	Visor, or ball cap with neck & ear coverage	$15	$25	Full-time, to keep sun, sweat, precip, and hoods out of eyes, and to protect head
Head insulation	Beanie, balaclava, warm hat; versatile pick: buff	$10	$35	Brisk daytime conditions. Personally, ears get cold first. If only cold camps, wear hooded jacket
Liner gloves	Fleece, poly, or wool	$5	$25	Cold camps; daytime temps below about 50°F
Shell mitts	Waterproof, not insulated	$60	$80	Chilling precip or high winds, alone or over liners
Sunglasses	Polarized and/or transition	$15	$175	Sunny locations; generally west of 100th meridian
Rx eyewear	Glasses or contacts	$0	$0	Not a backpacking-specific expense
Bra	Pack two	$0	$30	Alternate regularly; wash & dry as needed
TOTAL		$105	$370	

footwear

For most backpackers, traditional footwear does not achieve the best results. Boots are stiff, hot, and heavy. "Waterproof" footwear fails in prolonged wet conditions and dries very slowly. And a two-layer sock system absorbs a lot of moisture and traps a lot of heat—two of the three contributing factors to blisters.

While I use this traditional setup when backpacking in the winter, I use an entirely different setup for the remainder of the year, even on my most rugged outings, as do many other experienced backpackers. That said, footwear is a very personalized category, and I would encourage you to experiment until you find the optimal system for your feet and your trips.

item	ranking	my pick or suggestion	weight (oz)	msrp	comments
Shoes	Critical	Breathable trail-running or hiking shoes	12.0	$125	Vs. boots: more comfortable, faster drying, lighter, cheaper; not as durable or protective
Gaiters	Suggested	Stretch nylon, no instep	3.0	$30	Keep out dirt & debris; less necessary with pants

Hiking socks A	Critical	Merino/nylon blend	2.0	$15	Liner-like weight; more odor-resistant than poly
Hiking socks B	Depends	Same as pair A	2.0	$15	In very wet conditions, do not take; otherwise, yes
Sleeping socks	Depends	Poly, wool, or fleece	3.0	$15	Guarantee dry feet at night. Pack only if (both) daytime socks likely to get wet
Camp wear	Optional	Travel or airline slippers	1.0	$15	Avoid wearing wet (and maybe cold) shoes in camp
TOTAL			**23.0**	**$215**	

sleep systems

A sleeping bag's insulation type is the primary driver of its cost, weight, compressibility, and life span. If you have the financial means, choose a premium down insulation (800-fill power or thereabouts) for the best long-term performance and value. You need not spend as much as listed in the winter system, but expect some sticker shock. For Boy Scouts and others with more limited resources, I have included a budget system that will provide satisfactory performance at a fraction of the cost.

A traditional mummy bag and sleeping pad is not ideally suited for hammock use. Mummies are difficult to slide into, and pads rarely fit or stay put. Instead, the consensus pick is a top quilt (draped over the sleeper) and an underquilt (attached to the underside of the hammock). The former can be integrated into a ground system, though a bivy sack or over-size shape (maybe with a hideaway hood) is helpful in minimizing drafts. An underquilt has no value outside a hammock system.

Winter & shoulder seasons

item	ranking	my pick or suggestion	weight (oz)	msrp	comments
Bag or quilt	Critical	High-end 10-deg mummy, premium down	32.0	$575	Take subzero by wearing insulated clothes at night
Sleeping pad	Critical	Full-length air chamber, 2.5 in thick, R-value 3.2	12.0	$160	Unrivaled warmth & comfort for weight, but loud
Pillow	Optional	Inflatable, 2.5 in thick	2.5	$25	More user-friendly than extra clothes
TOTAL			**46.5**	**$760**	

Budget 3 seasons

item	ranking	my pick or suggestion	weight (oz)	msrp	comments
Bag or quilt	Critical	35-deg mummy, synthetic insulation	35.0	$90	Heavier, less compressible, & shorter life span than down, but better price
Sleeping pad	Critical	Full-length air chamber, 3 in thick, R-value 1.0	20.0	$70	Avoid wet & hard packed ground on chilly nights
Pillow	Optional	Extra stuff in stuff sack	0.0	$0	Use clothing, backpack, soft bottles
TOTAL			55.0	$160	

Hammock 3 seasons

item	ranking	my pick or suggestion	weight (oz)	msrp	comments
Bag or quilt	Critical	40-deg quilt with foot-box, premium down	16.0	$225	Wider comfort range than mummy
Underquilt	Critical	Down-filled, 3/4 length	12.0	$175	Traditional sleeping pad not ideal for hammocks, if compatible at all
Pillow	Critical	None	0.0	$0	Head naturally supported in a hammock
TOTAL			28.0	$400	

shelters

Hammocks are an unconventional choice of shelter, but they are compelling in heavily forested areas with poor ground campsites (e.g., wet, overgrown, rocky, rooty, and neither flat nor level), such as the Appalachian Mountains, or in locations with heavily impacted designated campsites such as Rocky Mountain National Park. Hammocks are primarily a solo shelter and have a steep learning curve. The weight and expense of a bridge hammock system would be greater than the gathered-end hammock outlined below.

Elsewhere, I generally sleep on the ground. On weight-sensitive trips in benign conditions (e.g., few storms, low humidity, bug-free nights, and dry campsites), I run with a tarp and bivy, and on most nights never pitch the tarp. For more challenging scenarios, I'm willing to accept the extra weight of a double-wall tent for the enhanced environmental protections and condensation management. I may use the fly and inner tent together or independently, like in the wintertime, or on hot and dry summer nights.

Even in friendly conditions, tents also appeal to individuals who want more privacy and living space than provided by a tarp and bivy setup. The weight penalty is not insignificant, but it's worth a good night of rest.

Tarp & bivy

item	ranking	my pick or suggestion	weight (oz)	msrp	comments
Tarp	Critical	A-frame, 9-ft ridgeline, waterproof nylon	10.0	$125	Open sides vulnerable to wind. Cuben: twice the price, half the weight
Bivy	Critical	Water-resistant top, waterproof floor	7.0	$175	Protects from insects, some wind, & quilt draftiness
Ground cloth	Optional	Emergency blanket	2.0	$5	Extra waterproofness for soggy ground
Poles	Critical	Trekking poles	0.0	$0	Counted elsewhere
Guylines	Critical	2-mm bulk, 40 ft	2.0	$5	4-ft corners & sides, 8-ft ridgelines
Stakes	Critical	8x, aluminum, Y- or V-shape	4.0	$10	Titanium round stakes are stupid light
TOTAL			**25.0**	**$320**	

Tent

item	ranking	my pick or suggestion	weight (oz)	msrp	comments
Fly	Critical	Full sided, nonfree-standing	21.0	$300	More homey and storm-resistant, but heavier and usually less ventilation
Inner tent	Critical	Smaller but proportional to fly. Included.	13.0	$0	Lighter if integrated with fly, but user more vulnerable to condensation
Footprint	Optional	Emergency blanket	2.0	$5	Also protects floor from abrasion
Poles	Critical	Trekking poles	0.0	$0	Counted elsewhere
Guylines	Critical	Included with tent	0.0	$0	Improves storm-resistance & ventilation
Stakes	Critical	8x, aluminum	4.0	$0	Y- or V-shape strongest. Included.
TOTAL			**40.0**	**$305**	

Hammock

item	ranking	my pick or suggestion	weight (oz)	msrp	comments
Tarp	Critical	Hexagonal A-frame	12.0	$100	Great ventilation & coverage area
Hammock	Critical	Gathered-end hammock	19.0	$150	Lighter, simpler, & less expensive than bridge hammock, but not as flat
Suspension	Critical	Adjustable straps	6.0	$25	User-friendly but not the lightest option

sample gear kits

Spreader bars	Depends	-	0.0	$0	Necessary for bridge hammock
Guylines	Critical	2-mm bulk, 40 feet	2.0	$5	10-ft ridgelines, 5-ft corners
Stakes	Critical	4x, aluminum, Y- or V-shape	2.0	$5	Learn the trucker's hitch
TOTAL			**41.0**	**$285**	

navigation

How can you learn to navigate or become more proficient at it? Carrying some or all of the resources and tools detailed below is a good start, as is taking a course on reading a topographic map or using a compass or GPS. But to really learn this backcountry art form, you must spend time in the field and practice, practice, practice.

item	ranking	my pick or suggestion	msrp	comments
Guidebook	Suggested	Commercial or DIY	varies	For big trips without one, create your own
Maps	Critical	Commercial or DIY	varies	Carry two sets: small- and large-scale
Datasheets	Suggested	Commercial or DIY	varies	List of key landmarks, plus distances, vertical, etc.
Watch	Critical	GPS sport watch like the Suunto Ambit	$250	Dead reckon with any watch. Altimeter is a nice feature. Take training to next level with GPS watch.
Compass	Suggested	Baseplate, no mirror	$45	Adjustable declination convenient for extensive use
GPS	Suggested	Smartphone GPS app (monthly subscription)	$6	Vs. handheld GPS: less expensive, better screen, more imagery layers, less battery life
Storage	Critical	Gallon-size bag (2x)	$1	One for materials in use; one for storage
Writing	Suggested	Standard ballpoint pen	$1	Generally useful. I like to take route notes, too.
TOTAL			**$303**	

trekking poles

A few serious hikers eschew trekking poles, but most consider them a critical piece of equipment. The most expensive models feature carbon-fiber shafts and real cork grips, and are sold through the traditional outdoor retail market. But like down-insulated jackets, trekking poles have become more mass-market, and one particular brand—Cascade Mountain Tech—offers a solid product at an unbeatable price.

item	my pick or suggestion	weight (oz)	msrp	comments
Top-shelf	Stiff carbon-fiber shafts, lever locks, cork grips	18.0	$160	If you can afford & justify the best. Fixed-length lighter but less travel-friendly, fewer available.
Budget	Carbon-fiber shafts, lever locks, cork grips	16.0	$30	Available online & from big-box wholesalers. Shockingly good performance for price.
Adjustments	Remove straps & baskets	-1.0	$0	Straps restrict hands; more difficult to let go. Baskets catch vegetation & wedge in rocks.

stove systems

I have two basic solo stove systems: for 3-season use, and for winter (when I must melt snow for water). The 3-season stove, the Cadillac, can be converted for groups of two people (or three small eaters), by using a larger pot and by packing an additional eating container, spoon, and mug.

However, a group willing to trade fire-power for weight may take better to my winter stove, Hot and Heavy. Again, additional personal items would be needed.

For those on a tight budget, consider the Dirtbag, which is suitable for solo 3-season backpacking (not groups). I used this system for many years and many thousands of miles, but with a titanium pot for better durability.

As shown, these systems are fully functional, with no critical missing parts. To the contrary, a few items (notably the mug) could be left out to save weight and expense.

The Cadillac: high-end ultralight system for up to 2 people

item	ranking	my pick or suggestion	weight (oz)	msrp	comments
Stove	Critical	Commercial cottage, wedding favor tin	0.6	$13	A fuel-miser. Not fast: Get it going, do other chores, come back to it.
Wind screen	Critical	Custom to pot size, titanium, rolls into tube	1.3	$80	Pricey, but super efficient, wind resistant, and stable. Fits inside pot.
Pot stand	-	-	0.0	$0	Wind screen serves as pot stand, too
Cookpot	Critical	Titanium, 700-1,000 mL	3.4	$60	Extremely light & durable, but $$$
Eating bowl	Depends	-	0.0	$0	Rec'd for groups of 2+
Mug	Optional	Titanium, about 400 mL	1.3	$35	Slower & less satisfying meals without
Pot lifter	-	-	0.0	$0	No tipping risk. Pot rim remains cool.

Fuel container	Critical	Plastic drink bottle	0.8	$1	Budget 0.5 oz fuel per meal.
Fuel measure	Optional	Plastic medicine cups	0.1	$1	1-oz size. Improves pour accuracy.
Utensil	Critical	Durable plastic, big bowl	0.2	$1	Cut handle to make more packable.
Ignition	Critical	Lighter	0.7	$1	More reliable than matches
TOTAL			8.4	$192	

Hot & Heavy: powerful setup for winter or group use

item	ranking	my pick or suggestion	weight (oz)	msrp	comments
Stove	Critical	Remote canister stove	6.9	$100	Heavier than upright stove, but more stable. In winter, run on liquid feed.
Wind screen	Optional	Aluminum, incl w/stove	1.4	$0	Critical in winter, less so for 3-seasons
Pot stand	-	-	0.0	$0	Pot sits directly on the stove
Cookpot	Critical	Titanium, 2 L	8.8	$75	Aluminum will be more economical
Eating bowl	Depends	-	0.0	$0	Rec'd for groups of 2+
Mug	Suggested	Hard-sided, wide mouth	5.0	$9	Take drink to go, or put in sleeping bag
Pot lifter	Suggested	Aluminum	1.2	$4	Handle big pot more easily
Fuel container	Critical	Canister 8 oz (empty)	5.1	$12	Budget 3 oz per day for melting snow
Fuel measure	-	-	0.0	$0	Cannot "pour" gas in field
Utensil	Critical	Durable plastic, big bowl	0.2	$1	Keep full length for snow melting
Ignition	Critical	Lighter	0.7	$1	More reliable than matches
TOTAL			29.3	$202	

The Dirtbag: functional and economical solo system

item	ranking	my pick or suggestion	weight (oz)	msrp	comments
Stove	Critical	DIY: 3-oz cat food can	0.2	$1	Functional, cheap, easy to make
Wind screen	Critical	DIY: Heavy-duty aluminum foil	0.2	$1	With care, lasts 10-15 meals, cheap & easy to replace, store folded in pot
Pot stand	-	-	0.0	$0	Pot sits directly on stove
Cookpot	Critical	1-L "grease pot"	3.7	$10	Upgrade to Ti for superior durability
Eating bowl	-	-	0.0	$0	Eat out of pot. For heavy-duty cleaning, use water + dirt or duff as abrasive
Mug	Optional	Reusable plastic mug	1.5	$2	Find at Seattle-based coffee chain
Pot lifter	-	Aluminum	1.2	$4	Counters wobbliness of DIY stove

part 3

Fuel container	Critical	Plastic disposable bottle	0.8	$1	Budget 1 oz fuel per meal
Fuel measure	Optional	Plastic medicine cups	0.1	$1	1-oz size. Improves pour accuracy
Utensil	Critical	Durable plastic, big bowl	0.2	$1	Cut handle to make more packable
Ignition	Critical	Lighter	0.7	$1	More reliable than matches
TOTAL			8.6	$22	

hydration

The types and sizes of my water bottles, and my water purification system, are dictated by the frequency and quality of water sources. When water is readily available, I carry only a quart of water or less and have a second bottle available for camp. In drier locations, I carry more capacity and give greater consideration to the weight and volume of the containers when not in use.

Most backpackers settle on a single water purification technique, but I think that chlorine dioxide drops and a screw-on inline filter are wonderfully complementary. The drops are ideal for camp, arid environments, and communal water, whereas the filter creates potable water immediately.

item	ranking	my pick or suggestion	msrp	comments
Primary bottle	Critical	Soft-sided, 34-oz size	$9	Free option: recycled disposable bottle
Storage	Critical	At least one extra quart; more in arid locations	$9	Collapsible 70-oz bottles weigh just 1.3 oz and occupy minimal pack volume when not in use
Treatment 1	Suggested	Chlorine dioxide drops	$15	Best for large volumes & long dwell times
Treatment 2	Suggested	Screw-on inline filter	$25	Instant potable water, if viruses not a worry
TOTAL			$58	

small essentials

Do not be intimidated by the listed weight or expense of this category. First, you probably will not need at least some of the items. Second, you probably already own many of them. Because it takes a while to assemble all the items on this list, I store them together between trips to save prep time, rather than mixing them with general household supplies and then having to hunt them down again.

item	ranking	my pick or suggestion	weight (oz)	msrp	comments
Light	Suggested	100-lumens LED	1.0	$35	Sufficient brightness for camp & some night-hiking
Knife	Suggested	2.5-in blade & scissors	1.0	$15	For normal backpacking, large knives are overrated
First aid kit	Critical	DIY - solo kit (complete description on website)	4.0	$50	Meds: ibuprofen, loperamide, diphenhydramine, loratadine. Wounds: adhesive bandages, skin closures, antibiotic, Leukotape P, benzoin. Tweezers. Plus multiuse items.
Satellite comm	Suggested	Two-way messenger (unit cost & service fee)	8.0	$300	For low-risk trips, one-way messenger is okay. For groups & big wilderness, sat phone is best.
Fire starter	Critical	Lighter & food wrapper	1.0	$1	Mylar-backed wrapper is extremely flammable
Foot care kit	Critical	DIY - solo kit (complete description on website)	2.0	$25	Bonnie's Balm, Leukotape P, duct tape, Blist-O-Bans, benzoin, plus resourcefulness
Repair kit	Critical	DIY - solo kit (complete description on website)	2.0	$10	Needle & thread, Aquaseal glue, Krazy Glue, duct tape, Tenacious Tape, batteries, spare head net
Bug repellent	Depends	Picaridin spray tube	1.0	$3	Permethrin-treated clothing best for intense bugs
Head net	Depends	Mosquito netting	1.0	$15	Much better airflow than no-see-um mesh
Bear spray	Depends	8-oz size, capsaicin	12.0	$45	For grizzly-inhabited areas; better than a gun
Sit pad	Optional	Closed-cell foam	2.0	$15	Convenient for wet or cold ground
Foot traction	Depends	Studded cables	12.0	$70	Good bite; more compatible with flexible outsoles
Ice ax	Depends	All-aluminum	7.0	$120	Self-arrest on steep & hard snowfields or glaciers
Dental	Suggested	Brush, paste, floss	2.0	$5	Cut brush in half so it's more packable
Toilet paper	Suggested	Premium, 4 tiles per day	1.0	$1	Use natural materials to start; polish with TP
Assistance	Optional	Pee jar or director	2.0	$1	Convenience or privacy at night & in group
Sanitation	Critical	Hand sanitizer	1.0	$1	Especially important in group setting
Feminine care	Depends	Menstruation products	1.0	$1	Should be packed out; use extra baggies
Skin care	Suggested	Sunscreen, lip balm	1.0	$10	Avoid "monkey butt" with backcountry bidet
Trip recording	Suggested	Compact camera	8.0	$400	Also consider: journal, smartphone camera, & audio recorder
Entertainment	Optional	Music player	0.0	$0	Personally, not my style, & not always safe
Wallet	Suggested	Card-holder	1.0	$10	ID, cash, cards; do not leave in car at trailhead
TOTAL			**71.0**	**$1,133**	

part (3)

packing

Frameless packs are lightest and least expensive. But their carrying comfort is normally too limited for backpackers who aren't vigilant about the weight of their gear, who pack food for more than a long weekend, and/or who must store their food in a hard-sided canister. A suspension pack weighing two to three pounds is the sweet spot for most.

Review food storage regulations for the area(s) in which you will backpack and read the food storage chapter. In areas where hard-sided canisters are required, rentals are often available. Owning one is more convenient, as well as more economical in the long term.

item	ranking	my pick or suggestion	weight (oz)	msrp	comments
Pack	Critical	Suspension, durable fabric, 40–70 L capacity	40.0	$225	Frameless packs lighter & less expensive, but less capable. Many good packs are sub 3 lb.
Waterproofing	Suggested	Trash compactor bag, used as pack liner	2.0	$1	More effective than pack cover. Lighter & less expensive than waterproof stuff sacks.
Snack storage	Suggested	Quart-size slider bag	0.5	$1	Today's food. Keep at top of pack for easy access.
Food storage	Depends	12x20-in odor-proof bag or nylon stuff sack	1.5	$8	Bag quickly not odor-free, but see-through is convenient. Redundant with bear canister.
Food protection	Depends	Hard- or soft-sided, to deter bears & mini bears	41.0	$80	Required in many high-use areas. If not, use Ursack. Redundant with food storage bag, above.
Stuff sacks	Suggested	For sleeping bag & pad, pot, & small essentials	3.0	$15	To keep items together or compressed. Don't overorganize. Use loose items to fill voids in pack.
Eyewear case	Suggested	Included with glasses	2.0	$0	Minimal weight to keep glasses clean & protected
TOTAL			**90.0**	**$330**	

sample gear kits

glossary & list of hikes

Alcohol stove: An ultralight, reliable, and inexpensive backpacking stove, typically homemade from cat food or soda cans. Most often fueled with denatured alcohol or methanol (aka HEET). Ideal for 1–2 people; not suitable for 3+ or for melting snow.

Base weight: The weight of a full backpack, minus food, water, fuel, and clothing and equipment that is worn or carried on the body. This oft-cited measurement provides apples-to-apples comparisons of pack weight regardless of trip length.

Breathability: Layman's term for "moisture vapor transmission rate" (MVTR). Unfortunately, it presents MVTR as an absolute (i.e., a material is breathable or not). In fact, materials vary significantly in their level of breathability.

Durable water repellent (DWR): A fluorocarbon-based coating commonly applied to polyester and nylon (including the exterior layers of most rain gear) to improve water-resistance. When new, DWR will cause water to bead up and roll off. But it is easily degraded by dirt, body oils, and abrasion. Restoration efforts have limited effectiveness.

Environmental and route conditions: Temperatures, precipitation, daylight, ground cover, vegetation, sun exposure, water availability, wildlife and insects, remoteness, and natural hazards. One's gear, supplies, and skills should account for these factors.

Gear list: An inventory (best recorded as a spreadsheet) of every item that will be taken on a trip. Helps in virtually assembling a kit, calculating pack weight, the final pack-up, and preparing future trips.

Layering: A time-tested strategy for having a versatile and effective clothing system. Each layer excels in a particular function, with no intentional overlap or redundancy. I propose four categories: Go, Storm, Stop, and Sleep.

Polyurethane (PU): A polymer that is frequently used in backpacking equipment (e.g., to waterproof tent canopies and floors).

Stupid heavy: An item (or items) that does not improve one's on-trail or in-camp experience and/or that is unnecessarily heavy relative to other options. For instance, a dozen books instead of a Kindle.

Stupid light: The counterproductive sacrifice of comfort, safety, and fun to save weight. For example, leaving behind rain gear despite a forecast of 35 degrees and rain, or using toothpick-size tent stakes that easily pull out.

Select list of author's hikes

Tarp system: A tarp augmented by an inner bug nest, groundsheet, bivy sack, head net, or some other item to supplement the tarp and create a full-service shelter.

Three-season: The conventional backpacking season, when conditions are relatively hospitable and gear need not be winter-worthy. The exact months vary by location: In Colorado, it's June through September; in Virginia, it's April through November.

Ventilation: The transmission of air, which may contain moisture and/or thermal energy (heat). An extremely valuable feature in clothing and shelters, to maintain thermoregulation and to minimize condensation buildup.

Waterproof: A layman's term for materials that surpass a defined threshold in a hydrostatic head test. Due to abrasion, UV exposure, repeated folding, or extreme pressure, waterproof fabrics can leak.

Waterproof/breathable (WP/B): A common rain gear fabric marketed as—miraculously—impervious to moisture while also allowing moisture to pass through it. Often branded (e.g., Gore-Tex, Precip). More accurately described as being somewhat breathable. Wets out after moderate use due to failure of the DWR coating.

Appalachian Trail: 2,175 miles, Georgia to Maine. May–August 2002.
Colorado Trail: 480 miles, Denver to Durango. July 2004, August 2006.
Sea-to-Sea Route: 7,775 miles, Quebec to Washington State. August 2004–July 2005.
Ultralight in the Nation's Icebox: 385 miles, Duluth to Ely, Minnesota. January 2007.
Great Western Loop: 6,875 miles around the American West. April–November 2007.
Sierra High Route: 200 miles, California's High Sierra. July 2008.
Iceland Traverse: 550 miles, coast to coast (east to west). July 2008.
Hayduke Trail and Grand Canyon Traverse: 800 miles, Colorado Plateau. February–March 2009.
Alaska Mountain Wilderness Classic: 180 miles, eastern Alaska Range. July 2009.
Alaska-Yukon Expedition: 4,700 miles on skis, foot, and packraft, March–September 2010.
Guiding: 55-plus trips with 400-plus clients. 2011–present.
Kings Canyon High Basin Route: 125 miles, California. July 2015.
Wind River High Route: 95 miles, Wyoming. August 2015.
Ultrarunning: 2008 Leadville 100, 18:17, 2nd place; 2015 Run Rabbit Run 100, 20:12, 3rd place; 2016 HPRS Silverheels 100, 23:17, 1st place.

glossary

illustrations credits

All photos courtesy Andrew Skurka unless otherwise noted:

Cover, (knife) Courtesy Victorinox Swiss Army; (stove) Courtesy Trail Designs; (watch) Courtesy Suunto; (trekking poles) Courtesy Black Diamond; (shoe) Courtesy La Sportiva; (headlamp) Courtesy Black Diamond; (water container) Courtesy Cascade Designs.

4, (jacket) Courtesy Outdoor Research; (sleeping bag) Courtesy GoLite; (cap) Courtesy Headsweats; (headlamp) Courtesy Black Diamond; (trekking poles) Courtesy Black Diamond; (canister) Courtesy Snow Peak; (overboot) Courtesy Forty Below; (compass) Courtesy Suunto; (socks) Courtesy DeFeet; (backpack) Courtesy Mountain Laurel Designs; (shoe) Courtesy La Sportiva; (knife) Courtesy Victorinox Swiss Army; (bivy sack) Courtesy Black Diamond; 8, Frans Lanting/Corbis; 11, Michael Christopher Brown/National Geographic Stock; 14 (both), Ryan Day Thompson; 18, Danny Warren/iStockphoto.com; 21, Michael Christopher Brown/National Geographic Stock; 22, NOHRSC/NOAA; 23, Michael Christopher Brown/National Geographic Stock; 25, Alex Treadway/National Geographic Stock; 28, Matthias Breiter/Minden Pictures; 31, Noah Couser/Wild West Photos; 35 (LE), A. Syred/Photo Researchers, Inc.; 35 (CTR), SPL/Photo Researchers, Inc.; 35 (RT), Michael Abbey/Photo Researchers, Inc.; 37 (both), Courtesy Ibex Outdoor Clothing; 42, maigi/Shutterstock.com; 44, Anatol Jasiutyn/Panoramafactory; 50, Courtesy Outdoor Research; 51, Courtesy OutDry Extreme; 58, Courtesy GIPhotoStock/Photo Researchers, Inc.; 58, Courtesy RBH Designs; 62, Courtesy Headsweats; 64, Courtesy DeFeet; 66, Chris Christie/All Canada Photos/Corbis; 68, Paul Willerton; 69, andesign101/Shutterstock.com; 71 (UP LE) risteski goce/Shutterstock.com; 71 (UP RT & LO), Courtesy La Sportiva; 72, Michael Christopher Brown/National Geographic Stock; 76, MarFot/ Shutterstock.com; 77, Miriam Stein; 78, JuGa/Shutterstock.com; 79, Courtesy of DeFeet; 81, Courtesy of NEOS; 82 (UP), Courtesy Salomon; 82 (LO), Courtesy DeFeet; 83, Courtesy Forty Below; 84, Ace Kvale; 88 (UP), Jeff Diener/Wild West Photos; 88 (LO), Courtesy GoLite; 90 (UP), Courtesy MusucBag; 90 (LO), Alan Dixon; 92, Courtesy of Cascade Designs; 98, Tony Wong; 100 (RT) Adam Buchanan; 101, Courtesy REI; 104, Courtesy Sea to Summit; 107, Courtesy TarpTent; 108, Courtesy GoLite; 109, Tony Wong; 110, Michael Christopher Brown/National Geographic Stock; 113, Courtesy Gossamer Gear; 114-5, Courtesy Black Diamond; 116, Courtesy Warbonnet Outdoors; 121, Courtesy Nite Ize; 124, Patrick J. Bagley/NG Staff; 127, Michael Christopher Brown/National Geographic Stock; 132 (LE), Courtesy Suunto; 132 (RT), Courtesy Garmin; 137 (UP LE & RT), Courtesy Black Diamond; 139, Courtesy Black Diamond; 149, Bluskystudio/Shutterstock.com; 150, Courtesy MSR; 152, Ken Hoehn/iStock.com; 155, Jamen Percy/Shutterstock.com; 156, Tupungato/Shutterstock.com; 159, Jeff Diener/Wild West Photos; 162 (LE), ck./Shutterstock.com; 162 (RT), Courtesy Snow Peak; 163, Courtesy Jetboil; 164, Ryan Day Thompson; 165, Ryan Tansey; 166, Miriam Stein; 169, Floortje/iStock.com; 175, Courtesy MSR; 181, Courtesy MSR; 182, Courtesy Sawyer Products; 184, Courtesy Victorinox Swiss Army; 185, Courtesy Sawyer Products; 187 (LE), Courtesy Black Diamond; 187 (RT), Courtesy Mammut; 188, Courtesy Counter Assault; 189, kenkistler/Shutterstock.com; 191, Michael Christopher Brown/National Geographic Stock; 194, Courtesy ACR Electronics; 195, Courtesy Dr. Bronner's; 197, Courtesy Joby; 198, Courtesy Canon; 199, Alaska Stock Images/National Geographic Stock; 201, Ryan Day Thompson; 206, Ryan Day Thompson; 208, Jordan Siemens/Getty Images; 210, Courtesy Mountain Laurel Designs; 215, Miriam Stein; 216, Ocean/Corbis.

acknowledgments

Neither the adventures on which this book is based, nor the actual writing and production of it, would have been possible without the help and support of many others.

At the very top of this list are my wife, Amanda, and my parents, Bob and Karen. Amanda was a coveted sounding board during the writing process (again). Somehow, she also manages to support my evolving myopic obsessions, which seem to involve play as often as work. My parents never would have chosen this lifestyle for me, but they nonetheless have supported me every step of the way. They have sent me supply packages via general delivery and bush plane, consoled me over the phone when I could no longer internalize the stresses of solo wilderness travel, and offered practical life and career guidance when I've asked for it. My sisters, Kerri and Christine; brothers-in-law, Ryan and Matt; and niece and nephews, Anne Marie, Owen, Colin, and Nathan, are less hands-on but equally reliable supporters.

This book's first edition was based primarily on what I had learned through my solo long-distance trips, while both planning for and doing them, with some additional input from all-stars like Phil Barton, Buzz Burrell, and Alan Dixon. The improvements in this second edition are largely due to the 50-plus group trips that I have led since the original release, in that I now better understand the full range of preferences, abilities, and knowledge within the backpacking community. As I outlined the text and discussed gear, supplies, and skills, I did so with Albert, Cindy, Kolby, Krishna, Lisa, Nitro Joe, and Vic in mind, plus many others. In short, my clients gave me an audience. I hope I gave them more.

Finally, I would like to thank National Geographic Books—notably Bill O'Donnell, Callie Bonaccorsy, Katie Olsen, Mary Stephanos, Patrick Bagley, and especially my editor, Susan Straight—for taking this project to another level, as would be expected of anything that earns the yellow border.

index

part 3

Since 1888, the National Geographic Society has funded more than 12,000 research, exploration, and preservation projects around the world. National Geographic Partners distributes a portion of the funds it receives from your purchase to the National Geographic Society to support programs including the conservation of animals and their habitats.

National Geographic Partners
1145 17th Street NW
Washington, DC 20036-4688 USA

Become a member of National Geographic and activate your benefits today at natgeo.com/jointoday.

For information about special discounts for bulk purchases, please contact National Geographic Books Special Sales: specialsales@natgeo.com

For rights or permissions inquiries, please contact National Geographic Books Subsidiary Rights: bookrights@natgeo.com

ISBN: 978-1-4262-1784-5

Printed in the United States of America

16/QGT-QGL/1

LET US PLAN
YOUR NEXT HIKE!

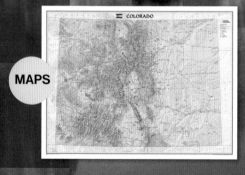